P9-BIL-011

LIFE
IN
A
NARROW
PLACE

LENDING POLICY
IF YOU DAMAGE OR LOSE LIBRARY
MATERIALS, THEN YOU WILL BE
CHARGED FOR REPLACEMENT. FAIL-
URE TO PAY AFFECTS LIBRARY
PRIVILEGES, GRADES, TRANSCRIPTS,
DIPLOMAS, AND REGISTRATION
PRIVILEGES OR ANY COMBINATION
THEREOF.

LIFE
IN
A
NARROW
PLACE

▼

Stephen
Hirst

▼

Photographs
by
TERRY
and
LYNTHA
EILER

David McKay Company
New York

LIFE IN A NARROW PLACE

COPYRIGHT © 1976 by Stephen Hirst and Terry Eiler

All rights reserved,
including the right to reproduce this book,
or parts thereof, in any form,
except for the inclusion of brief quotations in a review.

Library of Congress Cataloging in Publication Data

Hirst, Stephen, 1939-
Life in a narrow place.

Bibliography: p.
Includes index.
1. Havasupai Indians.   I. Title.
E99.H3H57   979.1'59'00497   74-6533
ISBN 0-679-20286-2

Manufactured in the United States of America
Designed by The Etheredges

10 9 8 7 6 5 4 3 2

We dedicate this book to the Havasupai people. It is a work of love. The author has been privileged to live in their midst as a friend for six years, during which time he worked as tribal teacher, sometime tribal secretary and publicist, and irregular editor of the tribal newspaper. The photographers have been familiar with the Havasupai people nearly as long and have also worked in their community as tribal teachers.

All of us came to know the Havasupai at a time when we were especially impressionable, and these gentle but determined people converted us to a view of the world and of man more humanistic and at the same time more rational than that we learned in our childhood.

Few persons could spend so much time among the Havasupai and fail to admire them for their quiet certainty in preserving a heritage they consider superior to that they find abroad in the recent years of their history. We sense here the conviction reported elsewhere among native Americans that the presence of the Europeans is a temporary phenomenon to be endured and that their own long-range survival depends upon preserving the wisdom they have acquired over the centuries. At times they apply subtle leverages to modify the European's peculiar behavior when it pinches too tightly. This is a world where even the Navajo and Apache are viewed as foreigners because they only arrived within the millennium.

The author has tried to be thorough in his research and conversations to capture the spirit of being Havasupai, of being 400 special people surrounded but not absorbed in a nation of 200 million. The photographers' cameras captured only what they saw; yet they record something printed in the photographers' hearts—and perhaps yours.

Finally, this book is in the nature of a repayment for the wisdom and strength our Havasupai friends have granted us. We chronicle here the magnificent, century-long campaign they waged to regain their homeland. It is from our own brief sharing of their long fight that this book grew. In its manuscript form this book provided some of the historical and legal underpinning of the long-sought reunion with their land which the Havasupai finally achieved January 3, 1975.

STEPHEN HIRST
Supai, Arizona

TERRY and LYNTHA EILER
Athens, Ohio

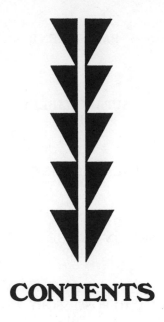

CONTENTS

viii

Contents

PREFACE

In the following pages, material taken from old records will contain certain spelling inconsistencies. "Yavasupai," "Yavasuppai," and "Suppai" have all been used to indicate the people whose name is today spelled "Havasupai." Likewise, "Walapai," "Hualpai" and "Wallapai" have been used to refer to the people who today spell their name "Hualapai."

Though we have now anglicized the Spanish word *cañon* into "canyon," the old spelling continued to be used quite freely until the turn of the century in English and still remains in use in certain local names, such as Cañon de Chelly and Truxton Cañon Agency. In such cases I have retained the Spanish spelling.

Many Havasupai family names are today spelled differently from my phonetic rendering of their original pronunciation. I cannot reconcile these differences; I can only try to be consistent in my spelling of each name where it appears. For example, the family name Watahomigie stems from an individual whose name I have rendered as "Wa tahómja." Similarly, Wescogame stems from the individual I have named "Wa tesgògama."

ix

Havasu Canyon appears on many maps and documents as "Cataract Canyon." They are the same. They should not be confused with the upper reaches of the Grand Canyon, also designated as Cataract Canyon.

The multiplicity of governmental agencies mentioned may perplex the reader somewhat. The Office of Indian Affairs of the first part of this century was simply renamed the Bureau of Indian Affairs during the Franklin D. Roosevelt administration. It remains an agency of the Interior Department. The OIA/BIA exercises jurisdiction over Indian trust lands [reservation lands].

Exercising jurisdiction over National Park and National Monument lands is the National Park Service, another agency of the Interior Department, but one whose purposes may conflict very basically with those of the OIA/BIA.

Finally, exercising control over National Forest lands is the United States Forest Service, an agency of the Agriculture Department. The U.S. Forest Service has no administrative connection with the Interior Department, and its directives differ as completely from either the National Park Service's or the Bureau of Indian Affairs' as those of the latter two differ from each other. While the Havasupai Tribe's lives and lands were parceled out among all three agencies from 1919 to 1975, the Havasupai people faced the impossible task of attempting to deal with all of them in coordination.

Throughout this book I use the term "European" to describe American society and the people who dominate it. The often-applied term "white" is inexact and misleading as a description of the culture which has come to dominate the Western Hemisphere, for it conjures up race as a decisive factor in the invasion and conquest of the New World. Such was not the case. The invasion of the New World which began in 1492 and the conquest which followed was led by European individuals motivated by characteristically European principles, but the impact of Europe's expansion into the Americas has been cultural rather than racial. The attempt has been to replace native cultures with Europe's culture rather than native peoples with European people, though that has sometimes occurred.

While United States society has by 1975 become multiethnic, its character remains firmly European. Europe's expansion drew non-European peoples into the New World for 320 years from 1609 to 1929 in considerable numbers. These non-Europeans took little part in the conquest of the New World; they were pawns of Europe's expansion just as surely as the inundated native peoples of this hemisphere were.

Certainly the dominant society of the United States is not "Anglo-Saxon" or "Anglo"; these terms provide much too narrow a description of a mode of thought and outlook generated by much more than England or Saxony. Europeans and Ashkenazim developed from the ruins of feudalism the thought, values and economic organization which still govern our actions today.

A very basic tenet of the European outlook is the tendency inherited from Christian philosophy to see man as a figure independent of his natural environment. Most of us remember some shock at learning the human being belongs to the animal kingdom. A second tenet so basic to European thought that most Euro-Americans take it for granted is individualism. The European-ized person expects initiative, welfare and salvation itself to be personal matters. The two concepts of individualism and of man as a supranatural being clash flatly with principles which many non-European societies follow, including those of the native peoples of the New World, among whom the Havasupai of course number themselves.

Europe's expansion was hardly unique in its inclusion of invasion and conquest of foreign areas. Roman legions had conquered northern Europe itself a thousand years before Europe undertook the conquest of the New World and, eventually, the cultural and economic conquest of all mankind. It is in this last conquest that Europe has, so far, proved unique.

S. H.

Preface

We used to climb a little hill at the end of day, all the work done, and look out over the land and just feel good to be alive.

—LEMUEL PAYA

I was born in a snowstorm in a brush shelter hut, wrapped in a rabbit-fur blanket, and my bedding was made from the bark of a sweet-smelling tree.

—LEE MARSHALL

Yul gesyó or Teyáva
"Daughter" of Baa 'nya j'álga

Courtesy Smithsonian Institution 1899

Lina Daughter of Hmány gejáa and Gwe gethgwáya
Wife of Duke Iditicáva

Courtesy Lorenzo Sinyella 1929

1.
1974: LIFE
IN A NARROW
PLACE

In the arid wilderness of broken plateaus where the Colorado River has cut its awesome canyon through northern Arizona, a peaceful group of Indian people were dwelling in 1974 on the bottom of the deep and practically inaccessible gorge of Havasu Canyon. Their community was situated on one of the tiniest, most isolated federal Indian reservations in the United States. Over 300 of these people lived on a total of 518.06 acres in this canyon. These people are the Havasupai. They were so crowded that, for many of them, carrying on daily life involved at least minor intrusions into his neighbors' resources. A hundred more of their people had to live and work elsewhere; there was not room for them in Havasu Canyon.

The people who lived in this canyon bottom did not choose such a way of life. Once they were the occupants of the lands along the Grand Canyon's south rim, ranging as far south as the present locations of Flagstaff and Williams. For more than ten centuries the Havasupai pursued a hard but rewarding life there.

They used the land with care and treated it with respect, believing they would stay in that place as long as there should be Havasupai. They welcomed visitors to their hard land and shared with them whatever it afforded.

One day a race of invaders appeared from the other side of the earth and said the Havasupai's homelands were so beautiful they should be reserved for viewing, and the Havasupai were made to leave. All that remained to them of their homeland was the narrow bottom of Havasu Canyon.

Though the government officially restricted them to Havasu Canyon in 1882, the Havasupai continued to use part of their old lands outside the canyon, but they were forbidden to live outside the canyon as a tribal community any longer, a situation they were to endure for nearly a century. The government had other plans for the three million acres over which the Havasupai once roamed. As one official wrote at the turn of the century:

> The Grand Cañon of the Colorado River is becoming so renowned for its wonderful and extensive natural gorge scenery and for its open and clean pine woods, that it should be preserved for the everlasting pleasure and instruction of our intelligent citizens as well as those of foreign countries. Henceforth, I deem it just and necessary to keep the wild and unappreciable [sic] Indian from off of the Reserve. . . .[1]

Yet the Havasupai remained industrious and hospitable people, for they believe good people must be industrious and hospitable. They claim none of them has ever killed any of the invaders from the other side of the world. Notwithstanding that, our government's actions up to 1974 seemed to indicate that we viewed the Havasupai as little better than a nuisance. But then the 425 Havasupai people came again to Congress—for the eighth time since 1908—in a last-chance appeal for the just restoration of their land. They found themselves plunged into their most desperate battle for survival since 1882 and, against all odds, they won. This is the story of their victory and of the terrible dark years they had to live through.

SUMMER BY THE BLUE CREEK

In the cool twilight stillness the stars fade one by one from the strip of lightening sky above Havasu Canyon. At first only the rush of the stream along the canyon walls breaks the silence. The smoke of little breakfast fires around the canyon begins to float tentatively into the coming morning. All at once, the first flash of the summer dawn illuminates the buff sandstone cliffs rearing 2,000 feet from their red sandstone base 1,000 feet above the course of Havasu Creek. Birdsongs lap and overlap each other in the cottonwoods sheltering the old iron beds outside. The children sit on the edge of the beds scratching their heads and swinging their feet, watching the reflected light of dawn. Down in the canyon one cannot see the rising of the sun itself. A few flies buzz aimlessly about. Across the canyon gentle laughter resounds over the hum of morning activity.

This canyon floor cutting northward through the upper Arizona plateau and into the Grand Canyon of the Colorado is home for the Havasupai people in summer. Even today many visitors to the Southwest learn with surprise of this community of Indian people living within the Grand Canyon. The people call themselves *ha vasúa báaja*—the Blue Creek people—and so number themselves among the few native Americans whom the Europeans called by anything close to their own name for themselves. Even "Havasupai" actually stems from their name in the related Hualapai (wá la pi) language: *ha vasú páia*. The Post Office Department long ago designated the isolated post office here—still served by horse and mule—as "Supai," and so the Havasupai community has come to have this name, though it has no meaning in Havasupai.

In summer, the floor of Havasu Canyon flourishes with cottonwood and streamside willow like some midwestern farming community, an oasis in the arid western intermountain basin. During the months of summer the Havasupai pursue their life as intensive agriculturalists along Havasu Creek, as they have for six centuries or more. Before the morning sun clears the canyon walls, families walk down to their fields to pull weeds and turn water into the fields; late in the day they may return to do some more work when the midday heat—usually over 100°—has let up.

At least two and perhaps six centuries ago the Havasupai constructed the two *ha yá gewa*—main ditches—which run along the base of the cliffs on each side of the creek. Many laterals branch in from these main ditches to feed the fields, especially on the west side of the creek, where most of the farming land lies.

The sandy, poor-looking soil proves fertile, and the Havasupai feel justly proud of the bountiful harvests on their tiny reservation. They grow here all varieties of corn, several varieties of melons, beans, squash and pumpkins. Besides the vegetable fields most families maintain a few fruit trees and some even small orchards to grow peaches, apricots, pecans, apples, pears, and black and green figs. As the fruits and vegetables ripen, the families send the children to the fields to bring home food for meals. When the family goes to the fields they may take their lunches with them and eat under the cottonwoods at noon and then go to the stream to cool off after a hot morning's work.

On the hottest afternoons the men participate in the health-giving ritual of the *to'ólva*, the sweat lodge. The Havasupai *to'ólva* resembles very much the Scandinavian *sauna* in being a small chamber in which one or several persons may steam themselves. The men use their visits to the *to'ólva* as an occasion for trading news and ideas as well as for purification and serious healing of aches and pains. Women also may use the *to'ólva* for healing, but rarely do they use it for pleasure as do the men. The summer *to'ólva* always sits by the stream, and after completing the *to'ólva* ceremony the participant plunges into the refreshing blue water. (See pages 141–142 for a description of the winter *to'ólva* ceremony.)

The Havasupai remained self-sufficient even until a generation ago. They raised enough fruit and hay so that they shipped a portion of it out to help

support the Indian school at Truxton Cañon. But by 1974 the foreigners had surrounded their use of the plateau for food with so many arbitrary restrictions on water storage that when dry years came, as they did in 1970, 1971 and 1974, Havasupai stock perished for lack of forage and water up above. More and more the Havasupai had to grow forage in the canyon itself, cutting further into what the land could provide its human inhabitants.

Formerly many families farmed other springs along the Grand Canyon's south rim in summer, but, with practically all of the tribe living in Havasu Canyon year round by 1974, the demands for space became acute. Less than a century ago people lived mostly at the edges of the canyon or right under the cliffs, leaving all the farmland unencumbered. By 1974 people had, out of necessity, begun locating their homes out in the fields, and the situation resembled medieval patchwork farming as the families divided the meager acreage further and further among heirs. A family's holdings scattered all over the canyon as they picked up and lost different patches through marriage. Fence lines as well as homes were slowly eating up the fields. Far less than half of the reservation remained arable; only half of the canyon floor lay within the irrigation ditches.

One of the most striking effects on farming and residential patterns in the canyon resulted from a recent Bureau of Indian Affairs housing program. In the 1960s the Tribal Council began to ask for some sort of housing assistance, and in 1967 the BIA proposed in response a plan to build fifty prefabricated homes in the canyon, all following a standard model. The material was to be pressed sawdust panels slid into grooved frame members; the buildings were to sit on concrete columns to leave a three- or four-foot crawl space underneath. These houses may have been satisfactory for air-conditioned desert living; in Havasu Canyon they provide too little barrier to heat flow and suffer too easily the effects of moisture. Houses built four or five years ago have holes rotted through the flooring from water leaks. The sawdust walls allow so much heat to pass through them in winter that the occupants must pursue every possible expedient for heating. It took six years to put up all the houses, and by the end of 1975 fifty of them will fill the canyon, some of them set but twenty or thirty yards from the next. Though the Havasupai's doubts multiplied with the number of houses, their erection also brought needed government money to the Havasupai families employed in putting them up. The need for work and for income outweighed the need for space.

Some people have stone and wood homes they built themselves, and at least one individual decided to build his own new home and obtained a loan to buy lumber and materials. He built and furnished it through his own efforts and even towed a new stove down the eight-mile trail from the canyon rim on a sledge. This last job took him two days.

Accommodating a growing number of tourists has become a primary activity for the Havasupai during the summer months. Below the Havasupai community Havasu Creek produces a series of breathtaking waterfalls and lovely blue pools which nearly 8,000 visitors a year come to see. Most of them hike into Havasu Canyon, but about a quarter of them prefer to ride the trail, as the Havasupai themselves do. There are no auto roads here; one goes about on foot or horseback along dirt trails in Havasu Canyon. Many visitors find it a refuge from the twentieth century. The Havasupai themselves, insofar as their situation allows them, resist what they view as the depersonalizing mechanization of modern America. These tourist riders provide the only locally generated source of income the Havasupai have at present. Individual families rent their horses to such visitors through the tribal tourist office and then guide them into the canyon. By this means the horse owners make enough to feed their horses and not quite enough to feed their families; yet they must keep the horses fed or some families would have no means of making any income at all.

The sometimes overwhelming numbers of strangers otherwise seem to leave no mark on the Havasupai community they pass through. Few of them pay much attention to the human inhabitants of this beautiful canyon. And yet, handfuls of young people have begun to sit in town in worn clothes and headbands, hoping perhaps to be taken as brothers here among these people, nearly forgotten by a society which even these young people who belong to it have come to find oppressing. Two or three days later these self-exiles leave again without having made contact. Other visitors come frequently, stay longer, and find warm friends among the Havasupai.

THE PEOPLE OF THE BLUE CREEK

The Havasupai Tribal Council is the local governing body of the reservation. Once the Council was an informal gathering of traditional headmen the Havasupai called *baa gemúlva*, or "bosses" (see p. 205). The Council is now a purely elective body with seven members who serve staggered two-year terms. One year four are elected; the next, three. The tribe holds elections on Christmas Day; then the newly elected and incumbent Council members sit together immediately after the election and select from among themselves a Chairman and a Vice Chairman. The Council holds a regular meeting the second Saturday of each month, and most of the town turns out to air grievances and voice suggestions. Other meetings the Chairman calls as necessary to dispose of pressing business. Meetings are generally conducted in Havasupai, with translations sometimes interspersed in English for the benefit of any non-Havasupai speakers present. Anyone may speak at Council meetings, and closed sessions are extremely rare. The Havasupai in its smallness and closeness observes an almost perfect democracy in its government. One person does not move without the others, for in the Havasupai world initiatives have meaning only as group initiatives. The tribal people consider those they elect as the people's property; few Chairmen hold any special charisma that could place them above the public that elected them.

The Havasupai run all their own businesses and hire all their own managers

for tribal enterprises, only a few of whom are not themselves Havasupai. The tribal businesses include a tribal store and a tribal tourism and supply-packing enterprise. There is a government-funded Native American Program (formerly the Community Action Program). The Havasupai have opened a tribal café, which serves as a comfortable gathering place for tribal people and visitors alike. They have placed local arts and crafts on sale inside and pictures of tribal life and old photographs on the walls. The atmosphere is cheery and energetic.

Among the crafts one may occasionally see some of the exquisite Havasupai basketry, among the finest and most highly developed in the New World.[2] Most often the collector must seek the best of these intricately woven and boldly designed creations at the homes of the women artists.

The tribe also manages a tribally controlled preschool, which is bilingual and bicultural. The Bureau of Indian Affairs maintains a regular local grade school, which now runs up through grade five. For years the parents have requested a new building to replace the present school, built in 1912. Until 1971 the local school included but two grades; that year the Bureau added two more grades as a result of the Havasupai parents' years of pressure. The results have been notable; the children in the local school, in strong contrast to boarding-school pupils, began to show much motivation, and their achievement levels began to improve noticeably. The parents, who formerly could consider their children as little better than temporary charges, began to take again the active hand in their development they had in the old days. Parents and grandparents began to involve themselves in the practices of the school.

Still, by age eleven or twelve every Havasupai child leaves his family in late August to attend distant boarding schools or stay with foster families until the following May. For the next seven years of their lives, unless they drop out of school, Havasupai children see their families only three months of the year.

Havasupai parents appear extremely permissive in bringing up their children; they are genuinely relaxed about them. Most of them believe striking a child is an unnecessarily severe punishment, and it is rarely done.

Until the age of seven months infants are snugly bound with soft cloth into cradleboards. The cradleboard has a hoop which surrounds the infant's head with flexible woven wands; if the cradleboard should fall forward when stood against something, the hoop takes up the shock and protects the child. In summer the parents may stretch a light covering of cloth over the hoop to protect the child from heat and insects. Parents and older sisters take an infant in his cradleboard everywhere with them, speaking to the child and giving him a close part in family life from the very first. The sensation of physical surroundment placates the infant, and it seldom complains in the cradleboard, even after the better part of a day in it.

At seven months most parents take the infant from the cradleboard, which is kept around for a while in case the child should feel its need. When the child reaches a year in age, some parents still mix the child's dried umbilical cord, saved from birth, with natural red ochre paint and paint it on the child in traditional patterns, as everyone used to do. This ritual coating with the umbilicus helps to link the child permanently to his ancestry and ensure that he will follow the Havasupai way on his journey through life.

Adults rarely use baby talk with children but speak to them in quite adult terms; children of five or six display unusual maturity and sophistication in their conversation. During summer, when school is out, most children of four or older simply leave the home in the morning and do not return until evening, spending most of their day among their peers. They eat at whatever house they find themselves, and any family feeds whoever is present at mealtime as a matter of course.

Despite the permissiveness, there is discipline, based primarily on constant admonition to follow the Havasupai way. Children are brought up to believe that one must share whatever he has to be a good person. Without thinking about it, a child given a cookie will break it into as many pieces as the friends accompanying him. Sometimes this is very difficult for the three- or four-year-old to accept, and the older children are patient and protective with such young ones. A five- or six-year-old girl may receive full responsibility for an infant brother or sister while her parents go to the fields. Older brothers and sisters never seem to resent the presence of younger siblings but seem instead proud of having a baby brother or sister along.

A young child is not permitted to swim or cross the creek unattended by parents or family until he is about five. Though most Havasupai children of four are accomplished swimmers, some very wistful-looking children of this age sit by the creek watching their older friends frolic in the water; you could not drag *them* in beyond a toe or two because they are there without an older brother or sister!

Quite commonly parents do not take full responsibility for their children after infancy but have the grandparents bring them up. This provides a satisfactory arrangement for both parties. The older people have the opportunity to have youngsters around when they most enjoy it, while the younger adults have their chance to pursue a less sedentary life with fewer encumbrances. This system also prevents much of the direct generational rivalry and conflict which our own nuclear families foster. Generally the parents and grandparents share the responsibility of the children, but the parents see the grandparents as a better source of wisdom and instruction because of their age and experience than they as young parents can be.

In part because of this relationship, children feel a relaxed sort of casualness around their parents, and many children address their parents by given name, just as they have always heard other people do. Formal relationship terms are known but seldom used to address anybody except for "grandmother" and rarely "mother" and "father." Even among adults one never hears "Mr. Paya" or "Mr. Watahomigie"; Havasupai has no equivalent for such formal address. All this stems in part from traditional usage when people used to bear but a single name. Not until the coming of the Europeans did single names pass to children as fixed

family names. The children of Hamdèq (Night Hawk), anglicized into Hamidreek, became Austin Hamidreek and Fred Hamidreek; Ijegáva's (Axe's) son the Europeans called Duke Iditicava. Some other children lost the names of these family heads entirely when they arrived at boarding school and received such names as Jones in place of their own Baa 'nyá (Sun Man), but most families still retain Havasupai surnames.

Names originally were a whimsical usage given to characterize some usually humorous feature of an individual, like our nicknames. Wa tahómja, for example, most people also called *Baqí ibè'e* (He totes a woman) because he physically carried home his wife Swejágeja. Today each Havasupai still bears at least one such "Indian name," usually irreverent, which his friends and acquaintances use in preference to his official name. Translated, they mean such things as "Mule," "Back," or "The Swallower." Many older people do not even recognize their ancestors' official names because they never knew them by any but their Havasupai names.

Sexual knowledge is widespread and quite casual from early childhood; the Havasupai view sex as a natural and integral part of their lives. However, they do not approve of sexual promiscuity. Havasupai women observe extremely modest habits and dress.

In recent years the position of Havasupai women in their community has begun to change greatly. The Havasupai, like many North American peoples, used to define sexual roles sharply: women made baskets and pottery; men tanned buckskins, hunted and traded. Farming they shared. Havasupai women were in many ways the property of their husbands, which gave rise to the tension Carma Lee Smithson pointed out in her *Havasupai Woman*:[3]

> Data pertaining both to past and present cases imply that Havasupai women have a basic ambivalence in emotional orientation toward men as individuals and as a class . . . Some women revealed feelings of insecurity and frustration apparently arising from two conditions:
>
> (1) feminine vulnerability to physical abuse by lovers or husbands by reason of inadequacy to cope with superior male strength as the decisive factor in the conflict situations, and
>
> (2) improbability of improving the feminine position, either in a particular relationship or by severing that relationship in favor of another with some other man of the tribe.

The frustration of which she wrote was a feeling certainly intensified by the period of contact with Europeans, when men in particular became morose and dissatisfied with their own lives and began to use alcohol. Traditionally, striking one's wife drew as little approval as striking one's children, but, like all people, Havasupai men soon tended to take out their growing distress on those closest to them.

In any case the demarcation and frustration of which Ms. Smithson wrote in the 1950s is lessening today. Many husbands now consult their wives and take them in as equal partners on important family decisions. No doubt this occurred informally in the past, but it is nearly a matter of course today. In part the increasing number of women's jobs and independent women has brought this change about. Women have been elected to the Tribal Council in recent years and served as its most active members.

The old people are the most prized members of the community, for they are the repository of skills and knowledge that keep the people alive and on the right way in this harsh but beautiful land. Some know dance songs; others know basketry designs or medicinal plants. An elderly blind man is a poet, storyteller, historian and singer of the tribe's songs dating back even to the Ghost Dance era (see p. 63). In him are stored over a century and a half of the tribe's genealogies and recountings of its past. Though he sits much of the day alone in his traditional lodge, yet he keeps current on each day's news from his daily visitors. He likes the old life, does not enjoy talking to the foreigners, and will not permit his photograph to be taken. Many parts of this book are based on his vast memory.

Many other old people were equally well informed but did not in 1974 seem to enjoy so much speaking of the past. They saw too clearly the changes forced upon them by their confinement to Havasu Canyon and found the past a painful subject, so they dwelled in the present.

WINTER BY THE BLUE CREEK

The changes brought during the last two generations had been hard ones, changes that threatened to change the Havasupai themselves into foreigners. The most serious change was the one which forms the subject of this book: the loss of their homeland on the plateau lands above Havasu Canyon. The canyon that summer visitors view as a landlocked Polynesia the Havasupai viewed in winter as a prison. The lack of winter sunlight stops all agriculture from November to March, and the canyon turns from a lush oasis to a barren place of confinement.

Until about forty years ago the Havasupai used to celebrate their harvest in Havasu Canyon with a festival of dancing and songs and foot and horse races and games in September; then they would begin preparations to depart. By October every family of the tribe would make its way to winter homes on the plateau, some twenty and thirty miles distant, and live as hunters and gatherers until March. There they used the snow for water and the juniper and piñon for fuel. This time was so important to the Havasupai they began their year at the time they resumed their winter residence on the plateau.

The Havasupai still carry on the Peach Festival but, until 1975, it no longer signaled the preparation for the winter residence on the plateau. It was even moved up to August, for it had come to serve only as an occasion to sing the old songs and remind the children who they were before they departed for boarding school.

Winter for the Havasupai used to be a time for living in the snow on the vast plateaus surrounding Havasu Canyon. It was the time for telling Coyote stories; by 1974 the grandparents were still reciting the tales of Coyote, but Coyote's trickery and occasional wisdom offered little meaning within the confines of the chill canyon. No longer could the listeners see from the lodge the endless spaces stretching away in which Coyote could work his feats, in which all things might be possible.

In winter, when all the families used to trek joyfully to the plateau for a season in the open, the loss of the past bore down heavily indeed. Fortunately, many who can remember those winters are still living today and able to revive them again. Since three or four families continued their traditional wintering on the plateau in out-of-the-way spots until the Second World War, a few who experienced the plateau winters are people in their thirties. By 1974 only one determined young couple was still able to continue winter-long residence on the plateau, but Congress's restoration of the winter lands held out hope that the Havasupai will once again be able to resume their age-old cycle in 1975.

After the government set up the absurdly small reservation for the Havasupai in 1882, the United States Forest Service and the National Park Service moved onto most of the Havasupai's plateau homeland and began to apply pressure to oust them even from that small part on top they still used. All but one or two Havasupai finally found it too onerous to face the restrictions any longer and interrupted their winter life and the maintenance of their long-preserved water-catchment basins (see p. 12) on the plateau.

In Havasu Canyon, cottonwoods now rise along every fence line. It was not always so; old people remember the canyon floor covered only sparsely with mesquite, desert ironwood and streamside willow, but the people were forced to tend cottonwood like a crop. A family owns each tree; only the few on school land remain open to dispute. About every three years a family would club a tree, cutting out all the limbs from the trunk. After several years' growth the fast-growing softwood will shoot out limbs fifty feet in length and six inches or more in diameter.

These cut limbs the Havasupai sectioned into fence-post lengths and replaced old posts with them. This allowed the new cuttings to dry out. Ideally, after three years those posts that had not sprouted into new trees were pulled out, replaced, and used for firewood. The Havasupai adopted this cycle when they were finally resigned to winter in Havasu Canyon, but there was not enough of the fast-burning cottonwood, and families constantly overcut the three-year cycle, cutting every other year and then every year until whole trees were taken.

The plateau foods that used to sustain them largely gone, the Havasupai were forced to alter their whole survival pattern; for, make no mistake, the plateau meant their survival. During the full summer days when the canyon could be turned to the growth of human food, the Havasupai consumed primarily a vegetarian diet; in the winter they ate primarily meat and wild plateau plants. Where the Havasupai diet once included primarily fats and protein and very little carbohydrates, today it contains much starch. Once the Havasupai shunned all foods but vegetables and mammals of the earth.

Lemuel Paya told it, "We didn't eat birds. I used to tell people at the store, 'I don't use birds because I'm not like cat or eagle.' I tell people that tuna smells like snake. Most of them used to say, 'Ay, I'm like you; you're telling true story.' But now I eat them, too—chickens, eggs. In my idea this will change us. It doesn't seem very good. Some of us act different."

Once subsistence from the available land was no longer possible, the Havasupai had to obtain cash to buy food at the tribal store at prices terribly inflated by prohibitive transportation costs. Even families with extensive farmland had to leave much of it idle or use it for forage in order to devote their time to earning enough cash to feed their families.

In winter, the change in Havasu Canyon is stunning: The sun clears the walls of the canyon by 10 or 10:30 and disappears by 3 or 3:30. The cold seems penetrating in the relative dampness of the canyon. The creek, maintaining its constant 70°, steams in the morning. Snow falls on the plateau above and layers the upper cliffs, but only drizzle reaches the warmer air in the canyon bottom. All birds disappear but the ravens, picking and fighting over shreds in the fields. Turkey-sized ravens line all the bare branches and perch on the fence posts, waiting. Naked branches scratch the air; acrid cottonwood smoke rises only fifty feet to level out against colder air and spread over the canyon floor.

Those brief winter days became a time of droopy horsemen towing cottonwood limbs along the dirt trails ahead of a little roostertail of dust. The canyon had lost its greenery to winter and most of its children to boarding school.

Winter became a time of long evenings by kerosene light and damp cottonwood smoke. A few families still slept on mats on dirt floors. Though new housing and electricity should have changed that for the better for most families, the harsh winters, flimsy houses and inadequate generating capacity often interrupted electrical service and left families plunged in darkness and cold for hours, sometimes for days at a time. When the electricity worked, the evenings were lighted and the homes seemed a place of shelter against the cold night. Then it seemed indeed more efficient to send electrons down a wire than to haul thousands of pounds of fuel oil into the canyon. Even then, on winter nights, everything was bleak and still outside. The cliffs, layered with snow, stood out in ominous threat on moonlit nights. On such nights, as the temperatures began to freeze the accumulated moisture in the rock, one heard the sudden reports of rockfalls all too frequently.

The outdoor life over, people spent the greater part of the day indoors in cramped houses. The young children remaining at home embarked on permanent colds and coughs for the duration; noses became crusted. The horses began to fade from lack of feed; everyone scraped to buy hay from Chino Valley or Bullhead City and hoped it could be delivered over the impossible winter roads.

Winter storms sometimes isolated the canyon altogether. In December 1967 a seven-foot snowfall on the plateau above cut off the Havasupai community for a week. To get through to Havasu Canyon, the Bureau of Indian Affairs finally had to send out a convoy of graders to break a road through to the rim. It took them nearly eighteen hours.

An old Havasupai man, Elmer Watahomigie, had brought a couple of tourists across the plateau from Grand Canyon Village in his pickup truck. The snowstorm began as he returned. Eventually he bogged down in the deepening snow and began walking. Helicopter search parties found his abandoned pickup truck four days later. Remains of Elmer's fires showed that he traveled in a straight line for the canyon, where his father, the subchief Wa tahómja, had long ago shown him some cliffside rock shelters in upper Havasu Canyon. For weeks after, Havasupai horsemen sought any further trace in vain, for no one else knew the location of the rock shelters he must have been bound for. Only seven years later did hunters come upon his remains huddled under a rock overhang in upper Havasu Canyon, only a few miles from an inhabited ranch.

In early 1973 an unusually wet winter cut off the Havasupai again, that time from February 8 to March 19, over a month. A crisis ensued, as the food ran out and then the fuel for the village generators located on the plateau above. Nearly the entire winter the generators had been breaking down, and then they threatened to cut out entirely. The Bureau of Indian Affairs and the Arizona Air National Guard began periodic flights to bring in mail, supplies and fuel to the generators. All this showed more than ever the necessity for tribal plateau land to live on in winter and for an improved road to the rim. The tribal people renewed their requests for improvements to the access roads leading off to their old areas to the east, toward Grand Canyon and Flagstaff. These roads, however, had been abandoned by almost everyone except the Havasupai, and no government agency expressed any interest in improving them because the Havasupai no longer owned the land they ran across.

Even Tribal Council meetings used to take place outside in winter; everyone would gather before the tourist office or tribal store, stamping and puffing in heavy coats and mittens, trying to shuffle papers with numb fingers. It was not until 1967, when a private citizen got the people of Santa Monica, California, to raise 20 percent of the cost of a community building for the Havasupai in order to make government matching funds available, that Council meetings were able to move indoors.

THE PLATEAU, 1974

Despite all obstacles, many Havasupai still managed to pursue some remnant of their dual life as farmers and as plateau people by being nonresident herders. For the government still allowed the Havasupai to keep their animals where they themselves could no longer live. The most enthusiastic farmers usually own the largest numbers of cattle. The Havasupai also keep the horses which they use for riding and packing up on the plateau. Usually each family maintains five or six horses or mules in the canyon and uses them until they run down; the trail is very arduous. They take the tired horses up to the plateau, turn them out to pasture, and catch fresh horses. Each family carries a brand on its stock, and certain stock goes to familiar water "tanks," which they are shown the first time they go to the plateau. At these "tanks" the horseman catches his stock by trapping it inside the fence built around the watering place.

Each wash has little earthen dams built across at several points to form water-catchment reservoirs, or "tanks." These dams both provide seasonal water for the stock and slow further storm erosion of the sparsely vegetated plateau. Many of them began as tiny, handmade water catches where the old people noticed the water did not percolate away. These were then enlarged with horse teams and some later even further enlarged with caterpillars. But one must know the country well to place these basins to avoid locating one over fractured rock where all the water would drain away in a matter of days.

To reach the plateau the Havasupai use their most ancient trails, those to the east, generally the Moqui Trail and less frequently the Topocoba Trail. Both these trails are precarious; at several points the rider must dismount and lead his horse.

Herding is primarily but not exclusively a man's work. Some wives ride along with their men to catch horses and round up cattle. Everyone cherishes the freedom of the plateau and the joy of riding freely in the open. Some of the women are quite apt on horseback and provide needed extra cattle herders. The fathers always make sure to take their sons and grandsons to the plateau and teach them where the springs and trails are located and how to find one's way and survive on the harsh upland.

One cannot fail to feel the release of the plateau. It fills the heart to see the stars sprinkle the magnificent bowl of the night sky with their hard light, to stand on a knoll facing east and watch the sun burst from the edge of the world, to drink coffee by a fire in the still morning, to see horses run with their manes flying, to see sleek coyotes, tentative deer and the fleet antelope, to see the bighorn sheep along the cliffs. The feel of the breeze parching one's face and the very expanse of the land defy description. Low juniper and piñon groves dot the plateau, and caverns honeycomb the limestone strata where old people are buried. Here and there one came upon the ruins of an old brush wickiup or a sturdy log cabin still in sporadic use by a Havasupai family. At Moqui Tank one found a little hamlet of homes, most of which were still frequently visited in 1974. At Wa tahómja's old place by Pasture Wash, his great conical house still stands, open now to the elements. The Havasupai say this was the smaller house; the large one must have been outstanding in size.

Up here nothing is wasted. Closed water barrels adjoin each house to collect rainwater from the roof. Piñon wood is used for pitch, fuel, building and incense, and the seeds for food. Juniper berries can be used for food and the wood for fuel and construction. The middle-aged and older people carry in their heads a cataloguing of the plateau plant life that would impress any botanist.

They can point out literally dozens of varieties and subvarieties of food plants, medicinal herbs and dye plants; they also know very exactly which are poisonous or worthless for human use.[4]

They consume the deer completely. The meat is eaten, the nerve tissue is used to tan the hide, and the hide is used for clothing. In the old days the bones were made into gambling sticks and the antlers used for flint knapping, digging and scratching. The Havasupai also used other game totally in this fashion. They treed porcupine and roasted and ate them. Their quills served as decoration or handiwork tools. Rabbits were probably the commonest source of wintertime food on the plateau, and their hides were sewn together with sinew into robes and blankets.

Nothing was killed and left unused, and nothing was killed when it could not be used. Even snakes were sometimes simply tossed to the side rather than killed. Nature, even in this harsh place, affords survival, but only with care and understanding. The Havasupai bitterly resented the public hunting which the Forest Service allowed within the Havasupai plateau grazing permit areas, for the foreign hunters took the deer of the land without respect for it. A Havasupai huntsman is not a killer; he is a brother to his quarry and takes from need only what comes to him. All the animals must be able to flourish and multiply.

The anthropologists Henry F. Dobyns and Robert C. Euler say Havasupai camps often sat atop knolls where the view was most satisfying,[5] and Lemuel Paya once said his people used to climb such knolls at the end of day and look out over the land, just feeling good to be alive. That satisfaction still floods over one staying at the old places. The Havasupai say this is their true home. Though they are among the most industrious farmers in the West, they believe their first calling is as hunters and herdsmen. They are gatherers who know how to live in a harsh place, and its demands make them as hard as the land they live in.

Up on the plateau, the old houses waited silently through the decades. Wa tahómja and Swèdeva lay in a quiet little cemetery among the juniper-clad hillocks on Park Service land. Short little graves covered children lost too soon. Young wives lay there, gone and returned to the beloved plateau, having left broken men and children behind.

And now the long years of separation have ended. Only by understanding the Havasupai's long attachment to these lands can one know the joy that burst upon them at their return in 1975.

THE PEOPLE

1. Summer Home,
   Havasu Canyon 1973

2. Loren's Home,
   Grand Canyon 1973

3. Amulets: Plateau 1973

4. The Trail to Havasu 1973

5. *Wallin Burro 1973*

6. *Leandra Watahomigie 1973*

8. Jóla 1973

7. New Family:
Roberta and Robert Watahomigie
with Bertina 1973

le

9. *Lonnie's New Face 1969*

le

10. *Marian Paya 1973*

11. *The Ditch 1969*

le

te

12. *After a Swim:*
   Byron Manakaja 1973

le

le

14. *The Avon Lady 1973*

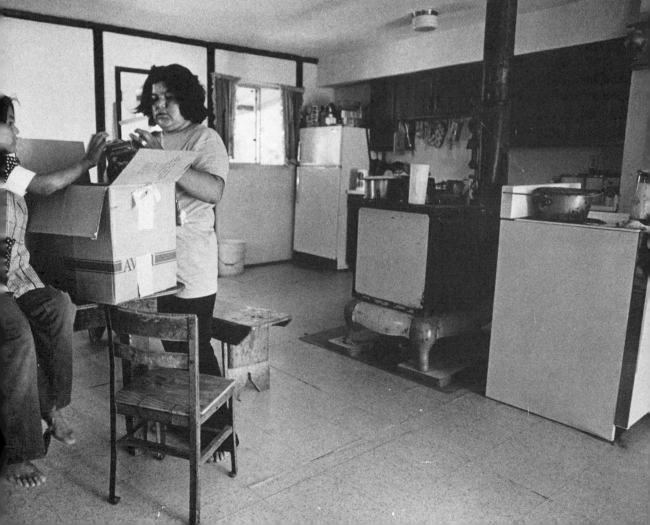

15. *Earl Paya: Plateau 1973*

16. *Grandma: Bernita and Lillian Paya 1973*

17. *Cousins 1973*

18. *Brothers: Gary, Cecil and
Claude Watahomigie 1973*

le

te

*20. Work Break:
Cordell Grounds and
Warren Sinyella 1969*

le

19. *Fydel Jones and Silver 1973*

21. *Valarie's and Carla's Babies 1970*

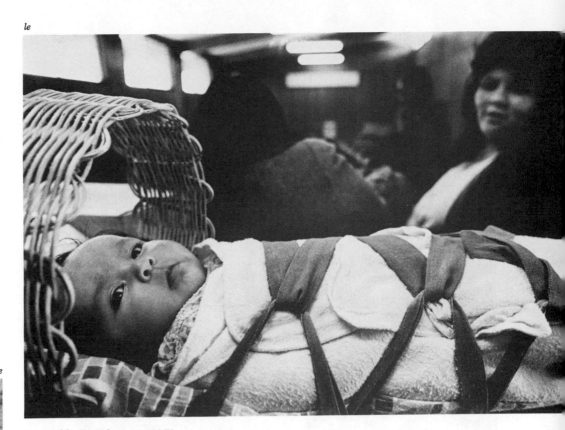

22. *Hilda Watahomigie 1970*

23. *The Parade:*
    Peach Festival 1973

24. *Lee Marshall:*
Havasu Canyon 1973

Burro tanning a buckskin

Courtesy Smithsonian Institution 1900

2.

THE PEOPLE
OF
THE PLATEAU

Although the Havasupai live in one of North America's most inaccessible villages, they are much visited, studied, and written about. At least thirty books and innumerable tracts, articles and theses have covered every aspect of their lives from childbirth to death. The accounts offer a long continuity, as one European observer passed through their territory as early as 1540 and another visited them and wrote of them in 1776. Others passed through on various recorded expeditions and surveys from the mid-nineteenth century on.

But long before they came, other Indian peoples had well-formed impressions of the Havasupai. Dobyns and Euler report that the Hualapai, their western kin, referred to them merely as *nyáv ko pai*, "the people to the east." [6] The Havasupai and the Hualapai speak dialects of one language, and Dobyns and Euler believe they are different bands of the same people, whom they call the Pai, artificially separated by the reservations established for them by the government in 1882 and 1883.

Far to the east, Cushing reported that in 1881 the Zuñi were referring to the Kuhni, as they called the Havasupai, as "little brothers." [7] The Hopi, who adjoined the Havasupai on the east and remained their closest friends for centuries, called them Co'onín and held them in special esteem. The Hopi feel, as do the Havasupai, that man issued from a southern tributary canyon of the Grand Canyon. Accordingly the Havasupai live in a sacred place, home of Masa'u the fire god, and the Hopi Kachina spirit pantheon includes a Co'onín Kachina who bears a stylized resemblance to the Havasupai in traditional ceremonial dress. This Kachina is a guardian and familiar of the sacred canyon and a bringer of corn in the spring.

European concepts of the Havasupai have necessarily grown from a very different experience with them. During the months of summer, most European travelers encountered the Havasupai living together in a village in Havasu Canyon. Few Europeans ever encountered them in winter when they lived as hunters of the uplands, scattered in bands over thousands of square miles. As happened with most North American peoples, the Europeans frequently used others' names for the Havasupai. The Havasupai and apparently the Hualapai as well often received the name travelers heard their Pueblo neighbors to the east call them—all the variants of Co'onín. Another name which appears on many maps to this day as an appellation for the upland Pai people was Yampai, which must have arisen from the Havasupai reply to the question, "Who are you?" or "What group do you belong to?"

"*Nyam báa jujij* (I'm a human being)" is the present pronunciation of the reply, which must have been dutifully taken down as Yampai and may in fact have sounded more like Yampai in an older variant.

Non-Indians' views of the Havasupai have been reflective, more than anything, only of the observers' alien viewpoints and brief contacts with this ancient people. The non-Indian descriptions of them as a canyon-dwelling people miss the essential character of the Havasupai, who conceive of themselves as a people of space.

Rather than canyon dwellers, the Havasupai were until quite recently inhabitants of the vast south rim lands of the great Colorado River canyon. Their lands stretched as far south of the Colorado as the San Francisco Peaks above Flagstaff, and as far as present-day Williams and Seligman. They hunted and traveled on their own lands as far east as the Little Colorado River, and as far west as the present Hualapai Reservation. (This western boundary was ill-defined, as the Havasupai probably did not consider themselves ethnically distinct from their neighbors and relatives, the rest of the Pai bands who today are lumped together as the Hualapai. They were culturally distinct, however.)

One can trace Havasupai history back over more than a millennium.[8] The Havasupai speak a language of the Hokan group, whose peoples apparently included the earliest arrivals to the New World over the Bering Land Bridge some 30,000 years ago or more. Hokan-speaking people, archaeologists think, originally occupied the Great Intermountain Basin north of the Grand Canyon, where they lived as gatherers and hunters of small game. Most of the Hokan speakers even in historic times remain desert and river-bottom dwellers as they were in the Great Basin.

Around 5,000 years ago a massive new migration began crossing into the New World from Siberia bringing new and somewhat alien peoples to compete with those already dwelling in the Americas. These new people included the Athapascans and resembled present-day Asians more nearly in appearance and language than did the long-separated groups of people who had come over earlier. These Athapascans began moving southward, pushing ahead of them such groups as the Shoshonean speakers of the Northwest.

By 4,000 years ago the Shoshoneans had begun to drift southward along the western slope of the Rockies, looking for a new home. As these new immigrants spread into the Great Basin to become the Utes, Paiutes, Gosiutes, Bannock and Shoshone, they gradually forced the Hokan people westward from their Great Basin home, and these Hokan peoples in turn began a long migration which was to leave their remnants all through California, Arizona and northern Mexico.

By looking at the locations of these groups, from the mountain-dwelling Washo, who still live on the rim of their original home, to the Tamaulipecs and Tonkawa, who migrated all the way to northeastern Mexico and Central Texas, we can follow that long migration.

Beginning with the Washo, who live just west of present-day Reno, we find their rivalry with the Shoshonean-speaking Paiute still reflective of their displacement by the latter. From there the Hokan migration left behind in southern Oregon and northern California the Karok, Shasta and the now extinct Yana.°

Farther to the south along the coastal valleys of California the migration left the Pomo, Salinans, Chumash and Diegueño. One group of Hokan people continued southward to populate Baja California. Another large group crossed the Colorado River somewhere near its mouth and divided on the other side, some going eastward into present-day Arizona and the others spreading southward into Mexico.

The group who moved into Arizona moved eastward up the Gila River valley some 2,000 to 3,000 years ago to form the Yuman branch of the Hokan peoples.

These Yumans dwelling along the Gila River became what archaeologists now call the Pioneer Stage of the Hohokám culture (the word is derived from present-day Piman people and means simply "those who have gone") of south

---

° One Yana individual became somewhat famous around the turn of the century. White settlers had killed every other member of his tribe years before, and he could no longer bear the loneliness in the memory-haunted hills. He walked into the town of Oroville expecting death at the hands of the Europeans. He gave his name only as "Ishi," which meant "man" in his language. The anthropologist Alfred L. Kroeber befriended "Ishi" in the cell where the Oroville authorities had placed him for safekeeping and arranged for him to live in The San Francisco Museum until his death from tuberculosis only four years later. Dr. Kroeber's wife later recorded the entire experience movingly in *Ishi in Two Worlds* and *Ishi: Last of His Tribe.*

central Arizona. These pioneer Hohokám lived in small groups, farming and gathering along the riverbanks, dwelling mostly in the pit houses which their forebears had begun building in California to escape the desert heat. The pit house was a shallow excavation with a brush cover nearly flush with the earth's surface. Some researchers suggest that the pit houses later inspired the ceremonial kiva of the Pueblo.[9] The early Yuman Hohokám farmed by using flood waters for irrigation; they made pottery and cremated their dead.

Around the year A.D. 600 a massive unrest began in northern Mexico. Within two centuries north Mexican expansionists had overcome the Yumans of southern Arizona and followed the generalship of the legendary Mixcoatl to the conquest of central Mexico and the foundation of the Toltec dynasty there. Some archaeologists theorize that the north Mexican invaders contributed to Hohokám life many of the Mexican cultural traits which mark the excavated remains of the later Hohokám—the plazas, ceremonial ball courts, irrigation works and truncated temple mounds.

Undoubtedly many of the Yumans stayed in southern Arizona following the Mexican conquest, but many of them fled north and west along the Colorado, where other Yumans already lived. It was this final migration north and finally east again which eventually gave rise to the various Yuman tribes we know today—the Maricópa, Quechán, Cócopah, Mohave, Halchídhoma, Huálapai, Yávapai and Havasúpai. Only the Havasupai among these Yumans developed into semisedentary agriculturalists, using irrigation and crop rotation—Mexican practices—centuries before the arrival of the Europeans. Despite their early departure from the Mexican conquest, the ancestors of the Havasupai adopted and retained these agricultural methods even though they had fled north to escape the people who practiced them.

The leading edge of the Yuman flight had begun to swing back toward the original Great Basin homeland of the Hokán people, and Yumans began to appear on the plateaus south of the Colorado River in north central Arizona by A.D. 600 or 700. Archaeologists call these early arrivals, who were the ancestors of the Havasupai, the Cohonína. The word stems from the response early researchers received from the Hopi upon uncovering abandoned Cohonína sites:

"Who made these?"

"Co'onín."

The word is the Hopi name for the Havasupai.

Unable to cross the Grand Canyon, the Cohonína began settling the uninhabited area they had found to the south of it.

It is worth noting that Havasupai tradition does tell of a northeasterly migration which began in the dim past from Moon Mountain, near Blythe on the Colorado River. The people began moving northeast, passing through present-day Kingman and staying close to the Colorado for water until they began to traverse the difficult canyon country east of Kingman. The people stopped in Matawídita Canyon, northwest of present-day Peach Springs, until a dispute broke out among the groups settled there, and everyone scattered to new homes, among them the people who would become the Havasupai.

Despite its emptiness, the area the early Cohonína/Havasupai had occupied had once supported others. Only a few centuries before the Yumans reached the northern Arizona plateau a group of people had lived there whom archaeologists have simply designated the Desert Culture. They could have been early Shoshoneans who followed the Rockies across the Colorado River and spread into the country of the San Juan and Rio Grande. These people had dwelled in simple rock overhangs and caves and lived as hunters and gatherers. They did not make pottery nor did they farm. The people of the Desert Culture left their tools and artifacts all through the area the Havasupai's ancestors were to make their home, at Red Butte and within the Grand Canyon itself. Some of the stick figurines left there by those early people date back nearly 4,000 years.

Immediately prior to the arrival of the Cohonína a new culture of considerable importance developed from the Desert Culture in the area just east of the Grand Canyon, a culture archaeologists have named the Anasazi. The Anasazi apparently developed around the beginning of the Christian era, and by the time of the Cohonína arrival six centuries later they were beginning to use bows, make pottery, live in pit houses, and follow the Mexican practices of agriculture, weaving cloth and making feather robes.

Apparently the influence of Mexican societies was reaching the Anasazi through the Hohokám to the south, who traded indirectly with the Anasazi through a group of people called the Sinagua living south of the San Francisco Peaks.

As the Cohonína arrived, the Anasazi were in the process of forming the Pueblo stage of their society, when the pit houses gave way to newer Mexican-type masonry houses. The incipient Pueblo apparently felt the venerable pit house represented a sacred form of construction, and the pit house became ceremony's dwelling place as the kiva. It was these Pueblo Anasazi with whom the Cohonína were most friendly and from whom the Cohonína absorbed many Mexican influences.

It now seems quite likely that the Cohonína/Havasupai had contact directly or indirectly through the Pueblo with societies as distant as the Mexican civilizations. Traditional Havasupai stories tell of traveling to lands where parrots and monkeys lived. George Wharton James also tells of "an interesting Havasupai basket in my own collection, the design of which is . . . horizontal zig-zags . . . these zig-zags, however, all start from near the center, and at the beginning of each is a sort of imperfect parallelogram, which is clearly a head. The weaver told me that these were four plumed serpents, and that the basket was used to carry the sacred meal which was sprinkled at a certain shrine, the serpent being the guardian of their sources." [10] This concept certainly stems ultimately from the south Mexican Quetzalcoatl, a figure who also appeared among the Hopi, the westernmost Pueblo, as Bálölökong.

Dendronologists believe northern Arizona once received more water than it does now, making agriculture possible, even on the uplands. Over the next four centuries the Cohonína took advantage of the more favorable climate and built many more-or-less permanent villages using the stone construction of their

Pueblo neighbors and at times even incorporating the kiva, whose inspiration they themselves had brought from California centuries before.

The Cohonína had brought Yuman pottery making north with them from the Gila River, and they left their plain gray-brown ware occasionally decorated with effaceable red ochre at many sites in the area. The potter created this ware by holding inside the unfired pot a piece of wood or stone to serve as an anvil, then striking the coils of the unfired clay from the outside with a flat stick to flatten them into a smooth surface.

By 1100 Cohonína society was well established in the area, with settlements well over toward the Little Colorado River. Archaeologists have found one of their villages as far east as Willow Spring, north of Tuba City. The Cohonína may even have accomplished the crossing of the Grand Canyon, for Euler tells of the remains of a Pueblo or a Cohonína bridge used to complete a trail crossing the Colorado River.[11]

For by 1100 some of the Cohonína had located the various springs and creeks flowing at the lower elevations of the washes and canyons falling northward into the Colorado River. Probably at that time they began to found seasonal settlements at some of these places, such as Havasu Canyon. Though Havasupai tradition credits Burro's father with being the first to settle at Indian Gardens east of Havasu Canyon, in 1830, more likely his Cohonína ancestors had long preceded him there.

Then, dendronologists detect that from 1100 to 1300 the life-giving rains dwindled over the northern plateaus, culminating in what they say they can discern as a terrible drought from 1276 to 1299. Desperate pressures and migrations began within the area. Only a century or two earlier the first of the Athapascans had begun moving southward into the land of the Pueblo, and now the failing climate drove many other invaders from the south and west to aggression. During this time of desperation the Cohonína may well have begun using the Mexican/Pueblo practice of irrigation and adopted as well the Pueblo ceremonial encouragements of the heavens to bring back the disappearing rains. When the spirits offered too little relief from the endless sun, the Cohonína must have turned more and more to irrigation farming, possibly constructing some of their present irrigation works at the end of the thirteenth century.

For a time the Cohonína had tried retreating to the well-watered northern slopes of the San Francisco Peaks to build their homes. About 1300 new Cohonína construction ceased. They seemed to have vanished without a trace. For years this provided researchers only an enigma until the work of archaeologist Douglas Schwartz in the 1950s and of archaeologist/anthropologist Robert Euler in the 1960s showed the Cohonína had indeed survived—as the people who call themselves *ha vasúa báaja*.[12]

What happened was this: By 1300 the drying plateau could no longer support summertime life. The competition for the San Francisco Peaks became too fierce for the apparently peaceable Cohonína, so to carry on their agricultural pursuits during the dry summers they began to retreat to the lower drainages they had discovered several centuries before.

Havasupai legend tells it that the people who departed Matawídita (see p. 40) continued their migration toward the sunrise until they came upon *Havasúa* (Havasu Creek). There they remained for many generations until their population grew beyond the resources of the canyon, and a large group of them elected to continue their drift to the east. Today some say this departing group was under the leadership of Hu gemáta (Mud Head). Before departing, Hu gemáta left a corn sign and a horse sign [visible as natural markings hundreds of feet up on the cliffs over Havasu Creek] for the people who were to stay behind so these things would always be available to those in the canyon [the horse sign is obviously a later addition to the legend, since the Havasupai would have had no horses at that time]. As Hu gemáta's group departed to the east, one couple among them regretted the departure; they looked back as they climbed over the rocks. They changed to stone and still stand today looking down over their beloved canyon. The rest of the group moved on eastward and was never seen again.

The People
of
The Plateau

Later, those remaining around *Havasúa* worried that they had still received no sign that their own long wanderings were to end there. They watched and watched for a sign, loath to leave, until finally they decided they themselves must move on. As the sad group started out, a child began to cry. When the group stopped, the child quieted and remained calm until they began moving again. The child had given them the sign; the long migration was over. The Havasupai were home.

Present-day Havasupai show little surprise to learn that tribes as distant as the Tonkawa speak languages related to their own. They say this merely explains what became of those who continued to the east with Hu gemáta.

In fact, the Havasupai/Cohonína were likely not the only occupants of Havasu Canyon during their early days of settlement there. Now-extinct groups from the west and south joined the Cohonína living in Havasu Canyon and other watered areas. Havasupai legend does tell of such a time of joint occupation of the canyon. By 1400 the visitors or invaders (it is not clear which at this distance) departed or were driven out except for some people archaeologists call the Cerbat, who had come from the area around present-day Kingman and who may well be the direct ancestors of the Hualapai. Some Cerbat stayed among the Cohonína and joined them to become what today we call the Havasupai. Certain Cohonína practices carried through the alliance unchanged; in 1900 the Havasupai were still making plain pottery in the same fashion as their Cohonína forebears had done so many centuries earlier.

On the whole, however, the Cohonína so revolutionized their life style by 1400 that they became all but unrecognizable to the archaeologist examining their earlier constructions. The plateau could no longer provide them year-round sustenance, and finally all of the Cohonína/Havasupai became seasonal users of the plateau, building only the temporary wickiups and hogans that the Havasupai build to the present day. The annual cycle of the Havasupai had begun.

In autumn, after the late-summer rains, the Havasupai returned to their old plateau home to live through the winter, when snow could provide water and hold game tracks for the hunter. During this frigid season the Havasupai could annually relive, for a few months, the lives of their ancestors. Indeed, one 1900 observer recounts poignantly their anticipation of this round:

> As jealously as the Havasupai guarded their canyon and as passionately as they loved it, the tang of autumn in the air turned their thoughts to a winter home on the mesa, and started them packing their possessions with a happy abandon. All summer they had planned for this—harvesting, preserving their food, and setting aside a portion to take with them . . . Nothing could be permitted to interfere with this jaunt to the outside . . . when I saw their childish delight as they made their departure, ponies loaded with cumbersome bundles, I knew that they were motivated by the very human desire for change, to get outside, where they could look about, with the full sweep of the vaulted sky above, with endless miles in which to wander.
>
> Not an Indian who was physically able to ride but longed for this trip to the mesa.[13]

Each family had designated spots where they wintered. We might even speculate whether these represented the ancient division between the Cohonína and the Cerbat; might those families who winter to the east of Havasu Canyon be descended from the original Cohonína and those on the west from the Cerbat? Of course any such division could no longer be traced among the people themselves, due to the frequency of cross-canyon marriages.

Since 1400 the plateau has remained dry, though large stands of ponderosa, juniper and piñon have survived the desiccation at higher elevations. As a result the Havasupai were unable to return to permanent life on the plateau. Before long another cataclysm stopped even much of their seasonal use of the plateau as well.

In the sixteenth century the first of the flood of strange-looking aliens from another world appeared on the horizon. In 1527 the king of Spain had sent an expedition under Pánfilo de Narváez into the continent from Florida. Four members of the expedition, which disintegrated before it even reached the Mobile River, lived through eight years of captivity and bewilderment before finally reaching another Spanish settlement near Mazatlán! Two of them, Alvar Núñez Cabeza de Vaca and the African slave Esteban, told of great and wealthy cities they had seen during their wanderings. Their stories excited the Spaniards, already inflamed by fables of untold wealth, and Antonio de Mendoza sent Esteban back to find the golden cities. Esteban reached the Zuñi pueblo of Hawikah, apparently the inspiration for his tale of riches, but the Zuñi put him to death upon his reappearance. Esteban's companion, Fray Marcos (Marcos de Niza), escaped and reported to Mendoza that Hawikah was certainly one of the seven golden cities.

Early in 1540 Mendoza sent an expedition under Francisco Vásquez de Coronado toward southern Arizona to seek the golden cities. Not until July did they reach Hawikah, but the inspiration for Esteban's boasts proved, in its dusty reality, unrecognizable to the Spaniards. The Zuñi, with tales of wealth beyond the mountains, encouraged the Spaniards to move on, but the Spaniards made Hawikah their base and merely sent forays northward.

Later in the year the Zuñi told of a wondrous set of villages called Tusayán to the north occupied by a warlike people, and Pedro de Tovar led a group of Coronado's men there. Pedro de Castañeda, a member of the party, recorded that they entered the area quietly and found the farms between the villages idle at that time of year. Finally they drew up under the edge of one of the Tusayán villages at nightfall and heard people talking. The next morning the villagers, who were probably Hopi but who may have included Havasupai, discovered the Spaniards and came out drawn up in regular battle lines with bows, shields and clubs. The Spaniards charged and scattered the inhabitants of Tusayán, who fled amazed before the Spanish horses. The people decided to make peace and gave the Spaniards buckskins, corn and piñon nuts of their own, and some cloth and turquoise gained by trade. They then told Tovar about a great river in a great gorge but a few miles distant and offered to lead García López de Cárdenas and a party to this place.

After an exaggeratedly long journey Cárdenas reached the river with his guides, who told him that a group of very large-bodied people—the Havasupai— made homes farther down the river. The Spanish tried unsuccessfully to reach the river while the people of Tusayán, who knew numerous trails to it, offered no advice. They did eventually point out to the Spaniards, from a distance, one salt deposit in the canyon.

After this expedition the Spanish party gave up their dream of gold and spent the winter of 1540–1541 in what is present-day Albuquerque. In the spring the Pueblo people there rid themselves of the Spaniards by telling of untold wealth far to the northeast, a tale that led Coronado's men clear into the Kansas plains before they finally gave up and returned to Mexico in 1542.

Though the Coronado expedition was totally unproductive from the Spanish viewpoint, this earliest European venture into the Grand Canyon country brought what was to become the mainstay of Indian life and a major source of mobility to the Havasupai and others—the horse. Some of the Spanish mounts were lost during the expedition, and the people who captured them were not long in learning how to use them well.

By 1598 the Spanish had colonized New Mexico and began to extend their rule westward over the Hopi. This eventually led to the great Pueblo revolt of 1680, when nearly all the villages of the Southwest rose up to slay the Spaniards and drive any survivors from the area for almost a decade. After that event some of the Hopi feared reprisal and fled to stay for a time with their Havasupai friends beyond the Little Colorado River.

A century later, in 1776, the Spanish priest Francisco Garcés traveled westward through Havasupai territory in the company of Mohave and Hualapai guides. He descended into their Havasu Canyon farms, where he wrote he was struck by the Havasupai's industry and fair appearance. Later Garcés departed eastward in the company of a *"jabesua"* guide and traveled out over the present Moqui Trail headed for the Hopi mesas, moving over the terrible waterless hills and canyons of the Little Colorado region. Garcés recorded that after crossing the Little Colorado and proceeding some eight miles up what must have been Moencopi Wash he came upon another Havasupai settlement of some 30 people, whose headman was brother to his Havasupai guide. This headman, Garcés wrote, affected a goatee, a usage found yet among the Havasupai. Later two Havasupai traders showed Garcés the trail to the Mohave all the way from Havasu Canyon. Garcés established a mission on the lower Gila, and it was there that the Mohave killed him in 1781.

All through that century northern Arizona had undergone a series of increasingly serious droughts. Finally a three-year drought began after Garcés's visit which lasted into 1780 and starved hundreds of Hopi people and forced the remainder away from their mesa sanctuaries. The Spanish governor of New Mexico reported in 1780 that fully 90 percent of them had left the mesas. Certainly some of these had trekked westward seeking refuge among their Havasupai neighbors in their watered springs and canyons.

Agriculture and especially irrigation farming had become increasingly difficult for the Hopi inhabitants of the dry country east of the Grand Canyon, for the rivers and washes had finally cut too deeply into the dry country to irrigate the fields, which now lay above the high-water level.

Undoubtedly during the 1780 Hopi visitation the Havasupai received the peaches which so many visitors to Havasu Canyon have remarked on. The source of Havasupai peaches seems obvious enough from the Havasupai word for peach: *thibála.* The Hopi word is *sipála.*

During the visitation the Havasupai may also have elaborated their irrigation works, where they were not already completed, with Hopi technical assistance. The 1780 visitation certainly reinforced a tendency of considerable importance in Havasupai life by that time—the growing Pueblo character of the Havasupai, which Garcés had already noted and later observers remarked upon as well. By the nineteenth century the Havasupai had already begun their own kachina dances and rain dances and told a number of parallel legends. In this sense the Havasupai became culturally, if not ethnically, distinct from the Hualapai.

Yet, close as the Havasupai and Hopi felt toward one another, they could not marry each other, because the newly married among the Havasupai, though they initially stayed with the wife's people, finally settled among the husband's people. With the Hopi they were to stay with the wife's people. A Havasupai-Hopi union would dictate that one partner would have to surrender his or her tradition in making a choice of where to live. Even today such a marriage is somewhat unusual, though both tribes continue to hold each other in the highest regard.

For the next half century the Havasupai saw little more of Europeans until a trapper or two entered their territory. But by the 1850s the invasion began in earnest, this time led by army river and railroad surveyors and newly arriving settlers. That begins another era in Havasupai history, one well recorded in written records.[14]

47

The People
of
The Plateau

3.
THE
INVASION
BEGINS

Until fully 1860 the Havasupai continued to live their traditional life with but few changes, one being the introduction of horses and cattle sometime during the seventeenth century, we would guess, via the Rio Grande Pueblos. Horses may not have been used as a primary mode of transportation until nearly the nineteenth century, however, with most people walking to get places in the arduous terrain. Havasupai informants can remember even in the 1890s walking thirty miles in a day as often as riding it. When the snow was deep, the Havasupai were often compelled to travel on foot.

The Havasupai still followed the time-honored annual round which they had begun around 1300. At the beginning of their year in late October or early November families departed the lower canyons for their plateau homesites, carrying with them enough foodstuffs from the summer produce to last them only a short while. They did not take all their food. According to Spier:

Hmány gejáa Havasupai headman: 1900–1942

Courtesy Southwest Museum 1898

When going up to the plateau for the winter, two small sacks of corn are carried along; they return for more as it is needed. The corn may be stored in three chambers: that in the first is eaten during the winter, that of the second during the spring planting period, and of the third only a little may be eaten, not all. "We don't eat it all; we don't plant it all." This remainder is saved against the contingency of flood, etc.[15]

Upon reaching the plateau many families would travel to Pasture Wash, an important plateau farming area to the east of Cataract Canyon, to harvest seeds placed in the ground at the beginning of the previous spring and brought to fruition by the summer rains. As the cold weather set in, families began to follow the piñon harvests about, primarily between Big Tank and Moqui Tank. By the first snows the game would be fat, and Havasupai informants say this is the only time one should kill a deer. Most families would kill but two or three deer a winter and live on the dried venison and rabbits and porcupine the rest of the winter. Birds were not eaten.

By February the thaw would begin; families would place seeds in the ground at Pasture Wash and return to Indian Gardens, Santa Maria Spring, Havasu Canyon, Mohawk Canyon and National Canyon. Some few families remained out to obtain red ochre paint used as a body paint for therapeutic and ceremonial purposes and salt. Then they traveled during this relatively moist time to attend the Hopi bean dances and trade baskets, buckskins, red paint, mescal, corn, salt and shells to the Hopi. The Havasupai obtained shells by trading with tribes west of them. The Havasupai red paint was held sacred by many Indian people for ceremonial body painting and often found its way as far east as the Mississippi. The Havasupai and Hualapai were especially noted for their soft white buckskins, and the Hopi used Havasupai baskets in many of their ceremonies. In return the Havasupai would receive jewelry, blankets, pottery and horses. Some of the Havasupai traders and their families would remain among the Hopi for as long as a year before returning. Havasupai informants say their parents and grandparents used to possess exquisite Hopi and Navajo jewelry, but the jewelry was buried with them. The Havasupai-Hopi trade tie has been short-circuited by the Europeans for decades now.

Meanwhile, the rest of the Havasupai, having returned to the lower, watered elevations bordering the Grand Canyon, had begun planting, and the time Spier called "the fullest of the year" began: "Morning finds the families in the fields; the heat of the afternoon (never excessive) is spent in the sweatlodge or at some favorite spot gambling and gossiping. Corn ripens throughout the summer, from the middle of June until September." [16]

Nearly all the tribe was gathered together in Havasu Canyon for the summer. Only gathering expeditions left the canyon for any appreciable time to obtain mescal, or agave, for roasting from the dry esplanade above their canyon and blazing star (silè'e) seeds for roasting and grinding into meal from the plateau in late May and early June. Late in the summer they harvested yucca fruit. Cushing found it "remarkable" that the Havasupai, proficient hunters, became almost exclusively vegetarian during the summer.[17] Havasupai informants say they also used to keep hawks and eagles in the canyon for their plumes as the Pueblo to the east did.

By the end of August nearly all the harvests were in, and the Havasupai would hold their Peach Festival, as they do to this day. To this they would invite their friends from the surrounding area, and contemporary accounts indicate the Hopi, Hualapai and even the Navajo regularly attended and sometimes even the distant Zuñi. The Havasupai occasionally used to affect a whipper kachina dancer to cajole any nondancers into joining the round dance, and a number of individuals still remember dancing as the kachina. The festival was secular and celebrated another bountiful harvest. In this regard Spier notes, "The Havasupai are inordinately proud of their abundant harvests and their superiority in this regard to the Walapai, Navaho and Paiute." [18]

Although Alfred Whiting has noted that the Havasupai considered themselves only secondarily as farmers, feeling that their home was really still on the plateau,[19] they were extremely resourceful at agriculture, as Cushing noted in 1882:

> The engineering skill and enterprise of this little nation are marvelous. Although their appliances are rude, they are able to construct large dams, and dig or build deep irrigating canals, or durable aqueducts, which often pass through hills, or follow considerable heights along shelves of rock or talus at the bases of the rugged and crooked walls of the cañon. The acequias, which have their fountain-heads in these canals and viaducts, are wonders of intricacy and regularity; yet on uneven ground are laid out in nice recognition of and conformity to unevenness and change of level in the surface they are designed to water.[20]

By October, as the weather began to cool and the days to shorten, the families prepared again for departure. Though the winters in the canyon were not in themselves unbearable, the high walls made the days as brief as five to six hours, thus limiting agriculture by lack of sunlight. The principal reason the Havasupai gave for abandoning the canyon in winter was the lack of firewood, which made departure imperative. Until 1900 few if any cottonwoods grew in the canyon, which except for the willows along the creek supported largely mesquite and sage.

During the nineteenth century the Havasupai had been subject to periodic raids from the Yavapai, their enemies to the south. Oral tradition repeated by Sinyella to Leslie Spier in 1918 placed one such raid, a small one, some time around 1840. Then a larger raid followed in 1855 where the Havasupai repulsed some 20 Yavapai raiders from Havasu Canyon. Finally a very large raiding party which Sinyella estimated at some 200 Yavapai attacked the canyon around 1862 by descending the present "Apache" (as the Havasupai and Hualapai frequently designated their Yavapai colinguists) trail at night. After some days of battling

within the canyon, the Yavapai retreated up Havasu Canyon and finally gave up the fight and went home.

By the 1850s the first groups of government surveyors and exploration teams had begun to move through Havasupai territory searching for a transcontinental railroad right of way. One man even proposed to locate a railroad along the floor of the Grand Canyon! The Sitgreaves expedition exploring the Colorado River in 1851 came through Havasupai territory. Captain Sitgreaves told of the theft of some of his mules by "Cosninos" and reported seeing a party of Havasupai in Deadman's Wash, northeast of Flagstaff.

In 1858 the army outfitted a small steamboat which they hoped could navigate the length of the Colorado River, one of the most interesting schemes to be attempted on the Colorado. The expedition, commanded by Lieutenant Joseph Christmas Ives, spent two months hauling the small vessel against the muddy torrent until they reached the present location of Boulder Dam and gave up the undertaking.

Partway back to Fort Yuma word reached the Ives party of a violent outbreak among the Mohave, one that was eventually to result in their confinement and the beginnings of the Hualapai Wars of 1866–1869. Ives split his men; one group continued navigating to Fort Yuma while Ives and the rest set out overland toward the Hopi country with Mohave guides. By the end of March 1858 Ives encountered the first Hualapai, who were very evasive about showing Ives and his men through their country. By April they had reached the Havasupai country and found it deserted, as the Havasupai had returned to their canyon farms for the summer. After a tortuous dry march from what were probably the Black Tanks, Ives and his men reached the place where the Hualapai foot trail began down from the rim toward Havasu Canyon. Ives found the mules could not pass and sent them back; the men continued on foot until they encountered Ii gesbéva [the Ladder], where the trail seemed to terminate in an abrupt, forty-foot precipice. Finally Egloffstein, the topographer accompanying Ives, discovered a wooden ladder under the lip of the precipice and attempted to descend.

The ladder broke under him, but Egloffstein fell without harm to the canyon bottom. He decided to investigate while the others waited. He shortly encountered a creek and a village of people with a little pocket of canyon-bottom farmlands. After a short visit in the village, he returned to the broken ladder and his companions hauled him up with a rope of knotted musket slings. The Havasupai who accompanied Egloffstein back declined to ascend the rope with him, however, and the party returned alone up the canyon in the dark. Later, upon leaving Havasu Canyon and heading on east, Ives came upon a vacant Havasupai winter camp over toward the Little Colorado River. In May the group reached Fort Defiance in what by that time had become Navajo country.

Jacob Hamblin traveled to the Havasupai's summer home in 1863, searching for converts to the Mormon faith. Hamblin's party apparently descended the Hualapai Canyon trail to the Havasupai village, where, according to Cushing, "The Indians received the little band of Saints suspiciously, and listened gravely to their preaching; then, rising, escorted them to the trail leading [eastward] out of the canyon, and directed them on their way, but assured them that their visit might be repeated only under penalty of death." [21]

On March 3, 1865, Congress set aside "all that part of the public domain in the Territory of Arizona, lying west of a direct line from half-way bend to Corner Rock on the Colorado River, containing about seventy-five thousand acres of land . . . for an Indian reservation for the Indians of said river and its tributaries." Former Arizona Indian agent Charles D. Poston argued before Congress that the idea was to remove all Arizona's Indians to this reservation, including the Hualapai and by implication the Havasupai. Poston reported he had called a council of the confederated tribes of the Colorado and told them "they should abandon" their lands and confine themselves to the place proposed for a reservation on the Colorado River. The Indians present, who did not include the Havasupai, made no agreement to this proposal.

By 1864 the raids of Kit Carson on Navajo homelands in Cañon de Chelly and elsewhere had begun to disrupt the Navajo most seriously, and they began to wander and flee outside their accustomed range. Sinyella first reported seeing the Navajo at that time, when a large party of them were camped on both sides of the Little Colorado in 1864.

The Navajo became more and more frequent visitors on lands to the west of their former range, and the trade values reported by Spier for Havasupai buckskins and foodstuffs to the Navajo reflect as much as anything the extreme destitution of the Navajo at that time. Two Havasupai buckskins and a little corn would buy a horse from the Navajo, as would a very large burden basket of shelled corn. It took seven or eight buckskins to buy a horse from the Hopi. Before long the Navajo had begun to settle permanently around the Hopi mesas and on the west-side desert flats and canyons sloping into the Little Colorado River.

Even then the Navajo were no strangers to the Havasupai, for around 1840 a party of Navajo had captured a Havasupai boy and raised him as a Navajo in ignorance of his real origin. Not until he was grown did a visiting Hopi trader tell him in confidence that he was really Havasupai. The boy let the Hopi know he wished to return to his true people, so the Hopi agreed to describe how to find the road westward to the distant Havasupai winter camps at Rain Tank. He warned the boy that he dressed like a Navajo and could speak no Havasupai, so they might kill him. The Hopi told him to approach the Havasupai slowly and remain on his horse with his arms folded across his chest and keep his head down and cry. Then the Havasupai would know him and take him in.

The captured boy later sneaked away from the Navajo and followed the trail to Rain Tank as the Hopi had directed him. He approached the Havasupai there as he had been instructed, and they understood he was their lost one. The boy stayed with Ákaba, and the Havasupai called them brothers. Many years later "The Navajo," as the Havasupai had come to call the lost one, was riding

across the plateau with some other Havasupai men. Their horses became so tired they were forced to stop for the night. There by the fire "The Navajo" began to sing a strange song the Havasupai had never heard before. "The Navajo" told them it had come back to him across the many winters since the days of his childhood among the Navajo. He explained to them it was a song to the horses to make them fast and tireless. The group stayed up all night while "The Navajo" instructed them in the song. The Havasupai still keep it today.

On July 22, 1866, Congress acted to convey to the Atlantic & Pacific Railroad a right of way across the west and the odd sections of land 40 miles outwards from the right of way. These lands were offered as an indemnity grant for the railroad company to sell to settlers in order to finance the railroad construction. Much of the railroad lay squarely through Indian territory in Oklahoma, New Mexico and Arizona. Where settlers already owned lands within the 40-mile place limit, the railroad company was to be indemnified with lands lying beyond the 40-mile limit. Through Havasupai territory the railroad was indemnified beyond the 40-mile limit with every other section of the Havasupai northwestern range in what would correspond roughly to the south rim portion of the former Grand Canyon National Monument. In Hualapai country the railroad was indemnified with every other section of Hualapai land right through the heart of it.

Around this same year, 1866, according to Sinyella, the Yavapai sent an emissary to make peace with the Havasupai, saying, "We will all be friends with one another. It is not right for us to kill each other; our language is nearly the same. It is not right; we ought to stop and be friends." Sinyella said the Havasupai agreed to this, and the Yavapai began to make trading visits.

In 1869 or 1870 a party of Havasupai was visiting Oraibi when a party of Yavapai arrived. The Havasupai group, which included Sinyella's father and Wa sgwívema, the head chief, used the opportunity to reaffirm their friendly intentions toward the Yavapai. According to Sinyella the Yavapai leader said, "We used to fight Mohave, Walapai, Havasupai, Navajo and . . . the Hopi. We will not do that any more." Apparently from that time all hostilities between the Havasupai and Yavapai ended.

Other pressures dictated this peace, for the so-called Walapai Wars had just taken place from 1866 to 1869. The beginnings of this conflict lay back in 1858, when the Mohave of the lower Colorado attacked a wagon train and turned it back to New Mexico. The army's Department of California dispatched a military expedition against the Mohave and confined them to Fort Mohave, along the lower Colorado. With the beginning of the Civil War regular army units left California volunteers in charge of the defeated Mohave. Some of these volunteers began to do some prospecting to the northeast in Pai territory. Apparently one of these prospectors murdered the Hualapai subchief, Wauba Yuma, in 1866. The Hualapai reacted by undertaking small reprisal raids against miners and prospectors within their territory. By this time the Civil War had terminated, and regular troops were released to meet this threat to white occupation of Hualapai territory.

The war went on for three years, mostly in the form of skirmishes but with a few actions that we would now call massacres.

The Hualapai organized themselves into a fairly formidable fighting force before their eventual defeat. Dobyns and Euler report that in one battle, in early June 1867, they engaged Fort Mohave troops for nine hours. The Hualapai force was estimated at 250 men. Despite their wide separation over a vast area and the dispersed nature of their political system the Pai were remarkably successful, Dobyns and Euler write, in amassing fighting forces that totaled as much as 25 percent of their total population.[22] After their eventual surrender in 1869, the army began, in 1871, to concentrate the defeated Hualapai in a one-square-mile compound at Camp Beale Springs, north of present-day Kingman.

On November 21, 1871, Major General Schofield, Commander of the Military Division of the Pacific, issued an order declaring all Indians not found on their reservation to be "hostile." Now the issue was forced. A number of Hualapai fled into the canyons of the Havasupai, as had the Navajo ten years before and the Hopi nearly a century earlier during a severe drought. Practically all the Hualapai were rounded up in 1874, however, and herded to La Paz (near present-day Ehrenburg), where Congress had established the Colorado River Reservation in 1865. Within a few months the Hualapai children were dying of disease and hunger, while the adults, lifelong mountain and upland plains dwellers, were weakening in the unaccustomed heat and humidity. This on what Poston had characterized to Congress as "one hundred and twenty thousand square miles, full of mines and rich enough to pay the public debt of the United States." Poston had also justified his failure to obtain an agreement to this reservation by informing Congress that at the Council to propose the notion, "These Indians there assembled were willing, for a small amount of beef and flour, to have signed any treaty which it had been my pleasure to write."

When spring 1875 arrived the Hualapai confined at La Paz gathered together and simply walked away, carrying their children and old people. They trudged for days over burning sagebrush flats until they reached the pine-clad hills of their sacred lands. Informants remembering the long walk said they began to run, laughing and shouting, as they neared their old homesites.

It could never be the same again; according to Dobyns and Euler, "all possibility of re-establishing the aboriginal economic patterns in their home ranges had vanished because of Anglo-American settlement during their absence." [23]

After the Hualapai pilgrimage the army's Department of Arizona pleaded with Washington to establish some sort of reservation for the Hualapai within their home range but could get no response. Finally, the military simply established a military reservation for them on July 8, 1881, until President Arthur finally recognized the *fait accompli* and established the Hualapai Indian Reservation by Executive Order, January 4, 1883.

And even then the whirlwind was preparing to descend upon the Havasupai, for General Wilcox, Commander of the Department of Arizona, reported in 1877 that the Havasupai had "never been under control." Adding to

his concern was the increasing number of prospectors and miners casting eyes on the Grand Canyon. Several prospectors began working in Havasu Canyon.°

Moreover, parties of Havasupai hunters and gatherers had already experienced a number of incidents with white cattlemen occupying their winter range. Billy Burro reported in 1950 that in his boyhood "these white would some time come, would bar the Supais from the water holes, the grazing lands, all of that . . . homesteaders and cattle owners put in lines, saying that they are not to roam that country any more." Mary Wescògame similarly reported, "all at once just out from nowhere there was white ranchers, homesteaders coming to this part of the country; just barred them against everything, water holes. They would even tell them to get out; wouldn't give them no time . . . The Havasupai people want to get back here to the country they thought belonged to them. They want to bring some horses here; the whites told them to get out, never to come back . . . They were driven out, but they kept coming back." [24] General Wilcox may also have been concerned to head off any Havasupai reprisals against the new white occupants of Havasupai territory.

In any case, Arizona Governor John C. Fremont added his voice to Wilcox's. On June 2, 1880, Fremont wrote the Commissioner of Indian Affairs to say that silver-bearing ore had been discovered in Carbonate Canyon along Havasu Creek and that the only approach to this ore would be through the Havasupai settlement. To prevent trouble Fremont suggested that the Commissioner establish for them a reservation beginning two miles downstream of the highest fall and extending ten miles upstream of it, with a width one mile on each side of the creek.

Within a week President Rutherford B. Hayes issued his June 8, 1880, Executive Order reserving a reservation twelve miles long and two and a half miles on each side of the creek. On November 23, 1880, President Hayes was forced to correct the June 8 order as he had inadvertently reversed north and south compass directions in the original order. The five-by-twelve-mile parallelogram enclosed only the farms in Havasu Canyon and a few surrounding headlands.

The army was ordered to send out a surveying party to place the boundaries of the new reservation, and one accordingly went out under the command of Lieut. Colonel W. R. Price to make its survey according to the 1880 order. The party arrived in midsummer of 1881, completed its work, and departed only a few days before Frank H. Cushing arrived for his visit. The army's report of the survey limns only a terrible compounding of the first injustice:

° A party led by Charles Spencer entered Havasu Canyon in 1875, and another led by the former sailor James Mooney visited in 1880. In attempting to descend the third and highest waterfall beyond the Havasupai village, however, Mooney fell to his death. Ten months later his companions returned to find him almost perfectly preserved in lime deposited by the waterfall's spray; they buried him on an island just below it. They then commenced silver and lead mining activities below this fall. George Wharton James reported in 1900 that other unnamed prospectors had started mining operations in the lower canyon as well.

To the Asst. Adj. General:

Sir:

I have the honor to report that, in compliance with par. VI, S. I. No. W. C. S., Hq., D. A., I have "established boundaries of such tracts of land as will secure to the Yavai Suppai Indians the continued possession of their present settlements with improvements therein."

These Indians occupy the bottom lands of a deep cañon whose walls, having a total depth of not less than two thousand feet, are of three cliffs nearly perpendicular, with two benches, or offsets, of varying width separating them. The mesa across which the cañon is approached, and the upper part of the cañons are very dry. A march of thirty miles from the "Black Tanks" brought us to the brink of the Cañon, and six miles up the cañon to our first water. The supply here being very small it was necessary to march thirty miles down the cañon to near the Indian settlements, where a plentiful supply of water was obtained but with little or no grazing. On the following day the greater part of the saddle and pack animals were sent back to the Black Tanks.

The lands occupied by the Yavai Suppai Indians extend from the head of the stream about two miles. Above this there is no water for many miles; below the succession in falls are so close to each other as to afford little or no available land.

The cañon is so narrow that no sight of the high mesa could be obtained from any point near the settlements. The crest of the first bench, at a height of almost five hundred feet, cut off our view.

Executive Order dated Nov. 23, 1880, gives to the Yavai Suppai Indians a tract of land extending twelve miles along Cataract Creek, and two and one half miles each way from the creek. The Eastern and Western boundaries of this tract lie upon the high mesa, in a country destitute of water at this season and said to present great difficulties in surveying. Its northern and southern boundaries, crossing the Cañon, cannot be directly measured. Such is the depths of the cañon and the forms of its walls that I believe at no point of the thirty miles of it which I have seen could monuments set upon the crest of the high mesa on both sides be seen from the bottom.

From the great difficulties presented by the conformation of the ground, and the scanty water supply obtainable at this season, I necessarily gave up all idea of marking upon the ground the boundaries as set forth in the Executive Order referred to although my sight of the country was a hurried one, I feel justified in saying that it is probably not possible to connect boundaries on the mesa with an initial point in the bottom of the canyon.

I therefore consulted with Navajo, Chief of the Yavai Suppai, as to the lands occupied or desired by him, and, in his presence, placed at the northern end of his lands two monuments of stone, one on each side of the

stream, marking a line which includes all that he desired in that direction. In the western one I placed a notice a copy of which is appended marked "A". Accompanied by his son, I placed, beyond the Southern extremity of lands used by the Indians, in a place already determined upon in consultation with Navajo, a simple monument of stone, containing a notice a copy of which is appended marked "B". Affected, probably, by a fear of encroachments and finally of removal, Navajo appeared to prefer having the boundaries close upon the lands he actually occupied. I placed the southern boundary to include more land than he desired, because it appeared to me that, also the natural head of the stream, water might be obtained by digging, to the detriment of the supply used by the Indians.

The improvements made by these Indians consist of their gardens, with accessories, and slight brush fences, and a few brush houses. Their use of the water, an essential consideration in this country, I believe to be fully secured by the southern extension of their lands beyond the head of running water, and by a fall of nearly one hundred feet which is included within the Northern boundary.

Within the boundaries marked are three small mining locations, close upon the northern boundary. About one quarter of a mile beyond the northern boundary marked, is the principal mining location of this group,—clearly within the reservation Declared Nov. 23, 1880. The prospectors and part owners, who were on the spot, declared to me their hesitance to relinquish all claim on account of the smaller mines within the boundary, in case that boundary should be accepted as the northern limit of the reservation, leaving them free to work their larger and principal mines outside . . .

From the samples shown me, and from the report of assay, I think it improbable that these mines can ever be profitably worked, access and transportation being peculiarly difficult and expensive. It is, therefore, in my opinion not probable that the Yavai Suppai Indians would in any degree suffer by the placing of the northern boundary of their reservation on the line selected by their chief.

I have the honor, therefore, to recommend that the reservation declared by Executive Order dated Nov. 23, 1880, be diminished to include only so much of the bottom land of the Cañon of Cataract Creek, bounded by walls of red sandstone on east and west, as is limited on the South by an east and west line (magnetic) crossing said cañon at a narrow pass marked by a monument of stone, almost two miles above the village of the Yavai Suppai Indians, and, on the north, by a line bearing N. 55D E (magnetic) crossing said cañon at the crest of the third falls of Cataract Creek, and marked by two monuments of stone, one on each side of the stream. [Cataract Canyon and Cataract Creek are often used, even today, to indicate Havasu Canyon and Havasu Creek.]

I have the honor to be,

Very respectfully,

Your humble servant.
CARL F. PALFREY
Lieut. Engineers
Engr. Off. Dept. Arizona

"A"

Yavai Suppai Cañon
June 12, 1881

This is to certify that I have this day placed this monument, with one on the opposite side of the cañon bearing from (magnetic) N. 55D E to mark the northern boundary of land occupied by Yavai Suppai Indians, being about one and one half (1½) miles within (south of) boundary of reservation declared for these Indians per Executive Order dated Nov. 23, 1880.

CARL F. PALFREY
Lieut. of Engr.
Engr. Off. Dept. Arizona

"B"

Yavai Suppai Cañon
June 12, 1881

This is to certify that I have this day placed this monument to mark a line of bearing East (magnetic) across the Cañon, as the Southern boundary of land occupied by Yavai Suppai Indians, being about eight miles within (north of) boundary of reservation declared for these Indians per Executive Order dated Nov. 23, 1880.

CARL F. PALFREY
Lieut. of Engr.
Engr. Off. Dept. of Arizona[25]

Why Navajo agreed to this shrunken reservation is abundantly clear; tales borne to the Havasupai by Hualapai friends and relatives returned from La Paz had instilled in them a thorough dread of a like forced removal. Lt. Col. W. R. Price's own July 1, 1881, report to the Department of Arizona makes this obvious:

Navajoe, the Supai Captain, was at first nervous and very suspicious—fearful that an effort would be made to remove them to some other reservation . . . There was some hesitation among them in accepting anything, food, and so forth, they being very suspicious that it might be the opening wedge toward their removal from their country. They had evidently been informed that the discovery of mines in their country would necessitate the abandonment of their lands as the whites would take them for their own use.[26]

Later, on about July 7, Navajo reported to his people that opposition "would be foolish for the reason that it could cause my children to be exterminated." [27]

On March 31, 1882, President Chester A. Arthur confirmed Lieut. Palfrey's recommendation by Executive Order.° Thus at the stroke of a pen, the entire Havasupai winter range and age-old plateau homeland became public property. It was some years before the Havasupai realized what had happened to them. Interviews and contemporary accounts indicate the Havasupai felt only that their canyon had been permanently withdrawn from all encroachments forever; no one believed the order could have any bearing on lands outside the canyon.

One subsequent government investigation concluded:

> it is clear that the Indians did not contemplate surrendering any claims whatsoever as a price for being permitted to continue cultivating the few acres at the bottom of Cataract Canyon which they had cultivated from time immemorial. On the contrary, they were specifically assured, according to trustworthy and unimpeached evidence [the testimony of Jim Crook regarding General George Crook's advice to them] that they would be allowed in the future to use land outside the canyon for the only purpose to which that land can be put, i.e., hunting, the grazing of livestock, and food-gathering.[28]

And Lemuel Paya recounted in 1972, "We felt we had more land up there to use, but the government claimed it and got tight with it, and we found we had nothing left to use up there."

Little time passed before the new occupiers of Havasupai land made the meaning of the order somewhat plainer. In 1950 Allen Ákaba reported on those days:

> White settlers, homesteaders, cattle owners, would come in here and the Indian would have a spring back in the hills, the cattle owner would come along, he would water his stock where the Indians were. He would stay with them; told them later on that this spring water hole was his. The Indian had nothing to do with it; chase them out. Gave them a few things and told them to go home, "Paid you for it." . . . This white owner would come along and help fix up the spring, and he told them he did all the work; "Indians get out, none of your business up here. My cattle water here. Go on home." . . . They were threatening them at the point of a gun . . . Bass threatened them with not just a gun, but sticks, away from water holes. . . . a white cattle owner . . . come and beat up a fellow by the name of Kit Jones . . . Hank Wood.[29]

° It is hereby ordered that the following-described country lying within the boundaries of the Territory of Arizona, viz, so much of the bottom land of the cañon of Cataract Creek, bounded by walls of red sand-stone on the east and west, as is included within certain lines, viz, on the south, an east and west line (magnetic) crossing said cañon at a narrow pass marked by a monument of stone, placed in the summer of 1881, by Lieut. Carl Palfrey, of the Corps of Engineers of the Army, about two miles above the village of the Yavai Suppai Indians, and on the north, a line bearing N. 55° E. (magnetic) crossing said cañon at the crest of the third falls of Cataract Creek, and marked by Lieutenant Palfrey, by two monuments of stone, one on each side of the stream, be, and the same is hereby, withdrawn from sale and settlement, and set apart for the use and occupancy of said Yavai Suppai Indians, and the Executive order dated November 23, 1880, withdrawing from sale and settlement and setting apart a reservation for said Indians, is hereby revoked.

And even within the new Hualapai Reservation were several areas that the Havasupai and Pai bands to the west of them had long used together and some Havasupai even claimed they had used exclusively. Pine Springs (*ha ge sáa*) and Mohawk Canyon (*hwal dovgyóva*) were two such areas. People who had always been neighbors, friends and relatives became adversaries under the new reservation conditions. One old man, Toby Uqualla, still was able to say in 1973, "The Hualapais are coming this way, the Navajos that way, taking our land. And nobody's saying anything." It is clear that, even today, the older Havasupai feel no doubt the plateau is still Havasupai territory, though occupied by temporary squatters, European and Indian.

C. C. Bean, Arizona's delegate to the 49th Congress, came to visit the newly established reservation and report on the tribe's situation; he wrote to the Indian Commissioner on December 12, 1885, that

> . . . the Havasupai obtain game in winter . . . their summer crops being insufficient. . . . Their hunting grounds extended from Pine Springs close to the Hualapai Country on the west to the mouth of the Little Colorado on the East and from the Grand Canyon of the Colorado on the north to the San Francisco range of mountains on the South, but the introduction of herds of cattle and flocks of sheep, of miners, prospectors and tourists have all combined to render this vast hunting ground useless—and the time has come when the United States must extend some assistance to this tribe. . . .[30]

In the winter of 1888 Euler reports, "A party of Havasupais [which party probably included Navajo himself, as he normally wintered near Black Tank—Hirst] approached a group of Anglo-American cattlemen [at Black Tank] and ordered them away, ordered them off the area around this tank, claiming that it was Indian country and that the whites had no business there. Of course the whites complained about this, and the Bureau of Indian Affairs and Military got involved, trying to see what the dispute was all about."[31]

Two years previously, on July 6, 1886, Congress had acted to declare forfeiture by the Atlantic & Pacific Railroad of its title to indemnity lands. Under the 1866 act the railroad company had been obliged to complete 50 miles a year starting in 1868, and to complete the line by 1878. By 1871 the company had completed only 75 miles of line. The March 1871 military order regarding Indians found off their reservations allowed the railroad to recommence work through former Indian territory, where the Department of the Interior had formerly held it from working. In 1871 the government required the railroad company to execute a bond for a half million dollars, forcing it to mortgage a large share of its holdings. By July 4, 1878, the date for completion, the railroad had completed only 125 miles. The company began buying and leasing track completed by the Santa Fe and Southern Pacific but by 1886 there was still a gap uncompleted through New Mexico and the Mojave Desert. So the grant which had been filed was returned to the public domain.

It was with this and the Black Tank incident in mind that Lt. Col. G. N. Brayton wrote the Asst. Adj. General of the Department of Arizona on January 26, 1888:

The Suppai Reservation is too small for the support of even this small band. By reference to the map it will be seen that there is but a small strip of country between the Suppai Cañon and Hualapai Reservation, which country has been used for many years as a hunting-ground by the Suppais. There is so little water that no one cares to make a permanent home on it. To avoid possible trouble I respectfully recommend that the Yavai Suppai Reservation be extended with boundaries say as follows: Bounded north by the Colorado River; east by a line running along the course of and one-half mile east of Cataract Creek; south by the north line of the Atlantic and Pacific Railroad lands; and west by the east line of the Hualapai Indian Reservation.[32]

General Nelson Miles concurred with this recommendation and forwarded it to the Commissioner of Indian Affairs, on January 31, but nothing was done. In fact the problem of the released railroad lands was just beginning, for the grants made within the Hualapai Reservation and the Havasupai winter range had now become public domain, and claimants abounded for homesteads and mineral rights on those odd-numbered sections. (It was not to be until the fall term of 1941 that the case was finally brought before the Supreme Court of the United States in U.S. v Santa Fe Pacific Railroad Company.) Suddenly the Havasupai found themselves competing for their winter range and in many cases driven from it. They found themselves adrift in a sea of hatred and rejection in their own land, as Euler has found so pointedly expressed toward the Hualapai in contemporary local newspapers.[33]

On March 21, 1886, the *Mojave County Miner*, published at Mineral Park near present-day Kingman, reported, "Several Wallapai [Hualapai] Indians have visited the happy hunting grounds in the past few weeks, and have become better Indians than they ever were on earth."

On October 8, 1887, the same paper reported, "The Wallapai Indians complain of the quality of the flour served out to them by the government, and say it is full of weevils and has an intensely bitter taste. A plentiful supply of arsenic mixed with it would disguise the bitter taste. We offer this suggestion to the contractor and sincerely hope we will adopt it."

On September 7, 1889, the *Miner* reported, "It is evident that the 'medicine men' have stirred up all the superstitions of which a savage is capable, and if the ways of God are mysterious, the ways of a live Indian are more so. 'Music hath charms to soothe the savage beast . . .' And it is said that the most effective is the whistle of a well-directed bullet."

An observer commented in 1891, "In every sense the Havesu pais are a dying race." [34]

Another observer had written in 1882:

The game is all gone. In 1863 the valleys were filled with antelope and the hills with deer. Rabbits and hares were abundant. Now one may travel for weeks and not see any game save an occasional rabbit. The stock have eaten off the grass so that their harvest fields where [the Indians] used to gather grass seeds are destroyed.[35]

During the final decade of the nineteenth century and the first two of the twentieth, new diseases began to ravage the Havasupai population, diseases like smallpox, measles and influenza against which they had very little immunity. Women were particularly hard-hit, and death during childbirth became unusually prevalent; by 1906 the Havasupai had three men for every two women. Fannie Banahmída Sinyella, the beautiful Havasupai mother shown in a 1913 photograph holding her baby Lorenzo, died only three years later giving birth to her son Roy. On top of all this, Dobyns and Euler report that the white immigrants considered the surviving Pai women fair game for their forcible use.[36] Small wonder that the Hualapai at least felt inclined to kill half-white children.

By 1890 a repeat of the 1888 Black Tank incident (p. 61) brought a much sadder conclusion. In that year Hotauta, Navajo's oldest son, whom the Europeans called Suppai Tom, attempted to reclaim Rain Tank, just north of Red Butte, from two white men and a woman, saying his family had lived there for many years. However, Superintendent McCowan, the Indian Service official in charge, stated that the Havasupai had "no right to Rain Tank or any other spot away from said reservation."

Many of the Havasupai began to wonder by 1890 if they had in some way failed their land or their gods; in any case the gods of the Pai people seemed to have deserted them.

In this time of terrible loss and bewilderment the message of Wovoka, the Paiute Messiah, began to reach the Pai from St. George, Utah. Born in a vision in 1888 of a mixture of Indian belief in natural equilibrium and Christian eschatology, Wovoka's message taught that Indian people should dance to seek contact with the dead to return them to life and, in so doing, to restore the earth to balance and wipe the white scourge from it.

Already in 1889 Indian people were sending people hundreds of miles to learn from Wovoka the dance they prayed would release them.°

Both the Havasupai and Hualapai sent people to become disciples of a sort and to bring back the message of Wovoka. Even in the absence of major river crossings the Pai had long maintained minimal contacts with the Paiute on visits and hunting parties by crossing at Diamond Creek and Shinumo Creek. At least one Paiute woman even married into the Havasupai and her twin sister into the Hualapai. The Havasupai leader Navajo, who succeeded Wa Sgwívema upon his

° In a matter of two years his teaching had swept the West and led eventually to the tragedy of Wounded Knee, when nervous government troops fired upon and killed most of a group of some 300 exhausted and starving Sioux encamped along Wounded Knee Creek on the morning of December 29, 1890.

death in the 1870s, may have sent Baa gedegóva, and the Hualapai sent the man called Dho in Húka to learn the Paiute dance. Before long the Paiute people sent their missionary, Panamoíta, to the Pai, and Navajo himself may have gone westward to the Hualapai to learn the dance.

In the spring of 1889 the Hualapai apparently held their first ghost dance at Grass Springs. During the winter of 1889–1890 another large ghost dance may have taken place near Stockton Hill. The Pai began another ghost dance in June 1890 at Coara Springs, and finally the winter of that year another dance began in Free's Wash that continued over into early 1891. Apparently Navajo and Baa gedegóva attended the Free's Wash dance; shortly afterward a four-day ghost dance took place in Cataract Canyon which several Hopi traders witnessed.

In the spring of 1891 the Hualapai adherents of the ghost dance movement, led by Sherúm, attempted to use the dance to revive a man who had just died. The attempt failed, and the western Pai began to lose interest in the movement. The Hualapai apparently held their last ghost dance in early winter 1891 at Coara Springs.

The Havasupai carried on the ghost dance several years more, maintaining the movement into the twentieth century. They held dances during the winter months of 1892–1893 at Sheep Tank and Black Tank. Superintendent McCowan reported seeing a Havasupai ghost dance in Havasu Canyon in 1895, and Flora Gregg Iliff observed strong remnants of the dance in 1900 and 1901 in Havasu Canyon. Later Havasupai respondents said the few participants who climbed to the top of a central dance pole and touched eagle feathers tied there all died shortly after, so the Havasupai eventually gave up on the dance as well.

However, Dobyns and Euler report that the dance held much more lasting significance in that its adoption drove the first wedge into Pai aboriginal beliefs; from that time they feel the Pai began to faction in their social and religious beliefs.[37] Certainly the growing influence of Christianity among such men as Baa gemiijeva dated from that time. That individual used to dress up in his finest every Sunday and exhort his tribesmen to hear about Jesus.

The ghost dance affected even more notably the funeral practices of the Havasupai, who, prior to ghost dance times, observed very little ceremony in the disposal of the dead. Prior to 1890, they frequently, if not regularly, cremated the dead or disposed of them in caves or rock cairns. By 1905 the Havasupai had begun burying all their dead as they do today, with a rather elaborate ceremony stemming ultimately from the Great Basin bear dance. Centuries ago this dance had passed from the Shoshonean Chemehuevi to the Mohave people and there became a bird dance. The Havasupai then learned the bird dances indirectly from the Hualapai during the 1890s as part of the ghost dance. Already in 1898 the Havasupai buried their leader, Navajo, a prime sponsor of the ghost dance movement, with all his effects. Ghost dance theology taught that the dead must be preserved whole for their coming return.

The Havasupai claim to know of but one cremation after 1905 or so, when they cremated the rain maker Baa 'nyá j'álga [Man of the Rising Sun] on his lands at *way gvasú* [green water in the rocks], a location known only to the Havasupai. This occurred in the 1920s. The Havasupai held Baa 'nyá j'álga, or Rock Jones, as the Europeans knew him, to possess control over cosmic forces, and even today they avoid the cremation spot.

By 1892 the government and the Department of the Interior had begun sending a government farmer to teach them to farm (!), and by 1894 R. C. Bauer, the government farmer, began constructing stone buildings near the headwaters of the creek for a school to open in 1895. Contemporary accounts make it apparent that the school was to be a missionary effort as much as a school, as Mrs. Iliff, a government teacher at the turn of the century, reports leading religious and military exercises in the Supai and Hackberry Indian schools. A later teacher reported leading church services in the early 1930s in addition to her teaching activities.[38] Of course this was the general practice in other American schools of the time, too.

Near the end of the brief ghost-dance era, the government presented the Havasupai with a new problem regarding their winter range. President Benjamin Harrison on February 20, 1893, signed an Executive order setting much of it aside as the Grand Cañon Forest Reserve. This was apparently going to be the government's only response to General Miles's recommendation of Lt. Col. Brayton's 1888 report on Black Tank.

Though the Havasupai now found their plateau lands further offered to the public at the expense of their own use, they were not about to give up, and they gained a staunch friend and ally in their new Superintendent Henry P. Ewing. In their June 30, 1896, report to the Indian Commissioner, Ewing and Bauer wrote:

> The boundaries of this reserve should begin at the southeast corner of the Hualapai reserve, thence east to the southwest corner of the Coconino Forest reserve, thence north to the Colorado River, thence west along the Colorado River to the northeast corner of the Hualapai reserve, thence south to point of beginning. The tract described is nearly all desert and "bad lands," and is worthless but for the little "water holes" on it at which the Indians keep their live stock. The country I have described is to-day actually occupied by the Yava Supais and is necessary for their support, as they can not keep stock in the canyon, which is only large enough for gardens for the Supais. The boundary question should be settled.[39]

By November word reached Ewing that the government was instead considering removing the Havasupai to La Paz, and he hotly wrote the Commissioner on November 17, 1896, "They ask nothing except to be allowed to live in this cañon, they love the spot as no white man ever loved his native country, and so sure as the sun shines they will never be peaceably removed from it, . . . and should force be used, then every man and boy, who could carry a rifle must first be killed."

In his June 30, 1897, annual report Ewing again wrote strongly, as the situation had not improved for the embattled Havasupai. But his words also indicate again that the Havasupai would not surrender without a fight:

> They . . . fear no living man. . . . They are the most industrious Indians I have ever known, being good irrigation farmers and horticulturalists, and as a matter of fact the most progressive agricultural community in northern Arizona. They are expert horsemen and hunters, and from the farm and chase procure, without Governmental assistance, their food and raiment. . . .

> The Indians have little "water holes," some of them 40 or 50 miles distant, at which they have kept their horses from time immemorial. These springs will not sustain many head of stock but white men are gradually encroaching upon these springs, and unless protection is afforded it will not be long before the Indians will have neither springs nor live stock. Last winter these Indians built about 12 miles of good log fence, stake and rider, from the cliffs of the Grand Canyon to Cataract Canyon, hoping to save these springs, which are as much their property as any land ever claimed by any of the aboriginal inhabitants of the United States.[40]

The land Ewing described lies on the Great Thumb Mesa.

The Forestry Department persisted in their belief that they had somehow received authority to terminate Havasupai use of land outside Havasu Canyon. Grand Cañon Forest Supervisor W. P. Hermann wrote to the Indian Commissioner on November 9, 1898, to complain:

> The Indians boast and threaten to kill the deer and antelope so long as the "Government does not supply them with cow meat." The Grand Cañon of the Colorado River is becoming so renowned for its wonderful and extensive natural gorge scenery and for its open clean pine woods, that it should be preserved for the everlasting pleasure and instruction of our intelligent citizens as well as those of foreign countries. Henceforth, I deem it just and necessary to keep the wild and unappreciable Indian from off the Reserve. . . .[41]

The Office of Indian Affairs responded on December 2 by instructing Ewing that, "In fact it would be best to forbid their entering this reserve for any purpose; and should you learn of any of them being therein it would be well to cause their return to the reservation, even though they may not be detected in the act of hunting."[42]

Hermann continued to complain about Indian depredations on "his" game, though a letter he wrote February 8, 1900, makes it clear he drew no distinction among the various Indian people in the area. The large deer drives he complains of in that letter all took place around Fredonia, far beyond Havasupai territory and certainly beyond where they ever traveled.

On November 16, 1900, Ewing wrote to the Commissioner, again urging that he set aside land on the plateau for the Havasupai. Finally a private group interested in having Indians' lands allotted individually to make sturdy citizens of them, the Indian Rights Association, contacted the Secretary of the Interior May 21, 1901, on the Havasupai's behalf. In part the Association complained:

> The crowning wrong seems to have been the Executive Order of February 20, 1893, setting apart the Grand Cañon Forest Reserve, which completely surrounds their little home, and further curtails their right to pasturage of stock and the securing of game. The authorities in charge of the Grand Cañon Forest Reserve seek to deprive the Indians of the privilege of crossing the Forest Reserve, and have notified the official in charge of the Havasupai Indians that they should not be allowed to trespass upon or roam over said reserve. If this rule is enforced these Indians will be prisoners within the cañon walls. . . .

> We entreat for the Havasupai Indians your earnest consideration and early action and would respectfully urge that this be taken in the way which we recommend namely by individual allotment to the Indians. But if this is, for any reason, inadmissible, then the assignment to them of a tract of reservation adequate to their wants.[43]

Ten days later Ewing wrote the Commissioner again to complain of underhanded attempts by prospectors to gain a foothold within even the shrunken reservation left the Havasupai:

> Each party who has located these claims has also located all of the water power on the Havasupai reservation as alleged mill sites, and, from the methods and actions of all these parties, I am compelled to arrive at the conclusion that the sole object which these parties have in pretending to wish to work these mines is that they may gain control of and possession of the water power situated in the Cataract Cañon on the Havasupai Reservation. . . . One party even went so far as to locate a homestead within the reservation claiming all the water power and water, and but for prompt and determined action on my part would undoubtedly have secured from the Land Department a title to this land.[42]

Notwithstanding Ewing's efforts to protect even the infinitesimal reservation, apparently Hermann, the Grand Cañon Forest Reserve Supervisor, himself had prevailed upon the government to allow a firm to develop the water resources of Havasu Creek on the most sacred of the Havasupai falls, Mooney:

> With shocking suddenness we learned that the Blue Water was to be commercialized. Mr. Ewing wrote that an Eastern firm had been granted authority to harness Mooney Falls to manufacture electrical power for distribution to cities in Arizona and neighboring states. Engineers, surveyors and workmen swarmed into the canyon where so few white men had ever ventured. Miners had once worked the ledges on the walls for silver, but never had the Indians' authority over the Blue Water or its canyon been questioned. These white men who were now tinkering with old Mooney

Falls did not consult the Indians. They were authorized to complete the project, they explained to me, and, intent upon this, they kept pretty much to themselves.[44]

The whole area between Havasu and Mooney Falls where the construction was going on was the Havasupai's cremation and burial grounds, as Iliff, James and others have noted. This depredation of the place of the dead was only equaled later when the National Park Service turned it into a campground for the public. In the earlier case, the Havasupai's creek resisted use on its own terms; in the midst of the work a flood came down the canyon and destroyed all the equipment and trails the crew had been constructing. This type of project was abandoned, as it turned out, permanently. When an attempt was made later to renovate the wagon trail into Havasu Canyon constructed by the abortive power project, the Havasupai pushed an old car body over the cliff onto the work, laid logs across other parts of the trail and blocked the rest with a rockslide.

The Secretary of the Interior referred the Indian Rights Association's letter to Arizona Indian Service Supervisor Holland for comment. Holland commented in part:

> At the request of the Supai Indians, I met them in Council. The speakers . . . wound up with the request that they be given some increased school facilities in the cañon so that their children will not have to be sent away. . . .
>
> My information is that when the Indians had undisputed possession of these lands, about the only use they made of them was for hunting purposes, grazing a lot of worthless ponies and a very few cattle. . . .
>
> Death is doing a great deal toward solving the alleged troubles of the Supais, and my idea is that the decimation of their number by that cause should be further increased by getting as many as possible out to school. After being at Truxton and Phoenix for a while it is not probable that many of them will want to go back to their little hole in the ground where they seem to suffer from malaria or too much inter-marrying or both. They are generally weak-looking.

On September 30, 1901, Assistant Commissioner A. C. Tonner referred Holland's report to the Secretary and commented:

> In view of the facts, as reported by Mr. Holland, it would seem to be unadvisable to attempt to secure a part of the said forest reserve and the withdrawal of public lands contiguous thereto for these Indians in order to give them allotments in severalty or to disturb them in their present manner of living. Nor is it deemed necessary to use any of the fund—Support and Civilization of the Apache and other Indians in Arizona and New Mexico—in the purchase of agricultural tools, etc., as they seem to be

getting along quite satisfactorily in their primitive way, and it might cause them to expect other gratuities from the Government should tools be issued to them.[42]

By 1902 the government had apparently found some way to eliminate the embarrassing Mr. Ewing, according to Mrs. Iliff:

> Mr. Ewing had been removed from office and had gone to his farm somewhere out in the desert. I never learned the exact charges against him. He had bitter enemies—cattlemen and ranchers he had forced off the Indians' land, and others who accused him of being arrogant, rejoicing to see how the mighty had fallen. . . . No jury would convict him, but he died a broken and disillusioned man.[45]

The government had removed one of the staunchest and ablest friends the Havasupai had, and they were not to have another such for nearly forty years.

Signing the Declaration
Havasu Canyon: 1913
(Third man from left with
earring is Baa' nyá)

Courtesy American Museum of Natural History 1913

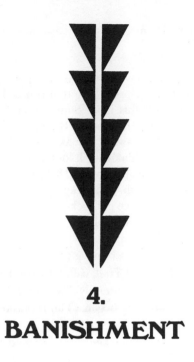

4.

BANISHMENT

In 1897 a group of promoters began construction of a spur line of the Santa Fe Railroad, by then completed across Arizona, northward to the Grand Canyon. After some reverses the Santa Fe opened the line all the way to Grand Canyon Station in September 1901. In 1905 President Theodore Roosevelt traveled on the line to view the Grand Canyon and rode down into the canyon itself. He found the Havasupai Ya nyemí ge swèdeva (Hanging Beard) living at his family home and Burro and his family at their home in what is now called Indian Gardens. Havasupai informants recount that Roosevelt spoke to Swèdeva, whom the Europeans called Big Jim, and informed him, through an interpreter, of the federal government's intent to locate on Swèdeva's and Burro's garden lands below the rim a park for the American people. To make such a park possible, he urged them to vacate the area. A man named Campbell may have accompanied Roosevelt, for Billy Burro remembered in 1950 that Campbell first told the Havasupai to leave Indian Gardens.[46]

The Havasupai Mark Hanna, son of Wa'agwánema, told of the visit in his autobiography:

Teddy Roosevelt said there was going to be a park place at Grand Canyon and there was going to be people there that run it. I asked Manakadja if we were going to get run off this land. Some other fellows asked him if the Supais would get money for the land for the Park. That is Supai land and we owned that place they took away. Manakadja told us to wait and see what they do. He said, "I don't think they'll kick us off that land." Capt. Navajo told us to wait, too [as Navajo died in 1898, this last must refer to earlier advice Navajo had given in 1881 regarding the establishment of the reservation]. We waited but we got kicked off the land and we didn't get no money for it. We just got kicked off.[47]

At Roosevelt's urging, Swèteva removed his family to a cave just below the rim along the present Bright Angel Trail, called by the Havasupai along with the entire South Rim *kathòdev hè'e*, literally "coyote tail," which refers to the spruce trees in which the trail once began. (The Havasupai name for a spruce is also coyote tail, from the resemblance.) Havasupai informants who know the spot can still point out the smoke blackening from Swèdeva's fires. He continued to farm Indian Gardens whenever he wished, however.

At this point a division arose among the Havasupai. Like the Hopi to the east, the Havasupai had their accommodationists, represented by Swèdeva, and their traditionalists, represented by Hmány gejáa. Hmány gejáa, who was formerly called only Wí maya (Little Mountain), had become the head chief at 50 in 1900 after his uncle Navajo's death and had at that time adopted his name, which meant "Who Looks After His Children." For more than forty years, until his death in 1942, he was to be one of the Havasupai's most respected leaders and spokesmen. According to Iliff, he "preached the doctrine that the white man and the Indian cannot live on the same ground; each must have his own, and there can be no encroaching, one on the other. The chief had decreed that no Havasupai blood should mingle with that of the white people, and never in the history of the tribe had there been such a marriage or mingling of blood."[48]

Within the space of two generations Mánakaja, as his name has come to be spelled, has already attained a sort of mythic hero status. For example it is said Mánakaja roamed the boundaries of the land whenever he wished and lived on the fruit of the earth. Still today one can see throughout the land the fire-blackened caves where he stayed. Once he decided to ride the perimeter of all the Havasupai eastern range and began from Havasúa, riding eastward by Moqui Trail to the Spruce Trees (the South Rim), where he stayed with Burro. Then he went on to Yaqui Point, Grandview Point and Desert View, where he turned back to ride to the Landmark (Red Butte), in the center of the land. From the Landmark Mánakaja turned again to the east toward the salty water of the Little Colorado. During his travel he obtained red ochre and turquoise. From the Little Colorado crossing at Moencopi Wash he turned southward to the Home of the Sun before the Snowy Mountains (San Francisco Peaks). At the Snowy Mountains he turned westward and rode to the Mountains of the Horse (Bill Williams Mountain), where he lived on the west side with Burro. From there Burro continued the ride.

The Havasupai considered Swèdeva a minor chief in those early days, but even then he was a respected figure in the Havasupai community and one of its ablest spokesmen. He worked for the Indian Service as the tribal policeman in the early part of the century and professed the Christian faith. He represented that side of Havasupai tradition which lays great importance on open-handedness and hospitality. He could afford to be generous, for he stood well over six feet and weighed over 200 pounds; not until he was eighty years old did Park officials tell him they wished him to stop farming at Indian Gardens as well.

In general, Swèdeva was a great favorite of government officials. His testimony to the Indian Claims Commission in 1950 is illuminating in the strong contrast it presents to the testimony of Billy Burro, Mary Wescògame and Allen Ákaba:

Q Why did you and your people leave these winter homes and never return there again?

A The reason they left this area is they do some planting each year at Supai. That is how we just leave this area . . . the interests of what they have to do with back home . . .

Q Did the white people allow the Supais to come back out in this area where they used to spend the winters?

A There is no objection among these homesteaders that comes in. They just friendly to each other and roam around this area just the same.

Q Did they let the Supais use all their water holes and all the land they used to have? All their old water holes?

A They all used the water holes peacefully. No objections.[49]

Not everyone was as fortunate or as imposing as Swèteva.

Despite the removal of Henry P. Ewing and the Forestry Department's continued pressure, the Havasupai determinedly continued their use of plateau lands on the remaining miles where they had been driven back up against the canyon. They even continued to construct their earth water-catchment dikes to catch storm runoff down the shallow washes. One can still see these constructions today, though some are now administratively withheld from Havasupai use. The plateau south of the Grand Canyon—which generally slopes *away* from the main canyon—is primarily underlaid with porous limestone, with impervious spots occurring only sporadically, so these dams and little reservoirs had to be very carefully located and laboriously constructed for the impounded water not to percolate into the rock below. The contemporary Havasupai leader Lee Marshall notes that, "The old people were good engineers. They knew where to put dams so they hold water. I've seen dams made of piles of rocks from long before we had horses even. I don't know how they knew."

Not surprisingly the Havasupai Indian agents who succeeded Ewing continued his efforts to have some plateau land set aside for the Havasupai, but with no better results. Finally in 1908 the Presidential Proclamations of January 11 and July 2 brought a considerable reorganization to the area by creating the Coconino National Forest and the Grand Canyon National Monument on the old Grand Cañon Forest Reserve. Immediately the Havasupai and the local Indian Service officials began writing to Washington that this opportunity should be used to withdraw some of the reshuffled land from the Coconino National Forest and restore it to the Havasupai. A letter of information written six years later by Second Assistant Indian Commissioner C. F. Hauke to Havasupai Superintendent D. Clinton West details the outcome of that attempt:

> Your predecessor suggested the necessity for setting aside a sufficient permanent and definite pasture for the use of the Indians out of the Forest Reserve, and said they had already fenced in a large pocket formed by the Grand and Cataract Canyons and constructed some six or eight good sized reservoirs in which to impound water. During the year 1908, the question of restoring a part of the Forest included in the Coconino National Forest to the public domain and withdrawing the land so restored for the use of the Supai Indians for grazing purposes, was brought to the attention of the Office. After some correspondence and consideration of the matter, it was decided that it would be better to get free permits from the Forest for the Indians to graze their cattle on the National Forest rather than have a portion thereof restored to the public domain and reserved to the Indians. This course was followed . . . the Forester has granted permission for the Indians to use a range at the head of what is known as the Topocobia [sic] Trail and also to locate some stock tanks within the range for the exclusive use of the Indians.[50]

The Havasupai had won a faint victory of sorts; though the attempt to restore this last bastion of the Havasupai plateau to its rightful owners and users had failed, at least the newly created Forest Service was prepared to devote more than 100,000 acres to the Havasupai for grazing use. The lands included took in the area around Topocóba, the Great Thumb Mesa, Moqui Trail, and as far east as Sheep Tank on the east side of Pasture Wash. Though the area was purportedly only for the purpose of grazing horses, the Havasupai continued to build homes on the use area, which the rangers referred to as the "Indian Pasture."

Then during these years a series of terrible influenza epidemics struck the tribal people and took a heavy toll, especially among the young children. In 1918 some families lost all their children in one blow. The Paiute woman Yu semè, who had married Mánakaja, died during one such epidemic about 1918. Spier reported that the effects of the epidemic were noticeable in the absence of a whole age group of children.[51] The tribal population even dropped below its historically constant level of some 250 persons during the first decades of the century from this cause.

Another cataclysm struck Havasu Canyon itself in the form of a disastrous flood. Havasu Canyon and indeed all the lower canyons draining into the Colorado are subject to flash flooding from storms above during the late summer. Usually these summer floods bring five to ten feet of muddy runoff down the creek, which subsides after three hours or so.° Winter floods are much rarer and less predictable. In 1910 most of the government buildings, including the school, and much of the village itself were located at the narrow confluence of Hualapai and Havasu Canyons, as the village had been for centuries, in the manner of medieval European towns. The best land below was reserved exclusively for farming, and people walked to the fields rather than living in them.

The winter of 1909–1910 had brought fairly heavy snow on the top lands. Then on New Year's Day came a sudden thaw and heavy rains. Lemuel Paya remembered he could hear water running under the snow, which kept caving in under his feet. A vivid record of the effects below in Havasu Canyon was set down by Richard J. Barnes, the supply and disbursement agent who was on his way to relieve Superintendent Coe and his wife on January 2, 1910.

Just before daybreak on the morning of the second, the few people staying in the canyon were awakened by a thunderous roar to see a terrifying wall of water bearing down on them. Coe estimated the wall at more than ten feet in height. After the passage of the initial wall, the water continued rising rapidly until it was twenty feet above the creek level. Everyone who was able fled to the talus slopes at the foot of the cliffs, where families maintained their pueblo-style rock storage houses, and set up housekeeping. One feeble, blind lady—Ilyewí'i, the Snake Woman—was unable to find her way to safety in time and perished in the roaring waters. About twenty horses were lost in the flood as well. The water filled the canyon from wall to wall, and Barnes arrived to find Coe and his wife in their night clothes, sitting on the roof of their half-collapsed house surrounded by the flood waters. Everything else had been washed away. The superintendent's house was apparently located on slightly higher ground at the mouth of Hualapai Canyon.

Most of the Havasupai farms were completely washed away, leaving only gravel in their wake. Every house in the village was gone; even the stone school building and agency house were destroyed. The only bright spot was that the flood had come in winter, when all of the tribe who were able still lived on the plateau. The threat of such sudden winter floods undoubtedly provided another reason the people had avoided winter residence in the canyon. Barnes rescued Coe and his wife, and they fled to Phoenix without staying to determine the fate of the people in the canyon or their homes. That was learned only later. Photographs that Barnes sent later to the Office of Indian Affairs detail the hopeless destruction that had befallen the Havasupai's summer farms.

On April 5 the government bought use of five acres of land in the wider

---

° However, a heavy summer storm on August 1, 1928, brought a late afternoon flood that began at 4:30 P.M. and continued until midnight. Mánakaja's 78-year-old Havasupai wife Gwegethgwáya was caught on a barbed-wire fence trying to flee the swirling waters and drowned.

section of the canyon formerly reserved for farming from Rock Baa 'nyá (Jones) for $50 and set it aside for a new school and agency site. These five acres are still withdrawn from farming or personal use by the tribe and today serve as location for the various public buildings of the community.

The government then began construction of the new school, which they completed in 1912; it was topped off with the old bell salvaged from the former school. That 1912 school is still in use in 1975, though the tribal people have been trying for at least 44 years to obtain funds to construct a new one. At the same time the government put up fifteen frame houses for local residents, who were to pay for them if they chose to occupy them. Disaster relief was apparently unknown in those days.

The government-built houses struck tribal people as incompatible with their life, and they remained unoccupied for years. By 1929 one observer said of them:

> The beauty of the valley has only one jarring note: the row of unoccupied ugly frame houses built by the Indian Service for the Indians over ten years ago. The Indians have refused to occupy them as too hot in summer and too cold in winter. If they are used at all, it is only for storage of grain or alfalfa.[52]

By that year (1929) tribal individuals had occupied three of them (one of these people, Jim Crook, still uses his today). The rest remained empty. The occupants of the three paid off half the cost of their houses, and the BIA finally wrote off the rest of their debt. Nine of the fifteen remain, five now unoccupied. One was burned in 1973 upon the death of its owner, and the others people tore down for lumber to make housing on their own.

In 1911 government officials came again to Swèdeva in his cave at Grand Canyon and this time ordered him to remove his family from the canyon and find a homesite somewhere on the plateau above back from the rim. There could be no people living in an area to be a park for all the people. Swèdeva again moved his family and relocated them at a point some five miles west of the Grand Canyon station, dug a well, and built a home there in a beautiful glade under the ponderosas. Farther to the west, near the head of Pasture Wash, he built an earth dam and a summer wickiup, for he farmed in Pasture Wash. The remains of this place are still visible today, but the Havasupai no longer have the right to use it.

Feeling more safely established with the new permit from the Forest Service, the Havasupai constructed two more earth tanks in 1911, and in 1912 the Indian Service spent $810 to make the first purchase of stock for the Havasupai and put a government stallion on the range. The Havasupai had some 400 horses on their range that year.

The Havasupai superintendent's narrative report of 1913 indicates he was again trying to have the Indian pasture set aside for the reservation, but again with no success. In 1915 the Havasupai constructed six more earth tanks, and the agent reported they now had 600 horses on the pasture and some 100 cattle. The Office of Indian Affairs spent $375 in 1917 and bought more cattle.

Under the urging of various private individuals and groups, the Congress in 1911 passed an act to permit erection of an Indian memorial in New York harbor. The plan apparently called for a sizable bronze statue on the order of the present Statue of Liberty.

In 1913 an expeditionary group under the sponsorship of department-store tycoon Rodman Wanamaker traveled to Indian reservations throughout the country bearing an endorsement of the project and a declaration of allegiance to the United States which each reservation's leaders were to sign. They also brought along a gramophone recording of Woodrow Wilson proclaiming the momentous event. In return for signing the declaration, the expedition presented each tribe with an American flag. Yet the United States did not even consider as citizens those who were signing their allegiance, nor did it allow them to vote in U.S. elections! The project never materialized. A number of excellent photographs have come down to us from that attempt, however, including one of all the Havasupai leaders of the time signing the declaration.

Banishment

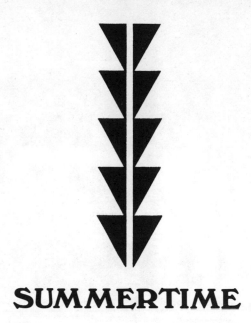

SUMMERTIME

25. *Horsepower 1973*

te

te

26. *Home from the Fields 1973*

27. *At the Store:*
    Paula Watahomigie
    and Haven Hamidreek 1970

le

le
te

28. *After School 1969*

29. *Easy Riders 1973*

30. *Galen Crook 1973*

le

31. *Havasupai Rodeo 1973*

te

te

32. Policeman:
Morris Jones 1973

33. Jack Jones Junior
and Senior 1973

34. At the Chute 1970

te   te

35. The Roper 1973

36. Alfred Hanna 1973

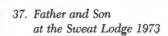

37. *Father and Son*
   at the Sweat Lodge 1973

38. *Sweat Lodge 1973*

39. Splitting Willow 1973

40. The Basket 1973

42. *Paya Sisters 1973*

le

41. *Glenda, Vivian and Barry Wescogame 1973*

43. *Paya Pout 1973*

te

le

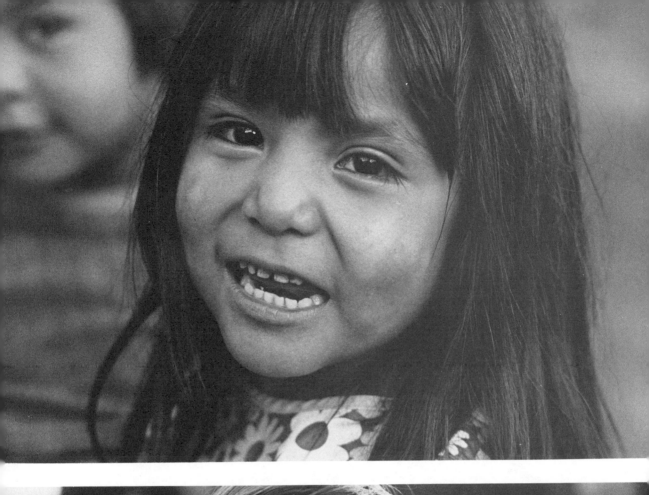

44. *Ethel Jack 1973*

45. *Marian at School 1973*

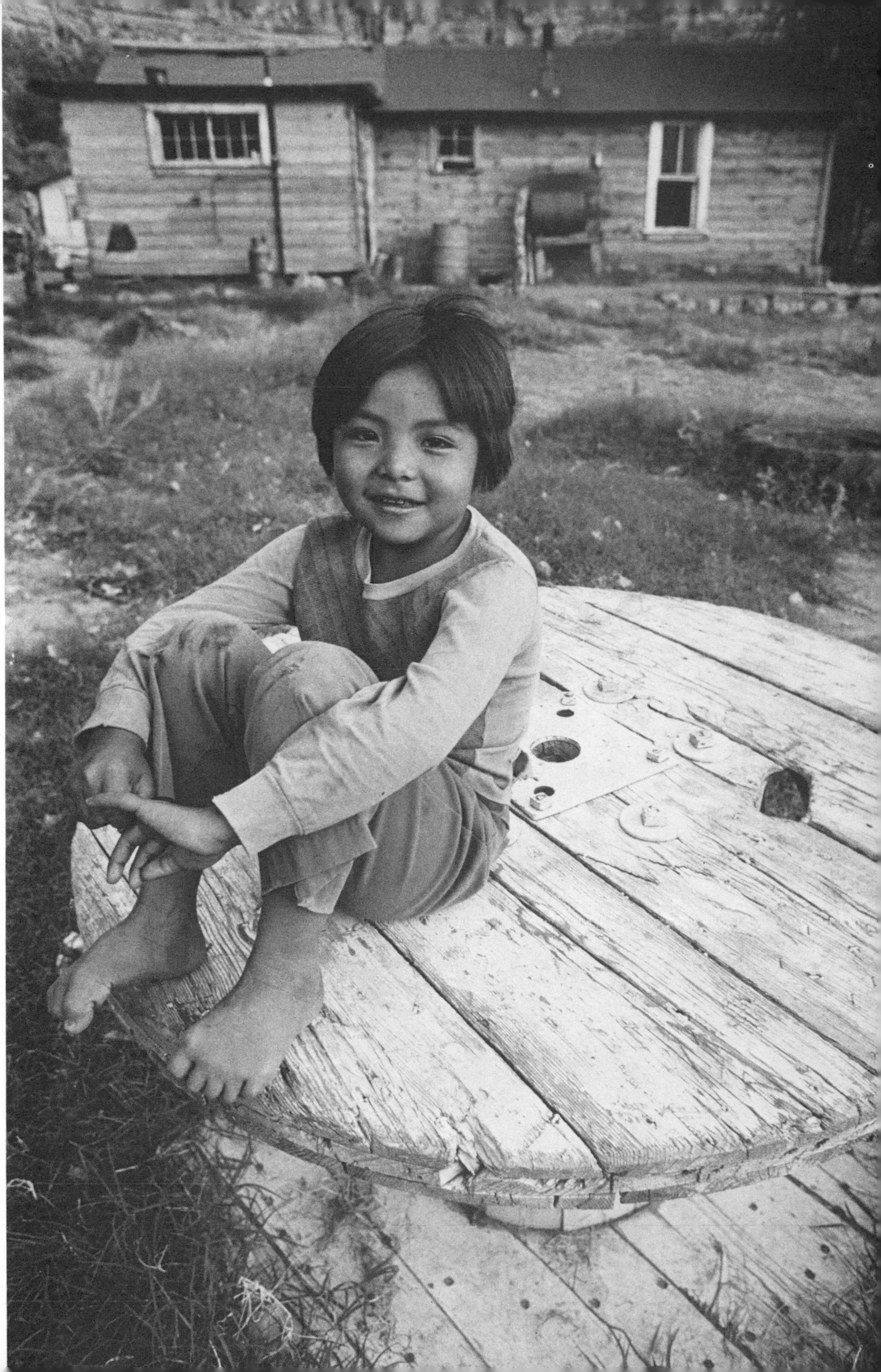

47. Nora Sinyella 1973

le

le

te

48. Glenn and Anthony Paya 1970

49. Suzanna and Daddy
    at the Rodeo 1973

51. Her Kitten 1973

le

te

50. *Sharon Uqualla 1973*

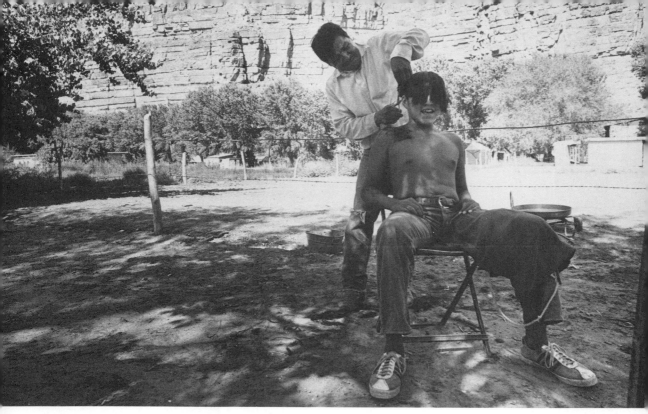

52. *Back to Boarding School: Richard Watahomigie 1973*

53. *U. S. Mailman 1973*

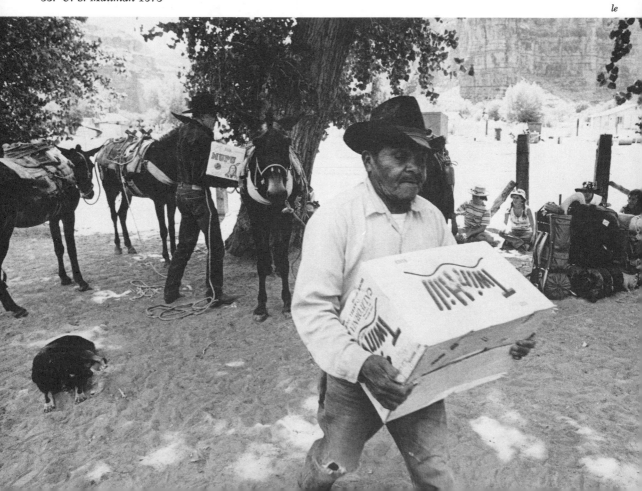

le

54. *Jennie Putesoy 1973*

55. *Bringing Home Groceries 1973*

le

56. *Rena and Ervin Crook*
with Valarie,
Galen and Carla 1973

58. *Marsha Watahomigie 1973*

59. *Suzanna on the Slide 1973*

60. Bubble Gum: Joe Watahomigie 1973

te

61. Cold Water 1969

62. *Gary in the Creek 1969*

63. *Augustine and Clara Hanna with*
    Harlan and Claudia 1973

le

64. *Lillian and Bernita Paya 1973*

65. *Leandra Watahomigie,*
   Sue and Nora Sinyella 1973

le

67. Main Street 1973

68. Barry and Vivian Wescogame 1970

le

70. Under the Cottonwoods 1973

69. *The Bridge 1973*

71. *Edward Hamidreek and Mules 1973*

72. *Nora Sinyella and Horse 1973*

te

le

Wa lúthema Havasupai subchief

Courtesy National Archives 1899

5.

SUPAI CHARLEY

Wa lúthema we called him. That means like "fire away," because he was always
the first one to kill a big buck when he saw it. You *hay gú* [white people] called
him Supai Charley. His younger brother was Baa nahmída; that means a man
who is glad all the time. His older brother was Teyáj gjáva, the corn eater.
Sometimes we called the older brother Soáta ke spó, because he was our great
songmaker. We still sing the fun songs he sang for our round dances at Peach
Festival time.

Their father had been the great one, Wa sgwívema, who made peace with
the Apaches. They were not like their father, these three brothers, but Nava hú
[Navajo] was. So we called Nava hú a big chief and the three sons of Wa
sgwívema we called little chiefs.

Wa lúthema and Baa nahmída used to go around just anywhere over the
plateaus and in the canyons off to the west of Ha vasúa in winter and even in
summer. Wa lúthema also used to go off far, far toward the sunrise and often

121

traveled to the Móga [Hopi] to trade. He liked to travel alone, for none of us could keep up with him, and he knew that hard country better than anyone else. Every time Wa lúthema had sat too long in the canyon, his eyes would begin to look far off. Before too long he would just go off along some game trails and follow the worst trails along the cliffs that most of us would not put a foot on. Sometimes he would go for months and sometimes for just a day.

Now it happened like this: Just before the snow melted in the year you call 1914, Wa lúthema took his wife, Desqídeva—that means somebody who's tattooed—and together they kind of drifted all the way to Seligman to see some friends there and accept some food and supplies from them. They stayed around a few days so they could see the railroad train go through and then they headed back up this way into our country. I guess it was just north of Black Tank they started feeling kind of hungry. Well, you know, by that year you hardly saw any deer out there any more, so he killed a calf. Some say that calf was his. He did keep some cattle around there, and he told us later that it was his own. Anyway, he and Desqídeva packed it onto one of their horses and rode on north to the Bar Four cabin just south of Hualapai Hilltop. They stayed around there a few days to eat the meat and cure the hide and just to look out the door and watch the winter sun rise.

Well, three days after they had stopped there a *hay gú* named Jim Black and several other cattlemen came there to the cabin. Jim Black claimed he owned the calf, and they were all pretty mad. Desqídeva said Wa lúthema tried to tell them the calf was his own, but that man Jim Black just yelled at Wa lúthema while another *hay gú* by the name of Bill Norton waved his gun at Wa lúthema. Finally they just pushed him onto a horse and tied his hands. Wa lúthema told Desqídeva just to stay there and not to worry; he would be back as soon as he could straighten things out with them. And then they took him off. He wasn't really worried, I guess. Those *hay gú* bothered us plenty, but they never really hurt any of us. We heard they had hurt some other people, but we had always believed it was because those people had fought with the *hay gú*. We never did that.

I guess those cattlemen took Wa lúthema to the Snowy Mountains, and they put him in jail there. Pretty soon a *hay gú* we were all friends with named Bill Pittz went down to the Snowy Mountains and talked to them there, and they just let Wa lúthema go. He came back then and told us about it.

But it wasn't any more than two or three days and Jim Black and Bill Norton were back with some others for Wa lúthema, and they still looked pretty mad. It was real cold, and they didn't give Wa lúthema any time to get a blanket or something to eat; they just took him off. I guess they took him back to the Snowy Mountains, because in a few days we got word from there that Wa lúthema was dead and they had just buried him there at the Snowy Mountains.

We felt pretty mad now, and some of us went after him. We went and dug up that place where they had put him. I was only a boy then, but some of the ones that went there said he was just stuck in some old carton. They had put chicken feathers on his head and painted red zig-zags on his face with some paint. And I guess after they got down hauling him back here to Ha vasúa, they found out somebody had, you know, castrated him. We couldn't do anything; we just washed the paint off and threw away those chicken feathers and buried him where he belongs. I can remember Desqídeva crying and crying. By then the first days of spring had come.

That was the first time any of the *hay gú* ever killed one of us. They never said any more about it. We were pretty mad, but we never did anything.

123

Supai Charley

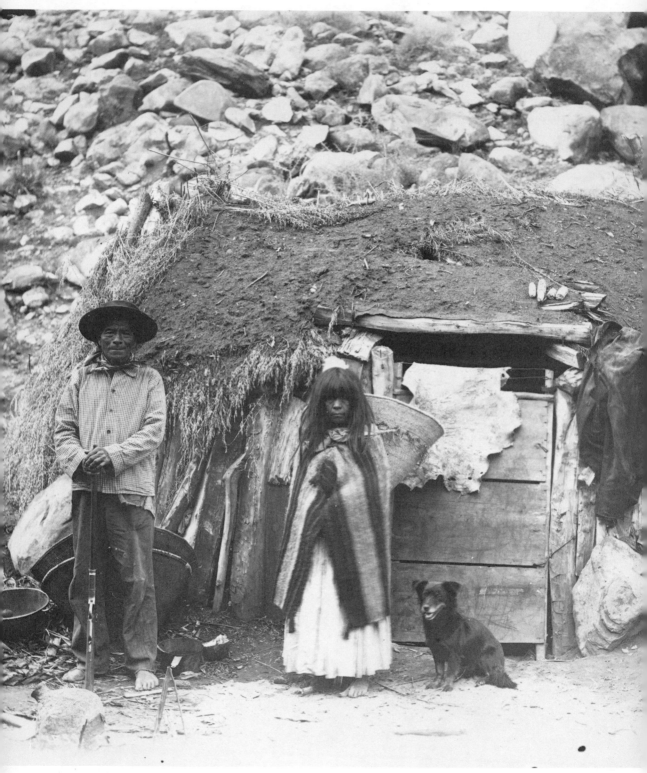

Burro and Desójva

Courtesy Southwest Museum 1899

6.

IN

THE PUBLIC

INTEREST

As early as 1914 talk began of setting aside the Grand Canyon as some sort of National Monument. Agent J. J. Taylor redoubled the efforts he had begun in 1913 to obtain plateau land for the Havasupai, writing Commissioner of Indian Affairs Cato Sells on May 11, 1914:

> It seems to me that with all the vast public domain which surrounds this Reservation, and which is apparently fit for nothing except for grazing and the gaze of the sightseer, and much of it not fit for grazing until water is developed, that these people who are so anxious for it, and have had so little done for them in the way of lands could be allowed a pasture. Out of this abundance it seems that these peacable [sic] and quiet people who have never opposed the approach of the whiteman nor disputed his progress might have enough on which to make an honest and plentiful living.
>
> They have with their own efforts and unaided, during the past winter

fenced in this large pocket formed by Grand and Cataract Canyons and constructed some six or eight good sized reservoirs in which to impound water. They hope to catch these full during the rains of August for stock purposes. They have built this seven or eight miles of good strong fence with the full expectation that the Government is going to set this aside for their use as a pasture. The fence was nearing completion when I took charge here. . . .

This land is within the Forest Reserve, but in so far as the timber is concerned is of no value whatever. I understand that this is wholly or in part within the proposed National Monument boundary, but it looks to a man on the ground and familiar with the circumstances that it would be a greater "Monument" to our Government to dedicate it to the use of these Indians. It is absolutely certain that they cannot carry it away nor tear it down. In a thousand years they could neither fill up these canyons, nor perceptibly enlarge them if they kept busy all the time.

It seems to one who is familiar with the amounts of money which has [sic] been spent on other Indians, supposedly towards their being placed on a basis of self support, that these people who do not ask for gifts from the Government ought to be allowed a chance to make men of themselves. It is my firm belief that if these people could have the money, in one tenth of the amount, that I have seen spent in one year on the improvement of Agency buildings used towards their assistance, that with proper and judicious supervision, in ten years, they would be self supporting.[53]

Taylor also wrote in his letter asking the Commissioner to permit credit sales of cattle to individual Indians, and he said he would vouch for their repayment, every one, within five to eight years. The Office of Indian Affairs replied on July 9 to say repayment of any loans for cattle "must be made by the Indians within four years after the date of the agreement." The letter then responded to the request for a pasture by noting that Taylor's predecessor had already brought this up, and the Forest Service was offering the Indians a permit, which was "better." The Office concluded that "It is not clear . . . just what further action is necessary. . . . It might be well for you to also communicate with the local Forester in regard to the matter." [54] The response was a strong indication that the Office of Indian Affairs felt inclined to wash its hands of the Havasupai since the Indian Rights Association annoyance had died down.

As interest in the proposed Monument grew with the passage of the National Park Service Act in 1916, the new Havasupai agency supervisor S. A. M. Young in his May 8, 1916, narrative report to the regional Indian office in Gallup said:

Since the Havasupai Indians are entirely dependent upon the land held under permit from the forest reserve as far as the live stock industry is concerned, and since they have expended much labor in an endeavor to develop water, which efforts will probably be successful, it seems only fair that steps be taken if necessary to protect the Indians in the use of the lands they are using. This tract comprises about 230,000 acres and is under fence. There is so little grass on this land that the tract is none too large for the Havasupai Indians. . . . If the arrangement is not fairly permanent it would seem useless to put forth much effort to develop the live stock industry among these Indians.[55]

The Government had committed itself very strongly to the idea of a National Park in the area by this time without any knowledge of or even interest in any prior claims to any of the area. The Havasupai had as their home what the government saw only as a scenic marvel to be opened up to the public. Opening it up seemed to hinge on trying to terminate the usages of the Canyon's original inhabitants in their own home. The establishment of this park marked the most damaging encroachment on their life yet dealt out by the federal government. At a stroke all the tiny gains made from 1908 to 1916 were wiped away.

By 1917 Arizona Senator Henry F. Ashurst and Arizona Representative Carl Hayden had submitted S 8250 to establish a Grand Canyon National Park. H. F. Robinson, the Indian Service's regional irrigation superintendent in Alburquerque read the report issued by the Chairman of the Public Lands Committee on the bill and the Secretary of Interior's opinion and wrote to Hayden on June 12, 1917, that these had made "no mention of any Indian lands or any desire to reserve a portion of this for Indian Use, but it is probable the Secretary . . . was unaware of the necessities of the little handful of Supai Indians who live in Cataract Canyon." Robinson continued that "It is apparent that if these Indians are required to remain in the bottom of this canyon all of the time, there can be little chance for advancement and the Indians are virtually prisoners on a small tract of ground entirely inadequate for their support as there is less than one acre of cultivated ground per capita." [56]

Robinson referred Hayden to a map prepared by Havasupai superintendent Gensler proposing lands that should be returned to the Havasupai and informed him of the Indian Office's hope to locate the agency office and tribal school on the mesa at Topocóba Hilltop. Robinson's letter also referred to Gensler's wish to have Pasture Wash included in the return.

In the middle of the proceedings the Forest Service decided to intensify the pressure on the Havasupai and in December of 1917 allowed white ranchers to begin using this very Pasture Wash farming area. This was probably the most valuable single area of plateau land the Havasupai had on the top; it was the location of many handmade earth dams and homes, some of which are still standing today. Pasture Wash was the only area on top that could support farming and living year round because it was possible to channel seasonal water into the series of small Havasupai reservoirs built there.

Agent C. H. Gensler again wrote directly to Hayden on July 30, 1918, and urged the return of the Indian Pasture to the Havasupai, as long as the land was to be reorganized again:

For some years these Indians have had the use of this "Indian Pasture" on an annual free use permit. It is good in so far as it provides the Indians with range for one year. It is not good for the reason that the Indian knows it is an annual permit and can be reversed at the end of any one year. . . .

Last year the Forest Service drew the lines in on this range by giving some white men a permit on some range the Indians had and advised the Indians to build more tanks or they would draw the lines in further. . . .

I should like to see this pasture made a part of this Indian reservation and to have the present eastern line moved east to include the west one mile of range 1 west or at least section 6, [Pasture Wash] township 31 north, range 1 west. Our Indians are farming section 6, and they need it. . . .[57]

Hayden's reply to the repeated appeals from the Havasupai people and their agency was to rewrite section 3 of the Grand Canyon bill. Originally this section had provided that the Park Service administration at Grand Canyon could lease out Park land for grazing purposes and the money derived thereby could be applied to the administration and improvement of the Grand Canyon Park. He reworded this to say

That nothing herein contained shall affect the rights of the Havasupai Tribe of Indians to the use and occupancy of the bottom lands of the Canyon of Cataract Creek . . . and the Secretary of Interior is hereby authorized, in his discretion to permit individual members of said tribe to use and occupy other tracts of land within said park for agricultural purposes.

And on February 26, 1919, Congress passed the bill including this language, once again failing to provide any material justice to the real owners of the new park.

Gensler had never received a satisfactory reply to his complaint about the loss of Pasture Wash and in his June 30, 1919, annual report to the Commissioner he wrote that the Havasupai were still farming upon the plateau in that area, but added that

The Forest Service are reluctant in granting a permit for farming up there, claiming this land is more valuable for grazing purposes than for farming.

Last winter the Forest Service issued permits to several white cattlemen to graze their stock on the Indian Pasture. There is not feed and water to justify this and other motives behind this place it in the light of a dirty piece of business.

It has been the result of stopping our development work there as the Indians now believe they will eventually loose [sic] this pasture and all the work they have done there in developing water which runs up into thousands of dollars.[58]

The Office of Indian Affairs made one final attempt to have 87,000 acres withdrawn from Tusayan National Forest—the remainder of the Coconino

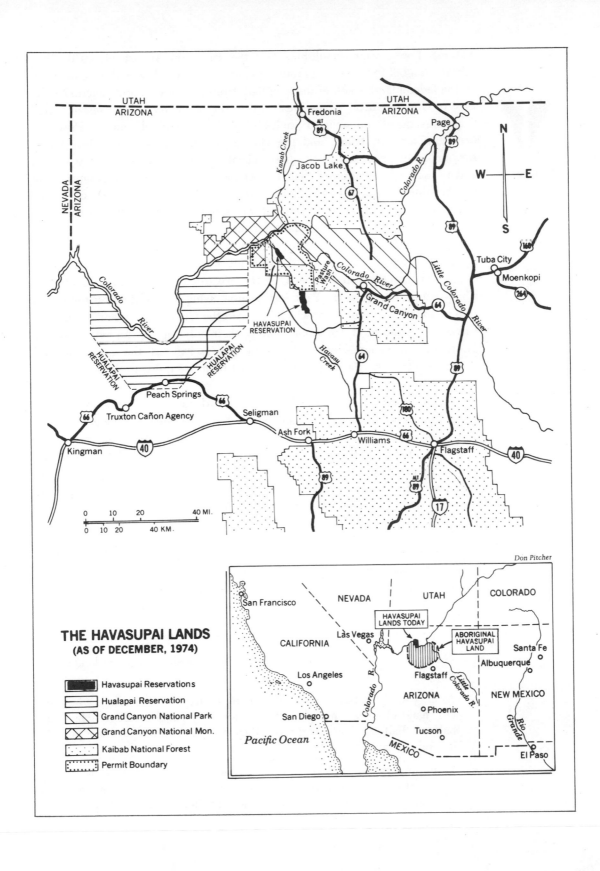

THE HAVASUPAI LANDS
(AS OF DECEMBER, 1974)

- ■ Havasupai Reservations
- ▤ Hualapai Reservation
- ▨ Grand Canyon National Park
- ▩ Grand Canyon National Mon.
- ⁛ Kaibab National Forest
- ⋯ Permit Boundary

Don Pitcher

National Forest after establishment of the Park—on August 14, 1920. They submitted a bill to Congress to return plateau lands which would have included all the federal lands south of the new Park from the present drift fence 17 miles west of Grand Canyon Village westward to the boundary of the present Grand Canyon National Monument 6½ miles before the Hualapai boundary. However, even this attempt failed, and the Havasupai now found themselves finally surrounded by a reorganization whose officials again proved to be hostile to them and to their attempts to use their former plateau range. The Havasupai agent was bewildered and wrote the Commissioner of Indian Affairs in October 1920 to ask just what rights the Indians had remaining to them on the plateau. The question was referred to the superintendent of the Grand Canyon Park, who replied in November that "it seems to me that the Indians are entitled to the use of this area, having constructed the drift fence some years ago under a special use permit from the Forest Service." [59] He forwarded to the agent four copies of a one-year permit to use the Park Service area "lying west of the drift fence," an area of 150,000 acres or more which included the Great Thumb and around the Havasupai trailhead at Topocóba Hilltop, their only link to the outside world. The Assistant Commissioner of Indian Affairs assured the agent he had determined that the Havasupai also retained their use rights to the area west of Cataract Canyon on federal land.

Yet it rapidly became clear that the new Park carried an even more callous attitude toward the Havasupai than had the Forest Service. Within a very short time, the Park Service informed the tribe they should build no more rain reservoirs on Park land. Certainly the accounts from the early 1920s in a book written by one of the early Park Service employees at Grand Canyon bespeak their resentment toward the Havasupai, who perversely refused to disappear so Havasu Canyon could be added to the Park as well:

> For some reason, even though it was a very severe winter, the Supai Indians had come up from their home in Havasu Canyon, "Land of the Sky-Blue Water," made famous by [the composer] Cadman and were camped among the trees on a hillside. The barefoot women and filthy children were quite friendly but the lazy, filthy bucks would have been insolent had I been alone. . . . the children filled sacks with snow to melt for drinking purposes. To be sure they didn't waste any of it in washing themselves.

> The Supai women are without dignity or appeal. . . . They begged for everything in sight. . . .

> At the end of the trail one stumbles upon the tiny, hidden village where the last handful of a once-powerful nation has sought refuge. Half-clad, half-fed, half-wild, one might say, they hide away there in their poverty, ignorance and superstition. . . .

> From a powerful and prosperous tribe of thousands this nation has dwindled down to less than two hundred wretched weaklings. Driven to this canyon fastness from their former dwelling place by more warlike

tribes, they have no coherent account of their wanderings or their ancestors. . . . They are held in low esteem by all other Indian tribes and never marry outside of their own people. . . . This last fragment will pass away within a few years and all trace will be lost. . . . It is a people looking backward down the years with no thought of the morrow. . . . Not many morrows for that doomed tribe.[60]

The Associate Director of the National Park Service warmly endorsed the book, and the Park quickly began to carry out activities designed to speed the departure of "this last fragment," as interviews with many Havasupai reveal. Park rangers finally broke the Havasupai use of their winter range by coming around and physically destroying their camps and telling the people they should stay in the woodless canyon in winter.

Lemuel Paya remembered in 1972, "The National Park was claiming this land. They refused us to camp up there and cut green trees. They was kinda stingy with land. They knew Supais used to live up there and they wanted us to stay put. The rangers would come around and tell camps to go back to the canyon. A government man came in here and said, 'You Indian tribe are not supposed to make a home in two places. Not down here and up there. In order to stop this you stay here and do your farming.' We found we had nothing left to use up there."

Lee Marshall tells, "Our people were picking piñon in the twenties at Grand Canyon. The rangers chased them out and told them, 'We want to save it for birds and squirrels.' But we've got just as much right; Indians are living things, too."

Some few individuals were able to continue their use of the plateau in very isolated areas, but even they tell of their eventual departure, suddenly struck by the strange loneliness on the deserted plateau.

According to Duke Iditicáva, "I was getting too old, and my eyesight was too poor, so I didn't go up any more."

Mack Putesoy remembers, "I finally stopped going up because there's too many white people up there, too close by. Too many cattle, no more game. So sometimes," he confesses, "we'd have to get a big steer."

To make the best of what amounted to confinement in the canyon the tribal people encouraged the spread of the few cottonwoods in the canyon. They quickly took hold, and the Havasupai began to grow them as a crop (see p. 10). Baa gelága (Morning Bird Man), the Havasupai gethië'e (shaman), whom the Europeans called Bob, had died in December 1918. Baa gelága had received his powers and his songs from his grandfather but at his death he said he wanted his spirit to leave him and so conferred his power on no one. Only Hotauta's son Tom Yunési carried on any of Baa gelága's songs; the rest of his powers died with Yunési.

Within a year or so Baa 'nyá, lying sick in a cabin on the plateau, died also. His powers were such that his people cremated him far out on the edge of the plateau. The songs which he had learned from his mother's brother may, even today, work their force when sung by the elderly grandson of that uncle. The two gethiè'e projected such personal force that contemporary observers estimated them to be more influential on the Havasupai than either Mánakaja or Swèdeva. The Havasupai could ill afford the loss of such men with the new trials ahead of them.

Up above, in 1926 the Park Service began constructing a sewer line to service the growing white community at the South Rim; they relocated and consolidated the two or three Havasupai camps westward to their present location astride the sewer line the Havasupai were helping to construct. The Park superintendent surveyed off a 160-acre plot and told the Havasupai they could stay on it. About three Havasupai families still live in this little camp under the big pines just west of the railroad station, but they are subject to continual pressure from the National Park Service to vacate. Sometime around the early twenties the Park Service made a big sign they placed on Swèdeva's house by the well which read, "Home of Big Jim, Chief of all the Supais."

The Havasupai say Captain Burro was still farming Indian Gardens in the twenties, much to the Park Service's annoyance. They tell that two rangers finally went down in 1928 and told Burro he would have to go and chased him out. They say Burro stood on the rim, looked down at the place and wept for it. He died the following year, and his wife in 1930. An era had ended for the Havasupai.

The loss meant rage, bitterness, tears and dejection. The loss still lives in the controlled tightness of old men's stories, in the indignant words of their wives.

Before she died, Mary Wescògame was asked if she had left her home at Grand Canyon voluntarily. Her interpreter heard her and replied, "No, she didn't give up the place voluntarily. Today she would come back and fight for it if she was given a chance." [61] Mary Wescògame was completely blind by then.

Here, it must live again for you, that last season on the plateau. You may place it at 1920 or 1930; it came to each person and finally to all.

The names which appear in "A Season on the Plateau" are the Indian names of real people, in many cases living individuals, whose recorded names may be more like Rock Jones or Pete Marshall. Two names are fictional: Baa vam nyuéva hija, *which means "Young Man Starting a Family," and* Baqí, *which means simply "Woman." These two, who are patterned after real individuals, must live for all Havasupai.*

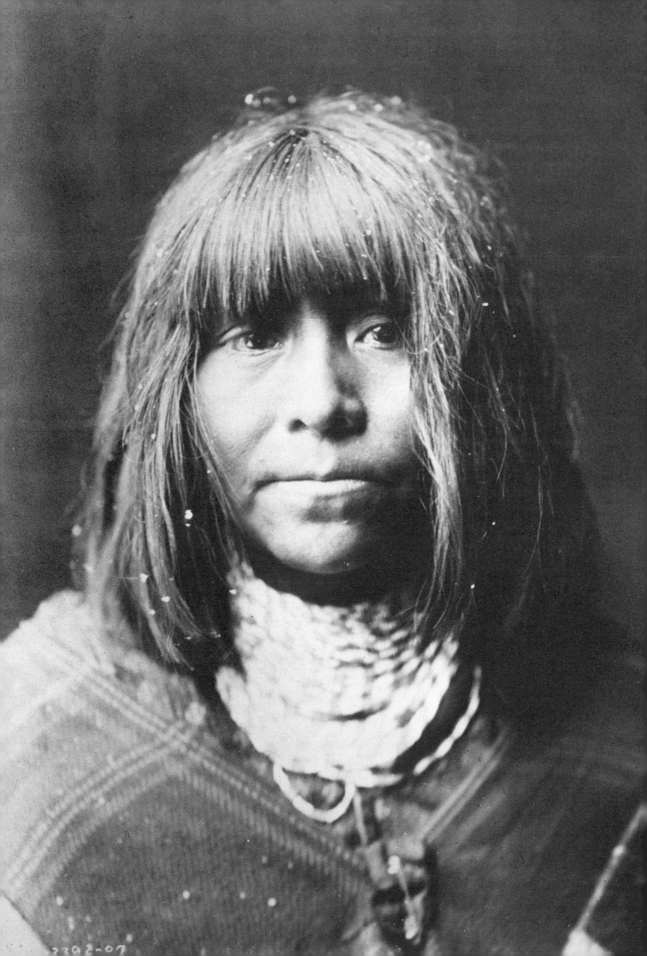

7.

A SEASON
ON
THE PLATEAU

The time is *sal j'ála'*; the five stars of the Hand, across the sky from the star that does not move, enter the sky. The year begins [November].

A man stands almost lost in the dry vastness of the plain, listening to the predawn stillnesses. He is lightly clad in a long buckskin shirt and leggings but seems not to mind the early morning chill. The first frost has yet to come. The man, Baa vam nyuéva hija, prepares his horse for travel and speaks to it as he cinches up the old, open-cantled, nail-studded saddle.

Close by, blue smoke rises thinly from Baa's *wa jemátv*, the low, earth-covered conical house he and his wife put up three winters before when they came to stay with her people. Their houses cluster nearby. Inside, Baa's wife, Baqí, feeds an occasional piñon knot and the slow-burning juniper into the fire, which produces no flame, only red coals that crack softly. She listens happily to her man preparing the horse outside and continues her work of smearing heated piñon pitch onto the willow water jug she has made. Their child still

135

Dotháamja Half-sister of Hmány gejáa

Courtesy Havasupai Tribal Collection 1907

sleeps in her cradleboard. Baqí dips her stick into the pitch, which she has already mixed with burnt yucca root, and daubs it around the inside of the jug. Soon she will carefully hold the jug near the coals, but not too near, and turn it slowly on sticks to soften the pitch and let it run into all the cracks and seal them. Too near, and the whole work goes up in flames; it takes a fine touch. She hears leather creak as her man swings onto the horse, and she listens as the hooves pad away.

Though Baa is only going over to his small field at The Farms [Pasture Wash], he carries his ash-wood bow and reed arrows with him. He chuckles to remember his fear, as a boy, at returning to Blue Creek to cut reeds for arrows. Then he had been haunted by stories of the boys who first cut arrows at their peril, for the canyon walls would close together and trap them. Even though he had been assured that the boys had shot their arrows into the walls and stopped them from closing again forever, his fear had made him cut rapidly and poorly. In later years, when he came to understand it had been but a story, he traveled quite eagerly to select the drying reeds by the spring; several of them would go together, racing on foot and stopping to swim in the warm afternoon. The summers in the canyon had really shown him the pleasure Blue Creek brings the people; he remembers wagering arrows with the other boys and standing among them chanting, "*Tenyã, tenyã, tenyã . . .*" while the winner would try to shoot the target from the air or else return all the arrows he had won. Baa thinks wistfully of that easy time when one could live openly.

With the passage of the early autumn rains and the onset of cold weather comes the best time to see a fat deer. As he rides, Baa sings to the sun to send him a deer today, which he will share with his friends.

After an hour's ride Baa reaches the gentle grassy trough of The Farms, where the seeds he set in the earth before leaving last spring have now matured after the autumn rains. He shuffles through the pumpkin vines and observes with slight irritation that someone has "borrowed" one of his ripening pumpkins. Let it be so; there are enough. He finds upon inspection that the corn has dried nicely on the stalk. The deer have helped themselves to no more than a few; the log fence keeps out all but the boldest. Baa plucks some of the colorful ears and holds them up to the sun a moment before taking them over to stuff them into the gunnysack tied to the pommel. The horse calmly munches a pile of drying cornstalks Baa lays by the tree where he is tied. Baa binds together a large sheaf of cornstalks with some quickly plaited corn fibers and slings them onto the saddle as well. The horse shall also eat well later.

He then takes up a horse shoulder bone lying nearby and begins to dig for some potatoes. He digs enough to fill his gunnysack and then sews it shut with the deer thong stitched into it. As he works, a light wind springs up from the juniper groves on the hillslope toward the rising sun. He removes his shirt as the sun warms the earth.

Baa is just knotting the thong when he catches a slight musky odor on the piñon-scented breeze. He continues working and fooling with the saddle while carefully slipping the bow and arrows over the horse's rump. Pressing these along his shaded side he casually walks back to the potatoes and retrieves the horse bone, bundling the bow and arrows with it in his hand. He digs around toward the sun and looks up carefully without stopping his regular digging movements. A deer stands at the edge of the piñon grove a hard stone's throw away. Baa quickly scans the horizon to see if anyone is in sight; his lips move as he sings to the deer, moving casually toward it. He stops, lays down the bundle in his hand and begins to dig on his knees, still singing. He is perhaps close enough to toss the horse bone to the grove. He rises to one knee holding the bow with an arrow fitted to the string, continuing to paw at the earth. Baa still feels the unmoving presence of the deer as he sings softly; he knows he must move well. He looks up smoothly and gazes an instant into the deer's eyes, unmoving, unblinking. The horizon is still clear. Nervously the deer breaks the charm and turns, presenting for an instant the broadside view Baa prefers. He raises the bow with the same motion he draws back the string and sends the arrow from one knee. His shot anticipates the deer's move to the right and strikes deeply behind the shoulder muscles. By the time the deer leaps from the blow, Baa has already sent another arrow for the neck and is on his feet running with the remaining two arrows as the deer crashes away into the grove. The second arrow strikes a shoulder obliquely and glances away into the brush. Baa sees the deer is already losing much blood; he will drop very soon. He turns aside toward the brush where his arrow flew and spends several minutes locating it near the base of a gnarled juniper. He then returns to his horse, climbs on and drops the corn and potatoes to the ground to set off into the piñon and juniper following the bright blood spatters. Soon he hears thrashing ahead and dismounts, tying the horse, who is always nervous at rustling in these low, dense groves. The deer has sunk to its knees and rolls its eyes at Baa's approach. Baa speaks softly to the deer, telling it death is necessary. It is no bad thing to die, as he will now provide for the humans. Someday, Baa promises the deer, he, too, will die and return to make the earth richer for the deer's brothers. We are linked together, he says, and plunges his knife into the failing deer's throat. Out of respect for the deer, Baa has concealed the knife from him. He then hangs the deer from a branch to let it drain so the meat will not be strong; by now he watches the horizon much more frequently.

After the blood stops flowing, Baa covers it with dirt. He ties the deer carcass across his saddle and then leads the horse back toward the flat wash to pick up the corn and potatoes at his field and tie them onto the saddle peg again. He selects one large, ripe pumpkin and tucks it under his arm. He smiles at the thought of pumpkin and venison stew and thanks Sun, the keeper of the deer.

He heads north along the wash's swale with the horse in tow, always moving fast and avoiding the ridges that are bare of trees. Before the sun has moved a hand he reaches Mugúlo's place and calls him out.

"Ho!" Mugúlo answers from within and appears at the door, a short muscular man with straight bangs and a wide mouth.

"How's it coming?" greets Baa. "I've got a treat for us—fresh meat. Give me a hand with it." Mugúlo helps him slide the deer from the horse, and the two of them set quickly to work flaying the carcass, folding the hide flesh side inward to preserve its moisture. They remove the stomach and intestines and empty them, and Baa slits the stomach and places the liver, heart and other delicacies inside. He and Mugúlo share some of the raw liver, still warm, while they rest a moment. Then Mugúlo lays open the large intestine and scrapes the lining out while Baa uses a stick to poke the nerve tissue out of the skull and vertebrae. He places this in the intestine and then ties it shut to keep it moist for tanning the hide later. Baa then hacks a haunch from the carcass and hands it to Mugúlo's wife, Tethèqeja, to take inside while the men stop their work to talk. Soon Tethèqeja rejoins them; this fine-featured woman is daughter of Hmány gejáa, the *baa gemúlva,* and she brings a new animation to the talk. She laughs in surprise when Mugúlo tells her Baa has killed the deer with an arrow; Baa says he still prefers the bow as it is quieter. They excitedly share news of other families. Mugúlo has recently seen Swèdeva, who stopped by on the way to his place near The Spruce Trees. Swèdeva was returning from Blue Creek with some herbs for Jóla's daughter, who is feeling quite sick. Wa tahómja has a new pinto horse for which he traded some shelled corn and red paint to a Hwamú [Navajo]. He, Mugúlo himself, wouldn't mind trading for such a one.

Baa chats awhile longer and then sees by the sky he must go in order to reach home before dark, walking as he is. Tethèqeja calls him to wait and eat with them before he goes on, and they sit before the door of the *wa jemátv* and eat piñon stew with flat píka bread. When Baa has eaten his fill the sun is half down and the day still warm; he feels reluctant to set off again but rises to go.

The walk is long and follows mostly flat clearings and threads around ridges on the eroded plateau. Always he stays close to cover. He notices during the warm afternoon how the flies have begun on the deer. As the sun nears the horizon he is winding down a wide, sloping wash which eventually leads to Blue Creek. The wash levels onto a flat before resuming its descent a good walk's distance off, and he sees his *wa* among those of his wife's people. The little earth-covered huts are all but indiscernible by the junipers; only the faint blue of the smoke betrays their presence. Baa is pleased at how well they blend into the trees and earth. Once they used to live on the ridges and knolls where they could see the earliest and latest signs of the sun, but now that means to be seen as well.

He is slinging down the remainder of the deer carcass when Baqí comes out; her wide-set eyes shine to see the deer. She brushes back her bangs and laughs, "Did you grow that in your garden?"

Her straight-bottomed eyes crinkle as she presses Baa's arm and tells him she is happy with him. The two of them carry the deer and the vegetables to the door. In the last light Baqí begins hacking the deer into pieces while Baa unsaddles the horse. He brings the buckskin and holds it toward her: "Here will be a fine buckskin. I'll take it to the spring tomorrow to soften it. You'll have some new boots, softer than before."

Baqí smiles and continues cutting at the deer. Finally she hangs the pieces on a rack behind the house, beyond the reach of Coyote and his friends. Tomorrow she will cut the flesh into strips and hang them to dry.

They stoop into the *wa* in turn and pull the blanket over the door. The early winter chill is beginning with the sunset. Inside, the earthen and timber walls seem faintly red in the crackling glow; the air feels warm and smoky, and the stars waver and flicker through the fumes leaving the smoke hole. Together they sit on the earth before the fire, and Baqí molds their child's legs straight while he tells her of the visit at Mugúlo's. After replacing the cooing child on the cradleboard she lays some liver on the flat rock over the coals where she has already smeared some deer fat. *"Laa!"* she exclaims as Baa slices a raw piece from the frying liver and swallows it. He laughs and tells her to wait; he is going to take some venison over to her mother and father.

By the time he returns the liver is done, and they give small amounts of it to the child after chewing it first to soften it. Now that the child is growing they will soon be going away to live with Baa's people. The liver is quickly gone. They sit talking quietly for a time and then lie down together under the rabbit-fur blanket.

▼

As the morning sun flashes on the horizon behind him, Baa rides along bearing the deer-hide bundle, the tied intestine and a piece of deer ribs. He feels very cheerful out here below the tops of the ridges, where the chances of being seen are slight and one can ride openly. His way follows the winding wash downward until the plateau abruptly gives way to a sheer cliff of stunning height. Here the trail becomes a serpentine track down the face of the white rock cliff to the canyon floor below. The canyon's gorge splits the entire earth it seems, and he has often heard that the beings of the underground still live in some of its depths. The canyon below still lies in shade as he begins the steep descent along a break in the cliff. Many mountain sheep signs dot the narrow trail, and he sees that another man has recently passed upward—probably Swèdeva. He rides in chill shade when he reaches the flat esplanade at the foot of the white cliffs where begins the gradual descent along a deepening watercourse winding toward Blue Creek. He stops by a large cottonwood at the base of the cliffs where a pool shimmers in a rocked-up basin by the tree. This is where humans drink. About twenty feet farther on another rock dam impounds the overflow where horses can drink, and his does. He could ride on down to the spring below the pine tree but decides to work here when the horse is finished.

After the horse has drunk its fill, Baa lays the deer hide flat in the clear water below the spring and covers it with rocks; the tied intestine with its moist contents he hangs by a sinew from a higher branch on the cottonwood. He then climbs back onto the horse and turns back toward the cliff he has descended.

At the top of the cliff he continues up the deep wash until he meets a shallow canyon coming in from the left. He follows that canyon higher and higher until he has almost regained the plateau. A gray breath of smoke shimmers in the air ahead, and he rides toward it until the darker mouth of the cave becomes visible. Dismounting, he walks toward the cave, where he can see people moving about.

"Father," he calls.

"Huh? Who's that I hear?" his father's hoarse voice replies.

"It's me," Baa answers, going in among the people sitting around the fire in the cave.

"*Jaa!* How's it coming?" exclaims the straight old man piling brush on the fire.

"Great!" Baa replies. Here in this place about six older people stay during the winter protected from the harsh winds of the plateau and from any need to move; one unmarried woman in middle life stays with them and cooks for them. It is quite pleasant here, sheltered from the weather. The cave is located on a slope facing the sun most of the day.

Baa's father is a leathery man with failing sight but still vigorous movements; he chuckles to see his son and presses his arm with delight. "What brings you this way?"

"I brought some fresh meat for you people here, something better than rabbit meat," Baa says and hands his father the deer ribs.

"Well, I think we know what to do with that," his father laughs. "And what more?"

Baa tells of his conversation with Mugúlo. His father nods as he mentions Jóla's daughter. When Baa finishes, his father says, "Yes, yes; Swèdeva stopped here and told me his grandniece is feeling pretty sick with aches and quite hot. I told him he should get some of the small bush that smells sweetly in the washes and boil that for her to drink and some of the bush that smells sharp suddenly on the rock slopes and boil that to rub on her, and it may help. She is a very pretty little girl who will make a fine woman one day. She likes to laugh and loves the sun," he muses.

Baa nods. They speak awhile more of one thing and another, and then he goes out to catch cottontails for them to eat tonight. He will stay here tonight with his father and then finish preparing the hide in the morning.

▼

In the morning he rises early to watch the first flare of dawn from the ridge above the cave. Soon the piñon and juniper seem to take fire from the sun, and the first pink edge appears on the opposite canyon rim. He returns for his horse and sets out for the spring. At the spring the air chills him thoroughly, and he sees the faintest crystals of ice on the edges of the stiller water pockets. Removing the hide from the water, he flops it over a small log he has propped against the cottonwood and squats before it. Taking the horse-bone beaming tool he has brought along he begins vigorously scraping the hair from the hide. This takes several hours and leaves him feeling quite tired when it is finished.

Now Baa opens the intestine and removes the brain and spinal tissue stored within. He places these tissues in a still rock pool below the horses' drinking place and pounds them into a fluid mixture. He takes mouthfuls of the mixture and sprays it onto the hide while rubbing it in, working circularly from the center to the edges. When all the mixture has been rubbed into the hide, he rolls up the hide tightly and rolls a blanket around it.

After a few minutes he takes up the hide and throws it onto his horse. He feels glad to let the horse carry him now.

Baa stops at the cave on the way back to spend that night. In the morning he and his father twist the hide dry and spend the remainder of the day by the fire in the exhausting work of stretching and working the hide until it is completely dry. When it is finished late in the afternoon they examine the hide in the light and find it soft and snowy white. They lie by the fire resting and talking for a while more, and then Baa rises to leave.

"Why don't you come back with me, Father? Stay with us. We have room for you."

"No, this place is warmer and safer for us old people. We can't all stay together so well any more; here no one bothers us. I can't get around up there well enough, but I do well here. I'll return with you to Blue Creek when planting time comes, and you'll come to live with your family again."

"I hear you."

Baa wishes him well and promises to return again before the deep snows. Baa knows his father will not return to the plateau again; that time is over for him. The plateaus are no place to be slow and dim-eyed. At the cave one can sing and drowse in the sun; on the plateau the arching sky and keen air demand clarity and speed, and now there is the new and ever-present danger.

▼

The first snow has come during the night. Baa sees its depth makes no more than the thickness of his foot, and the sun will be warm again today. He and Baqí fill every vessel with snow and scrape more into a trough by the house. Now there will be water. Four days have passed since the killing of the deer; in another four they will go for piñon nuts at the place where the Móga [Hopi] people come. Today he will make a sweat bath.

The sweat lodge stands near their hut, and Baa patches it where the summer rains breached the earth and brush cover. Already the sun feels warm on his face, and the chill earth begins to dampen under his feet. He takes juniper limbs from beside the *wa* and, using a coal from inside, starts a fire near the sweat lodge. When the fire blazes up hot and nearly smokeless, Baa begins raking rocks from the interior of the sweat lodge and placing them in the fire. The rocks that one uses for the sweat bath are the hard, white ones with sharp edges, about the size of his feet; they are further whitened by repeated heating.

When the rocks begin to take on an ashen gray, Baa lifts one from the fire with sticks and replaces it inside the sweat lodge. He repeats this until he has placed about a dozen large rocks inside. Baqí brings a large water basket full of snow from under the low shrubs and junipers nearby. Baa strips down to a buckskin breech cloth and backs into the small entrance, calling on the heat to keep him well. Baqí hands him the water basket and backs in herself, pulling the flap over the opening when she is inside. For a moment both squat in silence, getting accustomed to the heat. Baa finally perceives a faint red glow to the right of the entrance, which he is facing, where the hot rocks lie. He flips snow at the glow and begins to sing loudly, now sitting cross-legged in the low lodge. As the heat begins to prickle his skin he calls for it to cleanse him and sings for health for both of them and for their daughter. His breath seems to sear each part of his body as he blows on his skin. He can hear Baqí doing the same.

As he finishes his song the third time, the heat has gripped his body everywhere, and sweat pours from him. He begins to bend low to the ground to breathe for his fourth repetition and feels Baqí's hair against his face; she is already well down to the ground. Upon completion, Baa strikes the ground with the flat of his hand, and Baqí pulls the flap aside. They crawl out into the chill air, Baa crying, "That's good; that's good!" Baqí has pulled her buckskin apron to her waist, and sweat is streaming down her body. They both lie on the damp earth beside the fire; the sun feels soothing, and the early snow is nearly gone. After a moment Baqí takes the basket and refills it with snow from the shade; Baa lifts four more rocks inside the lodge. After that he backs into it again, followed by Baqí. Before closing the flap she hands him the water basket. In the quick light before the flap closes she smiles at him seriously, though they will avoid any physical familiarity during the process. This time the lodge is much hotter.

By the fourth time they enter the lodge, others of Baqí's family have come to take their turn in the sweat bath. Inside Baa and his wife bend quite near the ground, though he continues to sing quite loudly. The heat is dizzying, and they see sparkles of color before their eyes in the darkness. "That's good; that's good!" he cries at length and slaps the blanket flap. They crawl out rapidly, gasping as their sweat runs onto the earth. Both of them trot to the juniper and begin to rub snow vigorously on each other until each is cleansed. Baa shouts with joy at the cold which stings his hands and pains his skin. His head aches with the cold. He waits by the fire for Baqí, rubbing himself vigorously with a blanket; he hands this to her as she walks up to the fire, shivering. Her skin fairly glows. Now they are ready for the coming winter, and they return to the *wa*.

▼

After four days they set off on two horses toward the piñon groves; they have left the child with Baqí's mother. Baqí carries a large, conical burden basket on her saddle. The day is clear and cold, and the horses' breaths steam as they go. At the piñon grove beyond The Big Reservoir [Big Tank] they see several other families already moving among the trees; Wa tahómja, Mugúlo, Chikapánega, Sinyella and Wa tesgògama hail them as they ride up. All live near the grove. Several of the women rush up to Baqí to share news, and Baqí admires Chikapánega's wife, who is pregnant, and goes off laughing with the women to begin shelling piñon and filling the burden baskets. All around are ladies and children scouring the ground under the trees for piñon nuts; the men work slower, shaking trees and sometimes stopping to smoke. The families have set up a rough little camp, and the atmosphere is one of festival. The gatherers hail other arrivals, some of whom bring coffee and food to heat over the fire, which by now sends a blue curl through the piñon to the sky.

Suddenly one of the ladies on the sunrise side of the grove shouts to the others to look off toward The Farms. Everyone stops working and looks to see two riders on large horses coming their way. The riders wear the strange hats of the *hay gú* [white men] at the big canyon.

The families stand apprehensively as they approach; even the children stop playing. As the men approach on their fat horses, everyone sees they are, indeed, *hay gú* from the canyon. They appear odd and hairy, and their eyes, which look like those of blind horses, hold a tense look. Elmer, one of Wa tahómja's boys, walks out to greet them and put them at ease. He knows the *hay gú* talk from staying at the canyon and going to school there. The two *hay gú* remain on their horses while they hear young Wa tahómja. They don't return his greeting but begin to wave at the trees and sweep their hands toward Blue Creek. Other people begin to edge closer to the group and ask young Wa tahómja what they say.

"You know what it is: It seems as if they don't like us to be here." He returns to talking with the *hay gú* on their horses, who reply by turning their heads back and forth and sweeping their hands toward Blue Creek again and then moving their palms down toward the grove.

"What? What?"

"Well, they say this place is for the birds and squirrels, and we might take all their food. They say we don't belong here and should go back to Blue Creek anyway."

Someone groans. "Tell them there is always enough when one is not greedy. I know about these *hay gú*," another laughs.

"Tell them we live up here. We always do this."

Young Wa tahómja talks to them again. They lean forward to catch his words and then shake their heads again and point toward Blue Creek.

"They say this place belongs to them now. The big people in Wá senton have made a place for us to live at Blue Creek, and we're supposed to stay there all the time."

"Tell them there's nothing to eat there and no wood. This is always our place to get food."

"Tell them to chase fat deer down to us, and we'll stay at Blue Creek," one of the women laughs. Some others chuckle.

The two *hay gú* on the horses look nervous and say something more to young Wa tahómja.

"They say we can get in trouble if we don't go because we're bothering other people's land."

"Ask them what they mean. Land is just where people live. Tell them we have to stay here because we belong to this place, but they're welcome to stay here, too. We won't get stingy. Maybe that's what they're afraid of. Tell them if they get hungry or need anything they don't need to worry. Just come to us, and we can take care of them," Wa tahómja tells his son. Elmer speaks to them again, and the two men chuckle. Everyone feels relieved.

After listening to them for a minute, he reports, "They say they have plenty, since the big people in Wá sendon take care of them. They will take care of us and we'll have plenty, too, but we have to stay at Blue Creek. They say it's not their idea, but they have to tell us this because they don't want us to get into trouble. They say we're not supposed to use this place any more, and it doesn't matter how it used to be. They say they can put us into jail."

"Jail?"

"Jail. And you know how that goes. They might do to us like they did to Wa lúthema."

"How strange! These *hay gú* are hard people. They can put you in jail just for trying to eat."

The group peers curiously at the strange, hard people in silence when young Wa tahómja finishes. Old Wa tahómja suggests they head back to their camps so the *hay gú* will leave. The people begin to gather up their things and leave.

▼

The time for staying inside has begun, but Baa remains troubled for many days about the *hay gú*. One day he tells Baqí he is going to ride over to Swèdeva's place to see how Jóla's daughter is doing and talk with the old man.

He rides along toward the rising sun after leaving the *wa*, keeping the gray mass of The Snowy Mountains [the San Francisco Peaks] halfway to his right. When the sun reaches above The Mountain of the Horse [Bill Williams Mountain] on the horizon to his right, Baa enters the wooded canyon leading toward the sunrise and Swèdeva's place by the well. As he rides along he watches the ponderosa stands along the trail for signs of game, for he carries his bow in case he should be twice fortunate. Soon he rides by the spot where he passed once during summer, hunting horses during a thunderstorm. He grew thirsty and climbed up to the rock water hole off in the trees to the right. He can still remember the prickle on his neck as he bent to drink and saw fresh lion tracks leading from the hole and the splatter marks where it had shaken itself. He had left quickly without drinking.

Soon Baa sees the tall, middle-aged man out gathering wood near his place. His wife, Dasjígva, the Upright One and daughter of Yúta, shells piñon by the cabin. Swèdeva looks up and sees Baa approaching and stands watching him. "*Jaa!* How's it coming?"

"Great!" Baa dismounts and walks to meet him, this man who spent many years as the guardian of the Place Below The Spruce Trees [Indian Gardens] itself.

"*Baa gtáya* [old man]! I just thought I'd stop by and maybe bring you some meat, but no deer got in my way today." He hands Swèdeva some dried flank he has brought along.

"Oh, that's good! The keeper of the deer is generous!" he says and then laughs. "You didn't get caught either—twice fortunate." Baa follows him to the *wa*. Swèdeva holds the door for him, and he enters. Inside Swèdeva stands solemnly looking at the little pallet across the space inside where his grandniece lies. The girl, not more than twelve from the looks of her, lies on a bark and hide pallet covered with rabbit fur. Her eyes look dull, and she seems unaware of his presence. As Baa looks, she is wracked with a cough that weakly subsides. Swèdeva shakes his head in dismay.

"Only this year I made her first blood dress. And now . . ." Swèdeva stands for a moment and then touches his grandniece's face tenderly. Her hand comes up to press his hand against her cheek.

"Grandpa, I'm frightened."

Swèdeva sits by her and begins to sing of the health-giving earth and of the herbs he has brought her. Then he rises and motions Baa to lift the opposite end of the pallet.

"It's not too cold; let's take you out into the sun." They carry the pallet, which seems too light, out into the sun. They face her east for a second and then lay her facing south, her face and feet to the sun, which feels warm.

"My friend," Baa begins, "I know she will be strong again."

"Yes," Swèdeva replies abstractedly.

"Where is Jóla?"

"He and his wife are working at the Park, so I am taking care of the girl. Jóla may be able to come out later to see her; I think he will."

"I also come here to learn from you," Baa continues. "I have something to tell you about; you must explain its meaning."

"Go ahead," Swèdeva's gaze focuses now.

"Eight days before, I went with my woman to the piñon groves. Many of us were there, though we missed you. It was as always, with many of us there and much talk. Then a new thing happened—for me—though I guess it has happened to many others. Two of the *hay gú* came on fat, farting horses—large ones with big hooves—the kind that carry much weight but tire quickly. The men grew very fine, short hair on their heads but grew much hair on their faces—very coarse hair and unlike your own. They wore clothes that fit tightly and shine and look uncomfortable, just like a lot of us are beginning to wear now. They didn't seem to feel very easy about being there. One of them began to speak to us in their talk, which Wa tahómja's son understands. And in their talk they told us this: We have a home at Blue Creek, and that is our only home now. No longer are we to bother the trees or the animals up here; these things are no longer for us. He said we might get put in jail if we come here any more. This jail is a strange thing they have. Anyway we said we could give them our help if they are worried about having enough, but they were very serious and said no; they wanted nothing from us except that we leave that land and stay at Blue Creek. Often I have heard about this since I have grown up; when my father was young it wasn't that way." He pauses a moment and Swèdeva continues to look interestedly at a stick by his foot. "Now what does this mean?"

Swèdeva, who has maintained silence through the telling, now looks up and assumes a knowing look as he begins to speak. "Now it comes to you. I shall tell you of how it came to me and what I have learned of the *hay gú*."

Baa waits quietly for the telling as Swèdeva gazes quietly at the ground for a time. They hear someone coming and look up to see Jóla approaching on foot. They greet him as he approaches, and Swèdeva begins.

"We lived at The Place below The Spruce Trees. I was born at The Landmark [Red Butte] in the winter. There were always five of us—my father, mother, half-brother, my nephew here and me—and sometimes many more there. And there was Burro; he stayed in that place with his people, too. That's a good place, and some years we stayed there all the time. The Móga would come often to get *gwáta* [red paint] from us, and we liked to see them. They are kind people and very close to the spirits. We didn't have buckskins to trade with them because we didn't see much game down there. You yourself should remember how your father would leave a buck for us at the shelter on the top and call down to us so we could have meat. I remember when you came to stay with us as a small child when your family came for a dance with the Móga. It was only us then, but it changed.

"Before this girl was born by about twelve winters a man came to our place, one of the *hay gú*, with a lot of other people—all *hay gú*. This man looked almost like a gopher—lots of hair on his lip—and he carried bright, round-looking things on his eyes. He was their boss man, and they called him Tèdi Rósabelt. He gave me that tall hat I keep inside the house there. He is the big boss of all the *hay gú*, and they all must do what he says. I learned this later. I should say this now so you can understand them: The *hay gú* number many, many—more than we ever see here. Someday they will be everywhere, and we—who once were the only humans in this land—will be as nothing and forgotten." Swèdeva pauses to watch Baa for a moment before continuing. Jóla, who has taken his place with them, listens tensely but does not interrupt.

"That is why they are strong, and we shall go before them. One by one they are just like us, but for this one thing—they will let another one make up their minds, and one of them will go right ahead and tell you how another one feels. You see, they are quick to follow; even the two men [Kolb Brothers] who live by the shelter and make *denyúdi* [photographs] would wait on this Tèdi Rósabelt, and they hadn't seemed to be followers before he came. Because of their willingness to follow, many of them can act together in one way and do things that one man could never do. They say our brothers the Móga are this way in some things, but not in all things.

"What power this Rósabelt has I couldn't see. There are other things about these people I've observed which I'll tell you later, and more I have learned from the Móga, the Hwamú and the Paiute. Once, for example, the Hwamú came among us in our land to hide when the *hay gú* came and burned their farms. This was just after I was born.

"Anyway this man Rósabelt told me he wanted to make a place there for the *hay gú* to see the canyon, but he wanted it to be just wild there with no people, and he said it would be a good place for everyone. But we had to move out of that place because they couldn't have people staying there. I could see there was no use fighting it, especially if lots of *hay gú* would be coming and bothering us. So we all left, and many stay over in Coconino Basin now; I myself moved to a cave near the top of the canyon where I stayed by the trail for six winters. And it was as he said; many more *hay gú* began to come and the place was not so good any more. They began to break the rocks and leave their old things about. They chased the game away or killed it. They began to put up their big houses, and then the *hay gú* with the hats and shirts the same began to come. Three winters before this girl was born they came to my cave and told me to find a place on top. They needed all that place and didn't want people living there, because more of them were coming to live on top. So I looked around and found this place where there is a little water and made a well. Now the men with the hats and shirts the same come around to talk but they don't bother us. Sometimes people used to try making *denyúdi* of us, but we didn't like that always. Now the *hay gú* say they are leaving us all a place to stay up here not too far away, so maybe things will change."

At this point Jóla interrupts excitedly. "Here is what I see: These *hay gú* come and they move into a place, and right away there's no room for us people. Then they make little places for people to live like at Blue Creek and then keep us off the rest. After that the place all around is just for the *hay gú*—no more people unless the *hay gú* say so. What happened at the piñons the other day—I heard about it from some others—is like that: Now they want that place and soon they won't want people using the place any more. Already they say we are not supposed to be in The Farms any more. And the men who tell you will say they are only followers, and you can't argue or fight with them because somebody else is telling them. I was just a boy when Tèdi Rósabelt came to The Place below The Spruce Trees; I guess we had the man who tells them all, and maybe we should have found out why he does or tried to tell him about us. And now maybe we're the last ones. Already when even our children . . ." he turns sadly to look at his daughter and stops himself.

"But we are the people who belong here. What could this place do without us?" Baa says when Jóla is finished. "We can find a way to live."

"Perhaps. It is harder now. Those days may be gone and the earth different now," Swèdeva replies.

"We live by hiding like rabbits," Jóla spits.

From the hill by Swèdeva's place they can see The Snowy Mountains gleaming with snow. Baa looks at the distant mass for a while in silence. "How many days, *Baa gtáya*, to ride to that place?"

"Perhaps three or four. But now, who knows? The snow is deep in places near the mountain. This is not a good time to go there. When we tell of the days when animals were as people, we tell of Hawk and how he went to The Snowy Mountains. That place is the home of Hawk's people. At that time Hawk lived with his wife's people, the rock wrens, near Blue Creek, but up where it's dry.

"Now when it was this time of year Hawk had to fix the holes in his house because his wife complained the wind came in and blew the seeds away. Then after he had fixed it up well, Wren still complained, saying her grinding stone was too fine to grind up their seeds right, and she was always going to a neighbor's house to do her grinding. Even after Hawk roughened up her stone when she was away she continued to do this. One day Hawk decided to follow her and see why she would always stay so long to do her grinding. He saw her go into her neighbor's house and waited a few minutes before going up to peek through a hole in the wall. In there he saw his neighbor making love to his wife. He watched and then went back, saying nothing.

"When his wife came home he still said nothing, but he was mad. He decided he would just go away without saying anything, so the next day he took up his lion-skin blanket and shot an arrow out the door and followed it. He picked it up and went on. He walked all day and by evening he stopped and killed a few cottontails in that place. Early in the night his wife caught up with him—she had followed him all day—and asked him, 'Why are you leaving? You just left and said nothing. What are you mad about?' But Hawk acted as if he was still alone even when she came close by him. When she asked to get into the blanket with him, he said, 'Don't bother me. I want to sleep.'

"Toward morning, Hawk made a song: 'I am going on a long trip. You stay where we used to live. I am going to my relatives in a place where there is snow on the mountains.'

"Then he went off. After a while she followed him again. They kept on like this, reaching The Landmark in three days' time and near to the mountains in another three.

"His wife was getting mad now, too, because she hadn't got to his bed, but she kept on following him. The morning before going up to the mountains he sang to his wife, 'I might meet my relatives before evening, so you'd better go back. The clouds are on the mountain, and it may snow today. I don't want you in a dangerous place.' Then he left her.

"That evening Hawk found a little ravine on the foothills of the mountain and stopped in there by a pine tree taller than the others. He gathered a little wood for a fire, as it was getting cold, and began to roast some cottontails. He sat close by the fire until it was dying down. The wind was blowing very hard over the ravine, and snow was starting to fall. He looked for his wife to show up, as it was almost dark. By the time snow reached his camp and started blowing hard in his face, she still hadn't come, and the fire died out. And just then his wife came in. He said nothing to her but turned himself into a real hawk and flew up into the big pine where the branches were thick and protected him from the wind.

"His wife kept walking around down below trying to get out of the wind and kept asking him to take her up with him. She kept talking to him because she knew she was going to freeze that night. By the middle of the night she quit talking.

"In the morning snow was as high as the bushes. Hawk flew down and found his wife under the snow, frozen dead. She was pregnant.

"He made a fire and put her by it. Pretty soon her belly began to get warm and bloat up; then it split open. Many young animals ran out, and there was only one young hawk in the bunch. He took that one and left the others to freeze and went up into the mountain until he came to his relatives."

Swèdeva stops here, and they sit in silence for a while again. Baa asks, "Do people go into that mountain now, *Baa gtáya?*"

Swèdeva replies, "I went there once but not into the mountain."

"Tell me of that."

"It was in rainy time when there is water in the rocks [August] and traveling is easy. I started from The Spruce Trees and rode toward the mountain for four days. On the evening of the fourth day I came close to the mountain. The pines were very large and even then I could see snow high up above. From there I rode back again until dark, where I stopped. But I didn't go any closer after that but just came back because they say the rain beings in the mountain will make floods if we bother them too much."

"Sometimes I wonder, *Baa gtáya,* if there are truly such beings in that mountain," Baa muses.

"Consider this. When all the country around is dry, the mountain always has rain, does it not? This is also true of The Mountain of the Horse. When clouds appear they always appear on the high places, and the high places often have clouds when you find not even one anywhere else. See it now." Clouds shroud the entire upper half of the distant mass.

"Who is to say if these are beings?" Swèdeva continues. "Certainly the mountain contains forces that bring the clouds. I cannot truly say what these forces may look like, but you can hardly deny there is some force there. Is it too much to say the mountain is the home of the clouds? The Móga people say more, that the mountains are the home of the cloud people. This may be so; I don't know much about things like that, but I do see the power of the mountains to bring rain. I'm not the one to play with this power when water is so precious. We know that it takes water to live."

▼

The dreary sky appears as gray as stone. Snow stands above one's knees when a rider comes by Baa's camp, his horse plunging and fighting through the drifts. His approach, save for the horse's snorting, has been completely muffled by the snow, so his hail startles Baa and Baqí. They hurry out in surprise to see the rider, Chikapánega, coming into camp. He dismounts and leads his horse to the nearly bare area in the lee of the junipers. The horse stamps and puffs with exhaustion, and Baa hurries to get his boots on and help Chikapánega dry the horse. The two men wipe the sweat from the steaming animal with their hands. When they finish, Baa and Chikapánega hurry inside, where Chikapánega places his feet near the coals and leans back against the grinding stone, closing his eyes. He is nearly home now.

"I came to tell you," he begins after a time, "that Jóla's daughter has died." Baqí draws her breath in shock.

"I was coming up from The Piñon Grove [Moqui Tank] and met Sinyella. He had just come from Swèdeva's, and he told me. I am going there now, so we can bury her. Come on; let's try to make Jóla glad again. Let him know that he is still with us. Come to Wa tahómja's; that's where we'll be. There's plenty of room."

Baa feels heavy with sadness for Jóla and his wife and especially for Swèdeva, who has no children of his own.

"Eat with us before you go on, and we can travel together to Wa tahómja's place."

The three of them sit eating in silence for a while. Baqí feeds the child some of the piñon stew; she is older now and able to eat solid foods without much difficulty.

They prepare to go, and Baa rolls up eight buckskins he has saved over the past three years and ties them onto the horse. While Baqí rolls up two rabbit-fur robes and a lion-skin blanket in a Hwamú blanket, Baa starts his slow match of coiled and bound cedar bark smoldering and hangs it from his belt. Baqí bundles up the child for the trip and goes over to tell her family; they will wish to come, too. As Baqí is returning, Baa brings their finest Móga belt from the *wa* for the girl.

Outside, the snow glitters off in all directions, gently dimpled and dotted with bush tops. The black stubble of trees is scattered in sharp patches along the gentle hillslopes. The men tie the blankets and robes to the horse, and the group starts out on foot leading the horses. This way is easier in the deep snow. The walking keeps them quite warm, though the deep snow is cold on the feet. They keep their bearings in the trackless gray light through their familiarity with the land contours. The going is much slower than they had expected, and as the terrible chill of late afternoon begins to descend, they have yet to reach The Farms. The snow has begun to blow hard, and everyone is beginning to weep from the pain of the cold. The group heads for a large shrub projecting from the snow and they throw blankets over it and crawl under, forcing their way among the brittle branches. They break all the dead and dying branches off and peel some dry bark slivers to which Baa applies the cedar-bark match. Soon the tiny space under the shrub begins to fill with smoke and a little heat. The six adults and the child bend as low to the ground as their crowding allows them. They lay the child on the ground near the fire, where the air is freshest and warmest, and the rest of them sit coughing and rubbing their eyes, wrapped in the skins.

As the sky darkens they begin to nod, all huddling tightly against each other around the tiny, smoky fire and the child. Baa has many times made such quick camps while traveling after game and unable to stand the cold any longer. He has not made such a camp for so many people before, but they all keep each other warmer like this, he thinks, as he nods a moment again. His feet feel warmer now, and Baqí's buckskin boots are drying. He works them sleepily in his hands to keep them from stiffening.

He awakens repeatedly during the night to throw a branch on the fire; each time he feels stiffer and colder. The wind has quieted around the large bush, and a cover of snow closes them in now but for the smoke's vent. He believes he can see stars waver through the smoke at least. The time is *hamasí gedadía* [late January], when the stars glitter hard and cold.

In the first graying light everyone begins to groan and stir; the fire is only ash now. Outside, the horses face into the wind, dreaming and drifting. One by one they crawl out to find the snow dimly glowing under a lightening sky and nearly waist deep in places. The Snowy Mountains are lost in the gray light and distance, perhaps completely curtained by snow falling around them. They begin to shake the blankets and talk quietly, packing the horses again and eager to move and loosen their joints again. They are sure to reach Wa tahómja's place shortly after sunrise; and they start out, keeping to the ridges, which the wind has swept relatively clear.

The group stops moving for a moment to watch the clear fire of the sun burst over the edge of the world. Slowly the surface of the snow takes the sun's color and then Baa turns to see Baqí's face touched with fire, facing the sun. His heart rushes with the beauty of it; none of them can ever escape the magic of this endless drama. And every time, Baa thinks, it has a newness, like Baqí's face, turned to its fire now. He can't see enough of her this way; suddenly she holds the child up and lifts the blanket from her face to let the sun touch it. The child blinks and cries a moment, a whimper against eternity; then they all shake themselves and begin moving again.

The sun stands but three or four hands from the horizon as they catch sight of Wa tahómja's camp among the junipers above The Farms. Horses and people become visible moving around among the houses; a few fires smoke thinly. The people there call out as they trudge in; the area has been cleared of snow, and Wa tahómja's *wa* rises up huge above the junipers. Baa goes inside to greet Swèdeva and takes a moment getting accustomed to the darkness after the snow's glare. The huge juniper logs meet high above; the logs are so large a man could barely encircle one with both arms. This *wa jemátv* is legendary for its size, and the people often meet here in groups in the winter. Even now some ten people sit comfortably inside singing. Finally he can make out faces and sees Swèdeva sitting apart by Jóla, who looks drawn and mute. Baa goes around the group to them and takes first Jóla's then Swèdeva's hand and wishes them well. Others begin to enter, and Baa goes outside again. The girl lies against the snow, wrapped in a blanket. The last time she had been facing the sun; now she is still.

When the sun reaches The Mountains of the Horse Jóla comes out, and he and his wife tie the girl's body onto his horse. Everyone begins to follow as he leads the horse up the wash. After traveling until Wa tahómja's camp and even its smoke are lost from view, the group comes to a stop at a crumbling rock outcrop at the edge of the wash. Jóla unties the bundle and lifts the girl gently from the horse to lay her in the snow beside the white-laced rocks. Then Baa joins other men in rolling and lifting rocks away from the outcrop until they have formed a shallow depression below the surface of the ground among the rocks. Jóla lifts the girl and places her among the rocks with her head toward The Big River. Baa places the Móga belt with her, and others begin placing small blankets and gifts with her. Swèdeva places corn with her and takes some earth from around the depression and begins to sprinkle it on the bundle.

"This is your home now, my girl," he says. "You go before us, and it should not be this way. But you must leave us living now and go to your place. We must not look on each other again. Others wait for you there; go to them."

Then he motions the men to place rocks on her and stands aside, tears running down his face. When the men have piled the rocks into a cairn that must surely crush the frail bird beneath them, Swédeva begins to address those gathered around in a choked voice.

"Something is happening to us people. In my father's time the old went before their children, and the children could go on and have their children, and the people went on and on. But now when the children go first, what is going to become of us? One time we lived in the open and were strong; now the children get cold and sicken; now they cough and grow hot and die. Why? One time we thought we could dance the ghost dance of the Paiute and renew ourselves, and things would be as they were again. Many of us thought this, and when I was a young man many of us came together near here to dance and seek the visions of the Paiute dance. But nothing changed; even those who climbed the pole died soon after. So we did not dance that dance again. Many of us began to watch the *hay gú* and learn their power from them. They believe in a healer named Jesus who makes them strong. They say if we follow the ways of Jesus we shall take our place beside them. He will make us live forever, and we won't die any more. I told this girl of Jesus while she was with me, and now I tell you of him, too."

He breaks off, and a silence follows. Jóla still remains standing among the rocks. Without moving, he suddenly begins to speak to everyone loudly.

"We are weak. Everything changed with the coming of the *hay gú*. Once it was, indeed, different. My grandfather told of *hay gú* who came among us but just passed on. But now, within the time of my young life, the *hay gú* come again, and this time they tear us from our lands and push us into moving and hiding. We live and die like rabbits now, always on the move, followed, looking behind us in a land that was our home. The bear are gone; the deer are leaving.

Shall we follow them? Has the earth forgotten us, the people born here to walk upon this earth, the human beings?

"Getá gema, you tried the *hay gú* way and sang to the *jízes*. This girl here was not yet born when the *hay gú* sickness took all your children, and you left off from this *jízes* of the *hay gú* just as my uncle left off from the Paiute dance. The dance changed nothing; the *jízes* makes the *hay gú* strong while we get weak. Forgive me, my uncle, but I believe this.

"The *jízes* is strange; he tells the *hay gú* to go to other people's places and make the people there follow him. I see no pleasure in this *jízes;* he teaches us to turn away from our mother the earth and to turn away from being as people and to think always about death and the ending of things. Is this right?

"And more, the *hay gú* brings his *ha dáva* [liquor] to us, and we get weaker and grow crazy. There is nothing in here for us human beings.

"Once there were just enough men, enough game, enough water. Once dying and being born kept pace with each other. Once killing was only to keep life going, and the living stayed close to all the things of the earth. Now there's not enough of anything except people and *hay gú*, and there's too many of those. We die faster than we are born, and killing has become senseless. So we wait, and our lives run through our fingers like water. The land was ours, and we cared for it. And now these who care for nothing cover the land, and it dies under their touch. We, left with nothing, follow the bear and go with him. I am finished now. Forgive me, all of you. I am not so wise."

Jóla looks broken, the tears streaming down his face. Baa stands among the others, as silent as they. This talk leaves them no response. Instead of remembrance, Baa is left with desolation. People begin moving off through the snow, no one looking at anyone else. Jóla often talks so, but it makes them uncomfortable to hear these words. Perhaps at Wa tahómja's they can re-create some feeling of closeness and joy at being alive together.

At Wa tahómja's some of the women are preparing food as they await the return of the others. One by one the mourners return from the burial. When Jóla returns, he says nothing more but takes his place facing The Big River across the fire. A group of men take their places at his right facing a row of mostly older women across the fire. Facing across the fire toward the place of the sun's rising sits A'hmál and his assistant, Ákaba, who are to supervise the ceremony.

Soon Baa 'nyá begins moving the shaker, and the songs begin to flow into him, the cycle of songs which tell of man's birth and time and eventual disappearance from the earth. The songs continue, broken only by A'hmál's admonitions and short speeches of remembrance about the girl, until well after sunset.

Long after dark snow begins to fall again, and the singers and mourners move indoors to sleep. Some of the families have set up rude brush shelters, and the two great houses of Wa tahómja are ample to hold the rest. Wa tahómja, a tall, robust man with a slight goatee, invites Jóla, Swèdeva and their immediate family to share his larger *wa* with his family. The others move into the smaller one for the night; Baa is among these.

Inside the smaller *wa*, which is still larger than any other he has seen, Baa and Baqí pull their robes over themselves and lie around the crackling coals with their heads toward the door. The air is warm and stuffy with the smell of humans.

Baa lies thinking of what Swèdeva and Jóla have said; the words had almost disappeared during the singing, but now they return and go through his head in the dark. Baqí shifts about against him, and he knows she is thinking as he is. He thinks of what Swèdeva told him many days before—it was during the last moon—about the rain forces. Then he thinks of Swèdeva's words about this *jízes*. Do these go together? Swèdeva sees deeply into things, and his wisdom is not to be taken lightly. Yet Jóla's bitterness touches him.

He thinks back to the time when, as a boy, his father took him far out to the end of The Long Mesa with Nava hú and Baa 'nyá. The place had taken his breath away; the world fell away on all sides to depths below where the occasional glitter of The Big River caught his eye—a sinew winding among the rocks of the bottom of the earth. Rocks and cliffs dropped away from the little mountain on the end, Dead Squirrel Point, where they stood and tumbled into the chasm for a distance on all sides that would take days to travel on flat land. Truly this was a holy place.

Far over there where the land became flat again lived the Paiute much as they themselves live in canyons and plateaus. Far toward the sun's setting place they sometimes crossed The Big River by swimming a deep, quiet place, but otherwise they seldom saw one another on their opposite sides of this division in the earth. It was true, however, Hmány gejáa had taken one of the Paiute women as his wife, she who had borne Mugúlo's wife.

From Dead Squirrel Point the four of them had turned back through the dense juniper forest covering the vast, flat top of The Long Mesa and pressed farther north toward the great bend of The Big River where it comes around The Long Mesa. They had soon encountered a deepening wash cutting across their path toward the edge of the lofty mesa, and they turned and followed this until it abruptly emerged in the side of The Long Mesa several hundred feet below the rim.

They had turned and followed the cliff ledges from the left side of the wash's terminus until they could begin working their way down the dizzying sides of The Long Mesa itself. At its base they traveled on down the boulder-strewn talus to the foot of the cliffs and a dark spot of greenery.° While the horses drank from the pool among the mesquite there, his father had urged him to observe the source of the water. A small trickle of water issued from a pair of double vertical folds in the cliff; shrubbery crowded in on the spot. In that quiet, shaded spot amid the overwhelming scale of the canyon, it had seemed so right—the Spring of the First Woman!

° The journey described here is disguised to protect the actual location of these Havasupai shrines.

When they had all drunk and rested, the four of them hobbled the horses and walked several miles along the great mesa until they entered a large bay in the cliff wall. There, set at the top of the talus, they saw two black boulders streaked with white and larger than the *wa* in which Baa is now lying. Far above, near the top of the mesa, the two great Owl Eyes looked down from the cliff. His father had stopped him before he went any nearer, and Baa 'nyá went on alone toward the rocks while Baa had waited with his father and Nava hú. They explained to him that these rocks housed some of the titanic rain forces that only Baa 'nyá could deal with.

Baa 'nyá withdrew a large rock from his bag and struck the black boulder with it. The boulder gave off a queer, sharp ring when struck, and Baa had felt uneasy. Baa 'nyá had called out in a loud voice for the rock to send rain and described the rain and its effects loudly.

The winter had been an exceptionally dry one, and everyone had sought hopelessly for enough water; the horses had been thin and scarcely able to bear a man any distance. Baa thinks about this and remembers that the winter had continued dry anyway, following one driving snowstorm the next day.

"I guess we understand something wrong," he thinks, "certainly there is something to what Jóla says. All the old people tell us things are changing for us. I only wonder if the trouble comes because we misunderstand how things are in some way. I wonder if the nature of things has changed, and do we have to change our understanding now in some way?"

Baa feels more troubled than ever, and a great weight seems to lie upon him. He can feel that Baqí still lies awake, too. As he drifts into sleep, he consoles himself with the thought that winter always produces a time of closed-in doubt and lingering wistfulness.

▼

Dull, grayish light touches his mind. Somewhere beyond the edge of the world the sun is coming. Baqí stirs under the hide and then rises to blow on the coals. Baa rolls over on one elbow to regard her, smiling dimly. He sits up and scratches his head, then stands and goes outside. Baqí appears beside him in the cleared area among the junipers. Off to the south he can see snow rolling off to the blue horizon, dotted with juniper and piñon. Thin smoke rises from the camp shelters. The air smells of cedar.

Others begin to come out into the open, waiting for the sun. Everyone stands quietly, a few, like Baa and Baqí, standing almost touching. The sky shines whitely through a heavy cloud cover, brightened to the east by a dim glow. There will be no real dawn this morning. As the sky lightens to a nose-tickling brightness, several of the men begin to dash off toward the glow, plunging into the deeper snow beyond the camp and laughing. Baa is with them and then dashing and bounding past them until he falls in the snow. The other men catch him and push him. Someone rolls him, while they all shout and laugh.

"Baa! You're stopping to rest already?"

Baa jumps to his feet, breathless with laughter, while the others dance about him.

"No, no! I just saw something here I wanted to get a closer look at."

The others shout the more at this, and then they all return to the camp at a run, overtaking some of the younger women, who are trotting back toward the camp ahead of them. Baqí rejoins him, and they stand for a minute catching their breath.

"Baqí, let's go on east with Jóla and Swèdeva. I feel pretty bad now. Do you feel it?"

"Yes; I feel that. It is the little girl and what Jóla said yesterday."

"We can go with Jóla to cheer him up, and then I want to go on and go to the Móga. I thought we might do this, so I packed the buckskins, and we can get some *gwáta*. We can stay with them until the Bean Dance and then go back to Blue Creek when the snow is gone. It could be hard going, so we'd better leave the girl with your sister or your mother."

They bring their things out of Wa tahómja's place and begin rolling them together. As Baqí works at this, Baa gets their horses from the brush corral and puts the saddles on them. When he finishes, he goes over to tell Swèdeva they will return with him. Swèdeva grips Baa's arm for a moment.

"You will hear some more things from me. You're a good man and you can learn much. When we have such young men I feel pretty good about us. Some day you may tell these things to your own children. We mustn't forget who we are."

Soon all of them are ready, and they begin moving eastward through the deepening snow, keeping to the wooded ridges to avoid the deepest drifts. Before long they reach the ravaged wasteland of uprooted trees, where the *hay gú* have used great iron ropes to pull up the trees and leave their skeletons to die on the ground. Everywhere the torn trees reach from the snow. The going is much more difficult here.

"*Baa gtáya*, why do they pull these trees up?"

"The *hay gú* say their animals don't like trees."

"But the deer and other animals can't live without these trees."

"I know. It is strange."

When the sun stands above The Mountain of the Horse they are winding slowly through the shallow rock-margined canyon that winds through the big pines by the new iron trail. They take care to ride through the canyon now to avoid meeting one of the noisy fire wagons which would panic the horses. As they reach the wide place in the canyon, they turn and head north up the wash entering the canyon at that point. They climb out of the wash into the big pines, still moving slowly in the snow until they come to Swèdeva's lumber cabin in a large, level clearing atop a broad ridge.

They stay a day and a night with Swèdeva and Dasjígva after Jóla and his wife leave and ride on to The Spruce Trees. During their stay Baa checks the route to Móga carefully with Swèdeva, as he has not traveled there since he was

a youth, traveling with his grandfather. Baa can even now recall some of the
Móga tongue, but only words of it.

▼

The morning they set for their departure Baqí is up quite early, rolling all the
buckskins together while Baa brings the horses. She ties her baskets of corn onto
the saddles. The sun casts early beams through the tops of the dark pine glades.
Here in these tall trees one can see no distance at all. Game abounds in the
ravines here yet, despite the arrival of the *hay gú*. Here one can still hunt meat
for the winter months with very little fear of trouble.

The cloud cover is scattering overhead leaving an opening of brightened
layers toward the sunrise and Móga country. The snow still lies upon the land,
rather deeper here among these pines.

Swèdeva comes out to wish them a good journey as they ride eastward.
They urge him again to come with them, but he says he has to keep an eye on
things at home. The way continues to rise slowly until they come to the camp
where the Havasupai have just settled together. A big ditch passes through the
area, and farther on it appears someone is constructing some sort of bridge
across the neighboring ravine. No one is working today, however; the ground is
too hard.

Baa and Baqí stop for a time to share gossip with A'hmál, Wa tesgògama
Yum gwála, Getá gema and the others who live there. All of them are now
making *bes* [money] working for the *hay gú* here, who are building a waste ditch
through the camp. While Baa and Baqí chat, a *hay gú* drives up in one of the
iron wagons that runs with no horse. He wears the peculiar peaked hat of those
who work in this place. The talk falls off as he approaches the camp.

"Hi! Mrs. Smith said one of your kids was sick out here. He any better
now?"

The *hay gú* keeps looking all around among the *wa jemátv* as he speaks.
A'hmál replies finally, "She died three days before. We bury her now."

"Oh! Well, Mrs. Smith figured she probably would. You people ought to
bring those kids into the hospital where it's warm. Don't know what you wanta
stay up here for anyway when you got that warm canyon to stay in down there."

The *hay gú* walks around among the shelters for a minute or two while talk
stops. Baa's horses finally catch his eye. "Say, you're gonna have to move these
horses today." Then he goes back to his iron wagon and leaves.

"What was he looking for?" Baqí asks.

"Deer, rabbits, anything. We're not supposed to kill anything. They chase
us out and send us back to Blue Creek if they find any here. So we keep them
way back in the trees there. They want us to go hungry so we'll leave here, but
we won't leave here, ever."

"Why do they want us to move the horses?"

"They're afraid they might touch some of the grass."

"Who is Mrs. Semít?" Baa asks.

"Mrs. Smith? Why she came out here and married the big ranger they call White Mountain," Getá gema replies.

"White Mountain? He has a real name then. Is he a man then?"

"No, he is *hay gú*. So is Mrs. Smith. She comes out here sometimes just to look at us. She holds her nose and shakes her head and scolds us with big talk. She thinks we should live in lumber houses and wash ourselves all the time. She can't see there is no water. She wonders why we look poor, and she sits on our land and keeps us from living on it. They have all our springs and our game and tell us we should go back to Blue Creek, unless they need us to move rocks for them. Then they come around and look at us and shake their heads because we look poor and sad. Mrs. Smith comes out here and tells us to make baskets for her and then when we show them to her she holds them by the edge like they have shit on them and says she will give us one or maybe two *bes* for them and we should make good ones next time."

"How come they dislike us so much?" Baqí wonders.

"Because they have to see us and remember that we owned this place and they took it. They don't like to think about it and wish we'd go away and leave the place all to them. But we're going to stay, and our children shall stay, and their children, so the *hay gú* can never forget whose land they live on. These *hay gú* don't really dislike us; they fear us, they want to hide us from their sight, because while we stay they cannot leave the place and must keep watching always. They want to spoil this place; you see how they have, but when they see us they know they are spoiling the place. So we stay. Maybe get hungry and look poor, but we stay. It's our home." Jóla speaks this time.

One of the young men brings some fresh deer meat into the camp, and everyone gathers around to share the pieces roasted over the fire. They eat all the pieces clean to the bone and give the bones to the starving yellow dogs to worry and crack. After the dogs have chewed them and left them, the men bury the bones among the tin cans in the trash heap. No trace remains.

Baa and Baqí leave the camp as the sun passes between The Snowy Mountains and The Mountain of the Horse, both invisible from this location. Wa tesgògama travels with them.

As they ascend they finally come up to the rim of the canyon where The Big River flows far below. Now they see the *hay gú* town growing along the rim. In a way it is like a Móga town, all close together, except it seems ill-matched and dropped upon the earth instead of growing from it, like a Móga town.

They ride a few paces to The Spruce Trees, where the trail winds out of the spruce and down by the house where the *hay gú* make their *denyúdi*. At the rim Baa gives Baqí the horse. He will descend into the canyon and then return and catch up with her farther along. She will wait at the other camp for him and stay out of sight, for the rough *hay gú* men sometimes take a pretty woman alone by force or follow making suggestive hand motions, hoping for compliance. Baa tells her to be careful and says he will see her by nightfall.

He and Wa tesgògama then start rapidly down the snow-covered trail along the cliff. After descending to the bottom of the tan sandstone the snow thins almost to nothing, and they begin to keep a steady trot. In a short time they reach the spring at the place below The Spruce Trees where Burro and his wife Desójva live and keep a little garden yet, despite the disapproval of the *hay gú*. They give the old man some dried meat Baa has brought for them and stop to chat with them a few moments. They move on quickly and head back toward the place of the sun's setting and down the canyon until they have passed through the red rock and into the blue rock.° As the trail winds down a westward-facing canyon into the blue rock, they begin working their way along a barely perceptible track in the sharp-cornered rubble. They keep above the canyon bottom until they pass a drop and then slide down into the bottom of the watercourse. Baa's hands are whitened in the cracks from the cold, and the stones hurt his feet even through the thick *hay gú* shoes he now wears. His nose is running from the exertion and the cold, which otherwise he feels but little. Finally they round a ridge projecting into the canyon and find themselves on the beginning of a sheer cliff dropping into The Big River. A small ledge turns the corner from the end of the ridge along the face of the cliff.

They stop here, and Baa calls out, "Hear us. We come for *gwáta*. Don't hurt us. We shall only take what we need. We're not greedy. We bring something, too, so don't hurt us."

Baa goes first, with Wa tesgògama right behind him, and they begin edging their way along the ledge, facing the cliff. Baa tries to keep his mind on the finger holds ahead of him. They say little as they edge along now.

At a point where the ledge squeezes into the cliff, Baa takes a breath and reaches well ahead until his fingers meet a small projection on the wall ahead and around a little fold in the wall. He flexes his cold fingers and feels the projection carefully again. Then he grips it firmly and gets his left hand into a crack in front of his face. He swings his body around the fold, quickly placing his right foot sharply forward and meeting a small ledge. He then pushes his upper body around the fold, shifting his weight to his right foot now, until he is balanced on the other side of the fold. He closes his eyes and presses against the cold stone a moment. Below, the water roars through the rocks. Baa is shaking from the tension. Then he edges along the ledge some ten paces, and the cliff recedes into a shallow cave no wider than a man's height and so low he must duck down and crawl to enter. Inside the cave smells of roots. Baa takes a feather from his head that he had tied there upon a thong and, crawling to the back of the cave, sticks it into the clayey floor with dozens of others.

Baa then begins scooping the clay bottom with a stick that lies in the cave and collects four large mounds which he places in a sack tied to his waist. This completed, he stops. He wipes his fingers across his cheeks outward and down and returns to the cave entrance. Lying on his stomach he peers down at the

° The description of Pa's journey here is distorted to conceal any clue as to the actual location of his destination, which must always remain a secret of the Havasupai.

river. He rises and turns again toward the cave and awkwardly backs out until he can stand facing the cliff again. "Don't hurt us," he whispers and begins edging back to the fold again. At the fold he stops and detaches the sack from where it had tugged at his waist, hanging to the projection with his other hand. "It's me," he calls. This is a difficult point; he cannot swing around the fold with the dense overburden of clay behind him, and to place it in front of him would force him too far out from the cliff. Working the sack free, Baa carefully shifts hands, gets a firm hold and swings the sack, now in his left hand, around the fold. It hits the cliff on the other side and stays; Wa tesgògama has it. He releases it and feels for the crack on the other side. Wa tesgògama guides his fingers to it. Now he grips tightly and swings out and around, kicking for the beginning of the ledge on the other side.

He is back with Wa tesgògama. They stand a moment quietly facing the cliff while Baa recovers. Baa then reaches over and wipes his fingers along his friend's cheeks, leaving dull red streaks. Then he and Wa tesgògama retrace their sideways steps until they reach the mouth of the hanging canyon where they began.

After sitting a moment, both of them begin climbing out rapidly; the sun will set just before they reach the rim. During the ascent they trade the increasingly heavy sack of dense clay several times; it seems to resist the ascent from its birth place.

Just above The Place Below the Spruce Trees as they toil up the trail they see someone coming on a mule. Baa hangs the bag between his legs so his buckskin shirt conceals it and begins to walk with a spraddled gait.

"It is one of the *hay gú* they call a ranger," Wa tesgògama whispers as the man on the mule approaches. Baa goes over to one side of the trail and squats down.

"What the hell you fellas doin' down here?"

"We go see Burro."

"That son of a bitch is still down here, huh? Don't know what he lives on down here. He ain't supposed to be here, and this is the last year we're lettin' any of you fellas get away with it. We been nice to you boys too long now. A Park ain't no place for squatters. You fellas wasn't takin' any o' that red paint o' yours out, was you?"

"No. We go see Burro."

"What the hell's he doin' over there?"

"Him shit."

"Oh, for Christ's sake! Well, you boys get on goin', and I don't want to catch any of you takin' stuff outa here any more. I seen you comin' down here for it. That stuff is government property, all of it, so you boys leave this place be unless you got some business down here. And be sure you cover up what you're doin' over there."

The ranger casts a nervous look at the fading sky and turns his mule back up the trail. As soon as he is out of sight Baa rises and takes the sack from between his legs. They begin to trot along toward the top again. By the time they reach the rim, the small sack seems to weigh as much as a deer. Both of them are weary and sweating. The sun is just setting. Baa gives Wa tesgògama half the *gwáta* and then closes the sack again. Up here in the failing light the *gwáta* takes on a purplish cast and feels somewhat oily. Wa tesgògama departs on a trot for the Havasupai camp, and Baa begins to trot off eastward to catch up with Baqí. She will probably be waiting near the new campground where their people used to live.

▼

Baqí watches Baa descend along the snow-covered trail and then rides off when he turns out of sight around a corner. She crosses the iron trail and heads back into the trees toward the new campground. As she enters the trees, she looks back and sees some of the *hay gú* men across the iron trail. One of them appears to have seen her among the trees; he beckons to her urgently. She pauses for a moment to see if he has actually seen her. When she stops, the man makes [rude] gestures with his hands. The other men are all watching her now. Baqí feels a clutch of fear and kicks the little horse, holding tightly to the other one. As it starts and begins to plunge through the snow, she hears loud laughter following her and she kicks the horse into a hard run through the trees. The men can easily follow her in the snow, she knows, and hopes they believe she is going to her family, for they will not follow her then.

When she reaches the place where she is to wait, Baqí takes the buckskins from the horse and conceals them some distance off under the snow, brushing away her tracks as fast as she can. The snow is difficult to smooth. Baqí then takes Baa's knife and waits some distance off among some rocks. By darkness she is trembling all over with apprehension and from sitting motionless in the snow. One of the horses snickers and she tenses with sick fear. She sees someone moving silently about the animals in the darkness. She moves soundlessly up toward the animals until she can see the figure better. Suddenly a tiny glow breaks out, and she sees the white glow of Baa's buckskin reflected. She dives through the snow and catches his arms, breathless and shaking.

Baa only holds her tightly to him, saying nothing until she stops trembling.

"I saw their tracks. They started to follow you on foot but then they turned back, maybe to get horses, I don't know; but they didn't come back. Maybe they will come looking in the morning. But you are all right now; I am here. You did well to hide the buckskins; I couldn't even find them myself."

They make a small brush shelter around the fire, clear the snow away and wrap together in a rabbit-fur robe inside. Baqí clings to Baa tightly all night.

▼

As the first grayish line forms at the lower edge of the sky, Baa readies the horses, packing a deer-stomach bag with snow. Baqí roasts a freshly caught cottontail for them. The smoke from their fire is still invisible in the early-morning darkness. The sky will be clear today, and a terrible chill grips the land. Baa keeps moving, and the horses stamp in the snow.

By sunrise they are already into the low scrub oak and juniper. Their prints go through to the earth now. The land ahead will become fearful in its dryness. They ride on and on through the dry chill, and the hills of spotted vegetation turn to rounded rock, bare of anything. The traveling is easy in the cold, as they lose but little water. In the long days of summer, this trip offers some peril and is seldom attempted. The water is scarce and too quickly drunk. Now they can find water in rock depressions on many shaded hillsides. Neither of them uses the snow water they have brought. When the sun stands overhead they are passing the scattered hogans of the Hwamú. Once there were no Hwamú here, but they have begun to move into this area since Baa was born. Where once only his own people traveled, the Hwamú camp. Baa marvels at their tenacity in this waterless land. A thread of dust follows an iron wagon to the north, where the *hay gú* have built a trail for these wagons.

As the sun falls lower at their backs, they begin to sight the deep canyon of The Salt River [the Little Colorado] ahead of them and to the left. The air begins to chill again. As the sun nears the earth, Baa and Baqí begin descending toward the river crossing at the head of the Salt River canyon. They will make camp at *way temáti*, the water holes in the rocks on the other side.

They splash across the muddy river in the dusk. Baa disdains the *hay gú* road over the water. Before long they have the horses unpacked and have eaten well of the dried food they have brought along. Later, they talk aimlessly side by side as they lie in the open waiting for sleep.

"The trip is much simpler than I remembered it; we should have brought the baby."

"Next time we will."

"Yes, next time."

▼

In the morning a half day's easy ride brings them to the Havasupai camped at *va wîla* [Moenkopi], where they stop the rest of the day to pass on family news and notify the little camp of Jóla's loss. This is a transient community with most people staying only a year or two, farming in the wash. As some leave, others arrive. Usually some ten or twelve people stay here. In the days before the *hay gú*, and even coming here as a young boy, Baa remembers as many as thirty people here. All the people there are pleased to see them and eager for news of home, and Baa and Baqí stay up until well after dark talking with the others.

▼

The next day is again a long journey, and Baa is up moving around the horses in the chill darkness of predawn. In a short time they are under way again. By the time they have been riding long enough to feel hunger, the light begins to show the valley's dry winter brush and the terrible surrounding desolation. By this time they can see far ahead the blue line of the first Móga mesa, where they will sleep tonight.

Soon they begin to pass dry cornshocks amid the patches of snow. When they reach the foot of the mesa, a man with a red sash around his head is waiting to guide them up the trail to the top of the mesa. The man greets them, and Baa responds with *"Lo lo mái,"* which he thinks means "good." After that they continue up the mesa in silence.

As they top the mesa they see the piled stone and adobe village of Oraibi just ahead, lines of smoke rising from the homes. Another man greets them there and indicates they should follow him to his house.

"Nyá'a Humètkwa [I am Humètkwa]," he says, apparently in Havasupai.

"You speak our language?" Baa asks him in surprise.

"A little. You stay with us."

"Yes, we will sleep here. Tomorrow we want to go on to see some friends of my father's in Songópovi."

"Good; I go with. Help."

The man helps Baa unpack the horses, admiring the buckskins greatly. The sun is now touching the world's edge; the view is breathtaking, with haze filling in the spaces between prominences below. Humètkwa takes Baa with him to the mesa edge, and they watch the sun disappear from the chilled earth. Baa feels a familiarity of old things unchanged, except for one puzzling thing. As they walk back to Humètkwa's house, Baa asks, "There is another town down there now. Who lives there?"

"Us. But man trying be *ba hána.* You know *ba hána?*"

"Yes. We say *hay gú.*"

"Hay gú, hay gú. Man there want be *hay gú* and live there. We want be . . . just us, so we stay here. My brother there," Humètkwa says sadly.

"Why do they want to be *hay gú?*"

They are back inside now. Humètkwa puts up a hand and converses a second with his wife. Then he turns back to Baa and indicates bafflement.

"No know. They go sing *jízes* there. Leave Móki way."

This *jízes* again. Then he has come to the Móga, too. Baa and Baqí look at one another. Humètkwa's wife puts corn and mutton stew out for them, and they begin to crumble dry *píka* into it and eat lustily.

"You hungry. Go far today."

"Yes. Tell me, are there many of these *hay gú* among you?"

"Not here. There," he points toward the new town below, "plenty *hay gú.* Say we follow them. Here—we say no. So some leave, go there, follow *hay gú.*"

"But why? Who wants to be like that? We see maybe one or two *hay gú* in our place. They sing about *jízes* and say we should learn from them, but they don't have much to teach."

"Learn?"

"Learn—*follow.*"

"Oh."

"But we just listen. No one follows them. The *hay gú* ways to us seem wrong."

"There! Good! Stay . . ." Humètkwa gropes and grips his hands together. "You understand?"

Baa nods.

"But no be easy. You got kid?"

"Yes. A girl."

"You girl get big, be more *hay gú*. More, more. Maybe *she* follow them, *learn* them," he corrects himself and tries out his new word.

They continue their halting conversation, Humètkwa's wife asking Baqí through her husband how Havasupai foods and crafts have changed since the coming of the *hay gú*. While they talk, Baqí remembers and gives them some of the Blue Creek corn they have brought along; Humétkwa and his wife smile their pleasure. After a time he indicates a small chamber and says, "You sleep here. Tomorrow we go Songópovi."

▼

When Baa rises, the sky is lightening, and he hears a voice calling outside. He rises and goes out with Baqí; they see a group of people running to the east mesa edge to watch the sun rise. Baa and Baqí run with them, stopping at the mesa edge to watch the glowing line across the horizon widen and gather into a blazing spot. Some young boys race down the side of the mesa toward the sun. Baa's shoulder touches Baqí's; they feel at peace. Here the world is still in harmony.

As they ride with Humètkwa toward Second Mesa, they talk some more.

Humètkwa says, "One time we walk, you, we. Oraibi-Cohnina—three day. Hard way."

"My father tells me that, too. When he was young, he always walked here. The old people are strong."

"Yes. Young one leave the way. No good."

As they ascend Second Mesa, Nuvámsa greets them; he has already heard of their coming and invites them over to his house. Several people are gathered there in the plaza before his house. After they all eat, Nuvámsa takes them outside, and Baa unrolls the buckskins. The men gathered there begin to finger them. One man takes three and places a wide silver bracelet between them. Baa rubs his chin and calls for more with his hand. The man places another bracelet embellished with turquoise—a Hwamú piece. Baa looks at it very interestedly. The man calls for another buckskin. Baa instead pushes the silver bracelet back. Now they have the turquoise bracelet and three buckskins between them. Nodding, they grip hands and each takes his things.

Baqí is showing her baskets, and the women are trading their pottery and hominy for them. One woman wants Baqí's burden basket dearly, but Baqí indicates she must carry the hominy in it. The woman places a beautifully decorated water vessel from First Mesa between them. Baqí waits. The woman lays her intricately woven belt across the vessel. Baqí looks at it longingly and tries pouring the hominy into the pottery vessels. A little still is left, and the woman holds up her hand to wait and disappears for a moment. Soon she comes running back with a cloth bag. Baqí holds the burden basket for a second reluctantly and then slowly pours out the rest of the hominy and places the basket before the women. All the women clap their hands and gather around the basket, hefting it and admiring its weave. Baqí already has tied the sash around her waist, emphasizing her young, vigorous figure.

One of the men comes forward and says something like *"súta"* to Humètkwa excitedly.

"He want know you got *gwáta*."

Baa brings a bag from his horse and opens it. The men gathered there begin to talk excitedly, and the women begin to gather around, too. People begin laying jewelry down, and one man even indicates his horse. Baa shows no interest yet. He smiles at Baqí in surprise, noticing her strong figure and white buckskin set off by the Móga belt. He turns back to the array and sees a heavy silver and turquoise squash-blossom necklace on one of the traders. Baa holds out a questioning hand toward it; the man hesitates and then gives it to Baa to examine. After a moment Baa holds up the necklace and one fist-sized lump of *gwáta*. The man regards this a moment and then takes the *gwáta*. Baa takes the necklace and places it around Baqí's neck; the people there laugh their approval, and Baqí thanks him softly with her eyes.

When the trading is completed, Nuvámsa says Baa and Baqí will stay with him five days until the Bean Dance, and the group begins to break up, talking and comparing their prizes. As Humètkwa prepares to go, Baa stops him by his horse and gives him a piece of *gwáta* he has saved back.

"For you, my friend. I hope your young people come up to the mesa tops again."

"My friend," Humètkwa says simply and holds the *gwáta* in his hand.

▼

By the end of the second day of the Bean Dance, many dancers have presented Baa and Baqí with gifts of food in pots and tray baskets. One large basket is heaped with *píka;* Baqí wonders how the brittle rolled bread will travel and guesses it will look like dust before they reach The Spruce Trees. She smiles at the thought.

After the dance Baa spies their friend Humètkwa on an opposite rooftop across the plaza near the place the dancers had entered. They greet each other and Humètkwa invites them to stay on with him until they are ready to return for planting. They accept and accompany him back to Oraibi. There they stay for several weeks until the sporadic late-winter rains slacken, and they feel the first warmth in the chill days.

On that day, Baa knows it is time to return, and he and Humètkwa begin packing their various pots, corn, *píka* and Móga baskets onto the two horses.

After bidding Humètkwa's wife farewell, they wind down the mesa on foot, leading the horses behind them. Humètkwa accompanies them partway down the trail as they head toward Kyakótsmovi at the foot of the mesa.

Baa says, "I'm going to look at the new town; I want to see with my own eyes."

"Good-bye. I go here. I no go new town," Humètkwa tells him. They take each other by the arms and smile at one another. "Come see more. Good-bye," and Humètkwa starts up the mesa.

Baa and Baqí ride on toward the new town, a strange mixture of adobe and lumber houses. One big house has a pointed top on it; this, Baa feels sure, is a place where they sing of *jízes*. They hear a loud, blaring sound behind, and their horses begin to jump and dart sideways. An iron wagon clatters by while both of them strain to hold on to the horses. One of the clay vessels breaks during the commotion, and hominy spills on the ground. They scrape up what they can and place it in the cloth bag on top of everything else. They watch the iron wagon clatter on into town, leaving its strange, pungent odor behind.

They ride into town feeling very conspicuous in their buckskins and loaded with pottery. They see Indian people lounging in the dusty streets wearing white cloth shirts and black leather shoes. Some of them wear the shiny-looking things over their eyes, and most of them wear their hair cut short in the *hay gú* style.

"Let's leave here; I don't like this place," Baqí begs him. She feels watched and appraised here.

"I know. Let us see in their store what these people buy first. Then we may go."

Inside the trading post an Indian in leather shoes sweeps the floor at a measured rate. Two *hay gú* stand behind a wooden counter, one fierce-looking and bearded, the other unkempt and dissolute-looking. Baa suspects he suffers from too much *ha dáva*. Baa inspects the *hay gú* trade goods and finds them eye-catching and of a very regular appearance. Their even lines please the eye and the touch. How do they get such evenness, he wonders. While he is fingering a hat, he suddenly finds the fierce-looking *hay gú* standing quietly beside him, watching him closely. He starts.

The man chuckles in delight. "That's a beautiful necklace your wife's wearing."

Baa comprehends him not at all and just slaps his ears.

"*Ka-Hopi*, huh? I'd guess you're a Supai by the looks of you. We don't see many of you real wild Indians out here." He indicates Baqí's necklace with his hand. Baa shakes his head and goes on inspecting. Baqí knots up under the man's hard gaze and wishes to flee. Will Baa ever be done here? Baa himself feels nonplussed now. What was the *hay gú* indicating? He feels confused and threatened. Maybe their horses are not even safe outside; perhaps *hay gú* or these Indians in the white cloth shirts are even now outside picking over the pottery and baskets on their horses. He begins moving along toward the door, where Baqí waits impatiently.

"You know Hopi?" he suddenly hears at his side in broken Móga from across the counter. It is the disheveled-looking one. "You *ka-Hopi*. Cohnína?"

Baa looks at the man fleetingly; he looks as frightened as himself.

"You Cohnína? Havasupai?"

"*È'e,*" Baa answers.

"No. No speak Cohnína. You speak Hopi?"

"Little, little."

"No scare. You no like place. I see."

Baa says nothing.

"I be like you. This place no good. I need eat." The man rubs his thumb and forefingers together meaningfully. Baa fails to catch the meaning.

"You old-time man. Good. Him no good. Be *ba hána*." He indicates the slow sweeper, who continues his patient work deafly.

"I be this place long time." He indicates "this place" with a larger sweep. "Now more *ba hána* spoil it. Take all. No stop. You understand?"

Baa purses his lips and nods once, not raising his eyes from the counter.

"One time," the odd man stops, groping, "day come this all *ba hána*. You all die." He reaches across to grip Baa's arm, but Baa flinches back.

"You no do. No die, no go away. One time *ba hána* come see this no good," he sweeps around the store on this. "Then we be like you. One time. Remember." A strange light fills his eyes.

"George, what the hell you doin' over there?" the bushy one laughs.

"Why, hell, I'm still tryin' to talk him outa that necklace. He understands some Hopi, but he still says, 'no go.' I offered him anything in the store."

"Bullshit! You're just goin' on with more of your simple-minded red man talk. How about you go fetch in some spuds?"

Baa uses the exchange to take Baqí's arm and slip out the door. Their horses still stand outside. No one seems to have moved out there. The loungers still lounge where they were, their breath making small steam clouds in the winter sun.

They ride off hurriedly toward Móenkopi Wash. While Baa is still puzzling over the strange encounter, Baqí asks him what the man was saying. Baa reports the conversation verbatim. Baqí taps her temple and says, *"Ha dáv."*

"Maybe," Baa responds, "but do you suppose some of them could feel as we do?"

They stop at the Havasupai camp, where nearly everyone seems to be in preparation for return to Blue Creek. They decide to travel together and begin combining their loads and taking on all the water possible. The warming sun will already have dried many of the water pockets between Móenkopi and The Spruce Trees. As they work, Baa asks the others about the peculiar encounter at the trading post.

"Are there *hay gú* who do not talk of *jízes* but talk of our way, as friends?"

"You've met Crazy George at the trading post, haven't you? He's a fool and drinks too much. He was born among the Hwamú and lived here and there all his life, they say. He is neither a man nor a *hay gú*. He talks foolishness, but he hurts no one."

Baa still wonders, remembering the odd, one-sided conversation. Only the fools and drinkers of the *hay gú* see their way.

▼

The little procession makes its way toward the crossing of The Salt River amid the creaking of leather and clacking of pots and baskets tied onto the horses. Mounted atop the goods sit little children clinging to each other and laughing. Even the adults who are mounted go along at a walk to stay with the others who are afoot. They are soon winding down the lazy gravel curves of Móenkopi Wash until they see the rim of The Salt River ahead. Baa and the others stop and secure the loads on the horses better before splashing across the waning spring flow of the river.

Baa nahmída takes the lead winding through the sand bars and rocks across the insistent current; the others follow him in file. Everyone who is able sits up on his horse or on the rump behind the load, and the horses grunt and puff with the weight and the force of the river. A few are forced to walk behind their horses, holding onto the tails. Baa is one of these. Baqí carries his clothes, and he makes a great deal of complaint at the coldness of the water, to the great amusement of those on horses.

At the west side of the crossing the party stops to redistribute their loads for the long overland remainder of the journey to The Spruce Trees; some, like Baa, spend much time on drying off and warming up again by working very fast.

"Look at him; he's sweating so much over there! Did you run all day? The sweat is running from you!"

"No, I just came through a very heavy rain. Did you miss it?"

The good-natured talk goes on as the men work at putting the loads on the horses, while their women are spreading out their things on the ground and repacking them.

In a few moments they are winding up toward the great escarpment beyond The Salt River which marks the beginning of their home and which has also become home for many of the wandering Hwamú in recent years. The group will sleep there upon reaching the plateau. The early spring day grows dim as they top the escarpment and shout to see again the miles of low scrub stretching off toward The Big River canyon and finally to the rugged country of Blue Creek. Home!

Off toward The Big River canyon they see slowly moving lights leading a plume of dust along the iron-wagon road; behind them the gorge of The Salt River splits the vast depression dividing them from the distant Móga mesas, now filled in between with the rose haze of sunset.

While the men hobble the horses, and the women start some small cooking fires with the brush around, Toup spies the nearby fire of a Hwamú hogan and goes over to trade a little corn, so the people can drink coffee tonight to warm them in the chill night air. Toup understands the speech of the Hwamú, and spends a few minutes at the little Hwamú camp, consisting of a man, his wife, her brother and wife and three children.

"Greetings, brother," Toup calls out to them as he rides up.

The man comes forward and makes a sign of greeting and motions Toup to come share their fire.

"No one pass this way?" Toup asks around the fire.

"No one."

"You stay here long time?"

"Ten winters."

The children sit watching Toup curiously, listening to his strange accent. When he gives them a conspiratorial look, they quickly look down, but one of them giggles.

"You trade at crossing?" Toup pouts his lips down in the direction of the crossing they made earlier in the day. The *hay gú* now have one of their stores there where Toup knows many of the Hwamú go to trade.

"Sometimes."

"Maybe you got coffee then?"

The man continues to stare into the fire, which he is stirring with a stick.

"I bring corn. You got coffee, you take corn then." Toup opens the little sack of shelled corn he has brought out with him. The Hwamú motions his wife to go into the hogan, and she presently emerges with a can of coffee. Toup gives her a little sack of shelled corn and takes the can of coffee.

"Eat well, brother," Toup says as he mounts his horse. The family all waves as he leaves.

Back at the little temporary night camp the women have some water boiling in one of the iron pots of the *hay gú* that one may put directly into the fire without cracking it. Toup shakes about a quarter of the can into the pot, and the woody aroma of coffee begins to draw others to the fire. Soon everyone is dipping his cup into the pot and drinking the hot, dark coffee, saving the cooler dregs for the children to drink.

▼

Early in the morning the people make ready for departure while the sky grays before the dawn. The great bowl through which The Salt River cuts is lost in haze; only the distant line of the mesas is discernible against the lightening sky. A few children call out, but the adults work silently in the morning stillness, shivering against the cold. Far down the horizon to the south the dark bulk of The Snowy Mountains rises from its elevated base into the murky sky. Before long the first rosy light catches the snows atop the peak, and far off the Hwamú man stands by his hogan singing the morning song to the coming sun. Everyone stops working as the sun's fire breaks over the horizon and ignites the miles of scrubland they must still cross.

The procession all waves gaily to the Hwamú family as they ride by, heading for The Spruce Trees. Before noon Baqí's spirits rise, and the strange town below the mesa fades from memory as the scrub and semidesert of the edge of the plateau gives way to the first stunted junipers with the slowly ascending land.

By midafternoon everyone is beginning to laugh and talk animatedly as they reach the first piñon trees among the juniper; even the horses seem to quicken their pace, knowing they will be able to rest before long. The group has just passed The Cottonwood Grove [Grandview Point] and will reach the encampment in the big trees by nightfall. They ride south of the *hay gú* settlement and cross the iron road just by the Havasupai camp. The camp is fairly quiet, with only a few families cooking among the houses when they arrive. Those at the camp exclaim to see all of them come in, and several others rush out of the earthen huts to greet them. Immediately they fall to greetings and catching up on news as they unpack.

Baa decides they will stay only briefly and then ride on to Swèdeva's cabin for the night. Several families decide they will remain at the camp for the summer to work for the Park and make some *bes* [money]. Then they can buy some of the *hay gú* goods and take them to Blue Creek for the Peach Festival and show them to their families when the harvests are in. Those who are staying tell Baa and Baqí to take their horses on out to The Farms and leave them, so the rangers will not catch them in the camp when they come in the morning to start work on the waste ditch.

After sharing some food and conversation with the others, Baa and Baqí ride on to Swèdeva's place in the gathering darkness, leading a string of some eight horses. They feel safer once they have left the camp, for they have left the place where the men of the Park can come every day and lay hands on their lives.

Swèdeva is standing in the doorway of his cabin when they arrive, silhouetted against the lantern glow within. Jóla and his wife are also there, and he and Swèdeva help Baa unpack.

Swèdeva asks about a number of his Móga friends and is gratified to learn that Nuvámsa had asked about him as well. Jóla wishes he, too, had been able to go.

"They are good people, the Móga," Swèdeva remarks.

"And yet do you know, *baa gtáya*, that the *hay gú* comes to them just like he comes to us? They have built new towns where those who follow the *hay gú* go to live, and their people are dividing, even brother against brother, because of it. It is better for us than I had thought; the iron wagons travel right among the Móga, and the *hay gú* traders will soon replace our visits."

Swèdeva replies, "We change, too; more than you see. Did not some more of us remain at The Spruce Trees to work for their *bes* and eat their food? This may not be bad, you know. They bring much we can learn, and they bring much that we must turn away from. Take wisely, and you do not become less. After all, how can we survive among them if we don't understand their way? In this, we shall become the greater finally, for not many of them shall ever care to know our way.

"Before you travel on in the morning, expect to see other changes, unwelcome changes, ahead of you. Hear me: Shortly after you left, several men of the Park went out toward Blue Creek, we thought to make more of us leave. Behind them by several days came many, many—perhaps a hundred or more—of their *wagsí* [cattle]. We saw their big iron wagons go by and come back hauling the deer of our land away. When we asked about this thing, the men of the Park told us the deer got to be too many and were starving. Yet you yourself know they forbid us to hunt them."

"I can't figure it. What are they doing?" Baa asks.

Jóla replies, "Maybe this: We live by the deer. The deer live by the plants of the earth. They take the deer and send the *wagsí* to eat the plants of our earth, and the deer must disappear. Perhaps they believe that soon they may haul us away, saying that we become too many, and we, too, starve."

"Well, then we shall live by the cottontails and porcupines. We know how. There are more of those than they or their *wagsí* can catch or starve. They can get rid of us only if they destroy our homes, fill up our springs, and fence the earth against our return. The earth will always have a way to care for us.

"You have said it. Expect all this ahead of you, and remember that we can be stronger still.

Baa and Baqí ride on the next morning. The warming sun has already melted all the snow cover except for patches under the trees. The ground has turned to mud, and the horses labor to make headway, their hooves making sucking sounds in the sodden earth. At The Farms they turn the horses free that they have brought along. While they rest there a while in the sun, Baa tells Baqí he won't plant this year in the wash. Baqí says nothing, but keeps watching him worriedly.

All the camps they pass are deserted, but many appear damaged and broken. They see a number of *wagsí* around the hillsides but no deer sign. They begin to walk faster, pulling the horses along, as they near their camp among Baqí's people. Someone will surely have waited for them there, and they become animated and eager to show off their prizes. Most of all they cannot wait to see and hear how their girl has grown; she will be laughing and mimicking sounds by now.

As they top the knoll before their camp, they are both shocked to see only scattered wood and a few broken pots. They run the last distance and examine the ground carefully. The thaw has damaged the signs somewhat, but they see the tracks of shod horses and leather shoes all around, with the signs of unshod horses leaving toward Blue Creek at a slow walk half-obliterated under the other, fresher tracks.

Apparently the family had all departed for Blue Creek before or perhaps at the approach of the *hay gú*. Then the *hay gú* had broken up the place to prevent their return.

Baa looks at Baqí. She looks disconsolate in her beautiful silver and colorful belt, her eyes welling with tears. He takes one last look around: the deer killed and chased away, *hay gú* and their *wagsí* crowding in, muddying the springs and putting up fences across the earth. So this is how it will be.

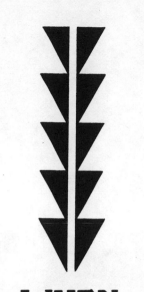

WHEN
THE LAND WAS
NOT OURS

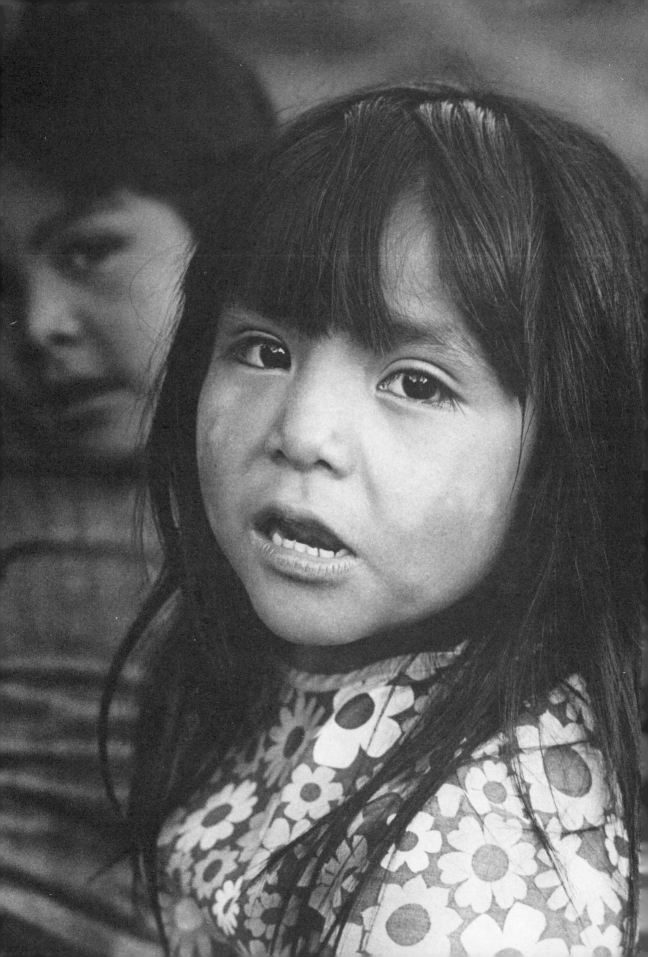

73. *Bernita 1973*

le

74. *Jóla at Home 1973*

te

75. Brenda Jones 1973

76. After the Storm 1969

77. *Father and Son 1973*

78. *Stanley and Alberta Manakaja with Shelton, Jolene and Hanson 1970*

79. *Flat Tire 1973*

80. *Firewood 1973*

81. *Going to Hilltop 1970*

82. *At the Indian Pow-Wow: Flagstaff 1970*

le

le

le

le

85. *Wa tahomcha's Home: Plateau 1973*

86. *Havasupai Cemetery: Plateau 1973*

le

88. The Plateau 1973

le

te

te

87. Abandoned Home: Plateau 1973

89. Five Horsemen: Plateau 1973

90. Lee Marshall: Plateau 1973

te

le

te

93. *Horn Catch: Plateau 1973*

92. *The Herdsmen: Plateau 1973*

94. *Guy Marshall Junior: Plateau 1973*

95. *Cattle Truck: Plateau 1973*

96. *Chick Putesoy: Plateau 1973*

97. *After the Round-up: Plateau 1973*

98. On the Corral: Plateau 1973

te   te

99. Moqui Trail 1973

100. Havasu Canyon 1973
te

8.

A VALID
POSSESSORY
RIGHT

The year 1926 began a new period for the Havasupai. The year before, the Havasupai Indian Agency was still able to report to the Office of Indian Affairs that the major portion of the tribe still left the canyon in the winter. That report commented further, "Several times attempts have been made to persuade the Indians to move out of the canyon, and it has also been proposed to erect new agency buildings on the high land at the top of the [Topocoba] trail." [62] But in 1926 the first telephone line was run into Havasu Canyon, and mail began to follow the route from Grand Canyon instead of the long overland route from Seligman. That year the Park Service gathered the various Havasupai groups into the 160-acre area just west of the Park headquarters where they still reside. In the beginning as many as ten families lived and worked at the village. They performed menial wage labor for the Park Service and Park concessionaire Fred Harvey. The Havasupai worked on the new sewer line, and others worked on the maintenance of Bright Angel Trail, the water line from Bright Angel Creek and the suspension bridge across the Colorado River.

Burro and Desójva: Exiles
Havasu Canyon

Courtesy Lorenzo Sinyella 1929

Early accounts indicate the Park Service preferred to use Havasupai labor for a number of reasons. In 1931 Park Superintendent Tillotson said the National Park Service usually employed 20 to 30 Havasupai and considered them better workers than other tribes of the area. For heavy pipeline work the superior size and strength of Havasupai men made them especially desirable, as Havasupai men can reach six feet and more and weigh over 200 pounds. It also seems likely the Park Service treated the Havasupai preferentially in hiring as a recognition of their special status in the Park. Havasupai women worked for the most part as maids, kitchen helpers and laundresses at Grand Canyon. Later, when the trails and construction were completed, the men were left with more menial jobs like washing and bussing dishes. One man was finally hired as a projectionist at the Kolb Studio and held this position until only a few years before his death in 1973.

During these years of the late twenties and early thirties the families at Grand Canyon still lived in their traditional wood and earth homes; only Swèdeva used a frame house, the one he had built at his well two miles west of the Park village. Even he maintained his traditional home as well, however, next to the earth dam he had constructed across the head of Pasture Wash. The Havasupai at Grand Canyon earned, most of them, too little money to survive in the cash economy, and with extreme skill and caution they still managed to hunt enough to feed their families without being caught. This must have been extremely difficult; former residents say the rangers came around to check their camp nearly every day.

In the spring of 1926 the Senate held hearings on a Park Service proposal to adjust the Grand Canyon Park boundary to include the Havasupai access road leading to Topocoba Hilltop. Notably, the Park went to some pains to avoid surrounding a private rancher named Buggeln and accommodated William Randolph Hearst, who owned a 160-acre ranch at Grand View, by offering him a clearance to the rim. They made no mention anywhere of the Havasupai, other than the vague concession that "some little question has been raised by the local people on the south rim." The Park Service's A. E. Demaray testified to the House of Representatives during their consideration of the proposal that no one had any grazing permits or livestock in the area to be added to the Park, and in a written recommendation made to the Senate the Park stated, "No lands in the national forests now utilized for grazing are added to the national Park." In fact the addition cut through the heart of the Havasupai grazing permit east of Havasu Canyon. Congress did not, however, approve of the addition finally.

By May 19, 1930, Havasupai superintendent Patrick Hamley was moved to comment to the Commissioner of Indian Affairs:

The area on this reservation is entirely inadequate for the number enrolled at this jurisdiction, especially so if we expect them to follow the livestock industry, as at present they do not own any grazing land. As stated before, they are more inclined to follow the livestock industry than farming and it is believed if they were given sufficient grazing land, which they knew to be their own they would prosper, but under present methods, in my opinion will advance very little if any. Many Indian families were at Grand Canyon and vicinity almost the entire year at day labor and it is believed the chief reason is that this reservation is inadequate as to area to accommodate them all.[63]

Hamley carried out his opinion by contacting Arizona Senator Henry F. Ashurst to make an actual request for an addition of plateau land to the Havasupai reservation along the lines of the unsuccessful 1920 plan.

As it happened, during this period of the late 1920s and early 1930s the Senate Committee on Indian Affairs was holding an extensive series of hearings on the conditions of Indian life. The committee scheduled a hearing with the Havasupai at Grand Canyon Village for May 21, 1931, and University of Arizona agricultural extention agent A. B. Ballantyne wrote Ashurst in April to say that Mánakaja had requested help in getting more land. He reported further that Hamley had worked out

an agreement with the National Park Service and the United States Forest Service by which it will be possible to have added to the Supai Reservation an area approximating 90,000 acres as a grazing ground for the livestock of this needy tribe. . . . From a purely humanitarian viewpoint it certainly appeared to me that the Supai were much in need of this additional reservation land, and . . . it would seem highly desirable that this additional land should be set aside for them.[64]

At the actual hearings Senator Lynn J. Frazier chaired the meetings and began by asking a number of questions about the canyon itself. Hamley testified that the tribe was able to farm no more than 100 acres in the canyon, and he added, "You will find Supai kept up pretty well. That is, the Indians themselves are very much interested in their own welfare."[65]

Frazier asked whether the tribe had need of more land for grazing purposes, and Hamley replied the tribe presently had some 80,000 to 90,000 acres for the tribe's stock on use permit from the Forest Service and another 95,000 acres from the Park Service. He estimated the tribe had 80 to 100 cattle and 400 to 500 horses on this area. He added the Havasupai could not develop more cattle because the Havasupai earth reservoirs provided too little water.

Senator Frazier inquired why the Indians did not develop more water, and Hamley replied, "Well, the Indians rather hesitated to make permanent improvements because of the fact that they did not own the land. These were tanks that they made temporarily, you might say, just for temporary use until they acquired this land and are able to get it."

Mr. Henry Scattergood of the Office of Indian Affairs noted that the Assistant Commissioner had commented favorably on transferring 90,000 acres from the Forestry Department to the Havasupai. Senator Wheeler inquired if the tribe would improve the land if they could have it, and Hamley replied, "I believe the Indians are so familiar with the land and the places that they could probably do the work themselves." The tribe maintained 18 or 19 farmhouses on the plateau, he noted.

Mánakaja then spoke to say the Havasupai needed more land, and Senator Frazier concluded by saying, "We will be glad to recommend more land for grazing purposes for your Indians."

Frazier then began to inquire about the school situation on the Havasupai Reservation, and Hamley said the tribe had but nine students in a school with a capacity of 34. Frazier somewhat incredulously asked why the Office of Indian Affairs did not add more grades then, and Hamley said the tribe would no doubt be heartily in favor of that, but he had instead recommended abolishment of the school. Hamley said there would be more students in the school, but "the flu of 1918 cleaned them out. We lost all the girls."

Hamley reported further:

> It is believed that pupils who attend non-reservation boarding schools have many advantages over these day-school pupils . . . this small day school . . . operates at great cost ($235 per capita) with little or no results obtained. It is considered a great injustice to these young pupils to retain them on this reservation . . . it is deemed a loss of time and money to maintain this day school.

When Mánakaja and West Sinyella then came forward both to ask for more local grades, Frazier expressed shock at the attitude of the Office of Indian Affairs and at the need to keep young children away from their homes and families for two and three years at a time. Hamley justified this by saying, "We have a lot of trouble when they do get away [from school] to get them back."

Despite Frazier's recommendations nothing came of the hearings for the Havasupai, except that their school was not closed for another 24 years.

Then on December 22, 1932, President Herbert Hoover issued a proclamation setting aside the relinquished Atlantic and Pacific indemnity-grant lands in the Havasupai's western winter range as the Grand Canyon National Monument. Though his proclamation was made "subject to all valid existing rights," Hoover said, "Warning is hereby expressly given to all unauthorized persons . . . not to locate or settle upon any of the lands thereof." Another bite of the Havasupai range became public. About this period the Havasupai ceased to make any further earth reservoirs on the plateau, as it seemed clear any improvements would simply be taken.

Shortly after, in February 1933, a heavy snowstorm completely marooned the Havasupai, now resigned to wintering in Havasu Canyon, and continuing snow and rain kept them cut off until the village was without food. For some reason the new superintendent tried to conceal the seriousness of the situation and telegraphed the Office of Indian Affairs to keep the matter quiet so newspapers would not "play up 'starving Indians.'" Others saw the plight differently, and finally after some three weeks the Park Service sent in sixteen pack mules loaded with food and supplies.

The next year, in 1934, the Park Service apparently decided the traditional homes of the Havasupai in their camp west of the Park Village were an eyesore and built ten sturdy frame cabins for the families there. Upon completion, the Park officials then tore down and burned the traditional homes, to the shock of the residents.

Mack Putesoy remembers, "They just burned them, with things inside. They're no good!"

Effie Hanna tells that she lost her marriage license and some old stone spear points she had been saving all her life. The Park carried out the "cleanup" operation in the summer, while the Havasupai residents were away farming in Havasu Canyon. The Park then began charging the residents of the new cabins five dollars a month, which included neither maintenance nor repair.

The initiative for this action becomes clear only in retrospect: By 1934 the Havasupai families resident at the South Rim had freely and continuously maintained and occupied their own homes at the camp since the creation of the Park fifteen years earlier. Unless the status of their presence could be changed, the Havasupai could take adverse possession—squatter's rights—over the camp. By moving the Havasupai families into rented cabins, the Park transformed them into tenants and erased their aboriginal status. No one warned the Havasupai they had any alternative to paying the rent; when they did so they entered an implied contractual relationship with the Grand Canyon National Park at the residence camp.

By 1935 the mail continued to come in once a week from Grand Canyon and down the eastern trail, but this route suffered periodic, serious flooding. That year the government began improvement of the hazardous western trail down Hualapai Canyon, at a cost of some $10,000. Further talk of relocating the agency headquarters to the plateau stopped.

This coincided with the political change brought to the Havasupai by the passage of the 1934 Indian Reorganization Act. The purpose of this act, fostered by Indian Commissioner John Collier, was to provide Indian communities with duly constituted and elected forms of government with whom the federal government could sign binding agreements. Many, if not most, North American peoples organized on a family or clan scale under subleaders. Such leadership divided functionally into religious, war, social and peace leaders; these were the persons the whites called chiefs or captains and the Havasupai called *baa gemúlva*—"boss." Among the Havasupai this division lacked sharp definition, and some individuals often embodied several functions. Havasupai leaders tended to approximate what we would call civic leaders in our smaller towns today—the persons of sufficient personal force and character to inspire confidence from their neighbors. No one elected such leaders to their status in any formal sense; they simply had a following that took them seriously. They would include such people as Mánakaja, Swèdeva, or Baa geláqa.

The Indian Reorganization Act encouraged tribes to adopt constitutions, hold tribal elections, and establish elective tribal councils. Many tribes adopted the expedient of appointing traditional leaders to the elective council as extra

members. Among such people as the Hopi, where religious authority was and remains very strong, the Indian Reorganization Act split the community between those who continued to follow traditional religious authority and those who chose to follow the new elective government. The elected Hopi government established itself in New Oraibi at the southeastern foot of Third Mesa, while the traditionalists remained upon the mesa tops following ancient Hopi tradition.

For the Havasupai the change brought less damage, for Havasupai leadership had always operated on a more pragmatic basis. The Havasupai adopted their constitution on March 27, 1939, and provided for a seven-member council under the first chairman, Arthur Kaska. Three of the members the council drew from the traditional leaders; four the tribal people elected by vote. In the beginning, the Havasupai felt hesitations about the alien arrangement; a Havasupai informant told one researcher in 1940 that he preferred the traditional chiefs to the new council. He claimed the chiefs took an interest in big matters, such as the tribe's land, while the new Council stuck to inconsequentialities and seemed not to know enough about anything.[4]

As it turned out, however, the second chairman, Dean Sinyella, led the council to take a very vigorous part in pressing the tribe's land complaints. Dean Sinyella's determination is hardly surprising, since he was among those the Park had dispossessed six years earlier. One can still find numerous records of insistent interviews with government officials at Grand Canyon, Valentine (site of the Havasupai and Hualapai agencies) and elsewhere, demanding something be done about the tribe's depressing situation. During this period a white rancher named Kirby had received a permit on some federal lands to the south, just above where the deep portion of Havasu Canyon ends and to the north of the present Babbitt Ranch. Kirby apparently constructed a trail down to a seep spring below the rim of Havasu Canyon and fenced it off in 1938 for his cattle to use. The Havasupai had long used this spring for watering their horses and newly acquired cattle, and the tribe began to raise a vigorous protest which quickly revived their larger demand for justice. Within a short time they had enlisted firm support from the Bureau of Indian Affairs and the Department of the Interior generally.

The question of forfeited Atlantic & Pacific railroad lands in the Havasupai and Hualapai range had never been satisfactorily settled, and private individuals and the Santa Fe, successor to the Atlantic & Pacific, continued to claim the checkerboard of odd-numbered sections within the Hualapai Reservation. The Hualapai took the matter to court, claiming the government could not have intended to convey to them a reservation encumbered by a checkerboard of conflicting claims. As the suit reached the U.S. Supreme Court the Havasupai and the Truxton Cañon Agency began to raise the question whether in fact the Havasupai had legal claim to railroad-grant areas as well. Within the Havasupai range these grants had been made and forfeited in the area between Cataract Canyon and the east boundary of the Hualapai Reservation, an area Herbert Hoover had already allowed the National Park Service to administer in part when he designated it as the Grand Canyon National Monument in 1932. The rest of the railroad grant area remained under the control of the Forest Service.

The Office of Indian Affairs approached each of these agencies to learn their views on transferring title to the former railroad lands back to the Havasupai, as the terms of the 1866 railroad grant had specified the grant to be subordinate to the aboriginal rights of the Indians resident in the area.

On May 1, 1940, the Regional Forester in Albuquerque, Frank C. W. Pooler, reported:

> In the event the Indian Service is able to work out satisfactory arrangements for the use of the National Monument and public domain areas lying between the Hualapai Reservation and the Forest, there is no objection on our part to the elimination of that part of the Forest west of Cataract Canyon. If and until such an arrangement can be worked out, the Forest Service has no objection to the continued use of the Forest area by the livestock of the Supai Indians.[66]

On May 6 C. E. Rachford, the Acting Chief of the Forest Service, concurred with Pooler's recommendation.

However, on May 15 A. E. Demaray, the Acting Director of the National Park Service, wrote the Commissioner of Indian Affairs a remarkable reply which concluded:

> At this time I am not prepared to recommend the transfer for reservation purposes of that portion of Grand Canyon National Monument south of the Colorado River. However, I am willing to begin consideration of a transfer. What likelihood is there of moving the Supai Indians to the Hualapai Reservation, and adding the Havasupai Reservation to the national Park?[67]

The only justification for such an offer would have to be that the Park Service felt the Havasupai were Park property and they were offering to surrender them in return for the land the Havasupai had been guaranteed by Executive Order.

Then, during that year, the Interior Department settled the problem of the rancher and the seep spring with a departmental order withdrawing four sections of land in the vicinity of the spring and around this dry upper portion of Havasu Canyon from private use and reserving these sections for Havasupai use. Kirby's permit within this area was terminated.

On January 28, 1941 the Hualapai lawyers filed their case before the Supreme Court, and during the October term of 1941, the Hualapai suit finally came before the Supreme Court as UNITED STATES OF AMERICA, as Guardian of the Indians of the Tribe of Hualpai in the State of Arizona, Petitioner, v. SANTA FE PACIFIC RAILROAD COMPANY.

Two questions of fact had already been established prior to the case: a) Intent of Congress to extinguish Indian title through statutory enactment is not to be lightly implied, all doubts in the construction of the statute being resolved in favor of the Indians, and b) Where the right of occupancy of an Indian tribe is not extinguished prior to the date of definite location of a railroad to which land has been granted upon condition that the United States extinguish the Indian title, the railroad takes the fee subject to the encumbrance of Indian title, the railroad's title attaching as of the date of the grant.

The great Indian lawyer Felix S. Cohen was one of the team of lawyers who filed the brief on behalf of the Hualapai. He argued, among other things, that "In the absence of express language to the contrary, a Federal grant of public lands does not constitute an extinguishment of Indian occupancy rights." The lawyers for the Santa Fe Railroad argued that Congress had the power to terminate the Haualapai rights to their aboriginal home and had in fact done so in conveying title to their lands to the Atlantic & Pacific railroad.

Justice William O. Douglas wrote the opinion for the Supreme Court, saying in part,

> . . . "the exclusive right of the United States to extinguish" Indian title has never been doubted . . . If the right of occupancy of the Walapais was not extinguished prior to the date of definite location of the railroad in 1872, then the respondent's predecessor took the fee subject to the encumbrance of Indian title. . . . Certainly prior to 1865 any right of occupancy of the Walapais to the lands in question was not extinguished. . . . If there was an extinguishment of the rights of the Walapais, it resulted not from action of the Surveyor General but from action of Congress . . . We are not advised that Congress took any such action. . . . We search the public records in vain for any clear and plain indication that Congress in creating the Colorado River reservation was doing more than making an offer to the Indians . . . which it was hoped would be accepted as a compromise of a troublesome question. We find no indication that Congress by creating that reservation intended to extinguish all of the rights which the Walapais had in their ancestral home . . . the rule of construction for over a century has been that "doubtful expressions, instead of being resolved in favor of the United States, are to be resolved in favor of a weak and defenseless people, who are wards of the nation, and dependent wholly upon its protection and good faith." [68]

The Court also cited ATLANTIC & PACIFIC RAILROAD COMPANY V. ROBERT MINGUS, in which Justice Brown in 1896 had written, "Under these circumstances it could scarcely be expected that the United States should be called upon to extinguish, for the benefit of a railroad company which had chosen to locate its route through this territory, a title guaranteed to the Indians by solemn treaties. . . . The railroad company was in no position to insist that the government should extinguish these titles, at least without affirmatively proving that the Indians were willing to make the cession. . . ."

The Court upheld the right of the Hualapai tribe to possess forfeited railroad lands within their territory, making title to their reservation clear and complete. The implications for the Havasupai were momentous, as the decision could well be construed as an affirmation of their rights to such lands within their winter range to the west of Cataract Canyon.

Following the decision the Interior Department sent out a team of legal examiners to the Hualapai and Havasupai to determine just what lands each tribe might have title to. During April 1942 the lawyers Abe Barber and Felix S. Cohen held a series of hearings and investigations on the question with each tribe and prepared their report in May which included the following conclusions:

> On the question of forfeiture . . . no record has been found from which it could be remotely inferred that the Army intended, or that the Indians agreed, to a curtailment of any aboriginal rights in non-reservation lands. . . . it must be concluded that the area in question is still subject to the aboriginal occupancy right of the Havasupai Tribe unless there has been, in fact, a voluntary abandonment of this land by the Indians themselves. . . . With respect to the question as to whether the Havasupai right of occupancy has been extinguished by any action of the Government, the examiners are of the opinion that no such extinguishment has occurred.

> By a number of Executive orders and proclamations and legislative acts various portions of these lands were included within a forest preserve, a national monument and park, and power site withdrawals. But all of these were intended to prevent the future acquisition of private rights in these public lands, not to impair existing rights.

> The examiners have found that there is no evidence upon which it can be said that the occupancy rights of the Havasupai tribe to the lands in the area have either been abandoned by the tribe or been extinguished by Executive or legislative action. The conclusion is inescapable that the Havasupai still have a valid possessory right to the land in question.

Based on their findings Barber and Cohen concluded:

> Since the surrender of all right and title in the odd-numbered sections of land within the area described, executed by the Santa Fe Pacific Railroad Company, successor in interest to the Atlantic and Pacific Railroad, on December 17, 1940, full and unquestionable legal title has been vested in the United States, the Havasupai Tribe retaining its exclusive right of use and occupancy therein.[69]

With the submission of this report, the Interior Department issued an administrative order on May 28, 1942, recognizing the claim of the Havasupai to the federal lands between Cataract Canyon and the Hualapai reservation. They began to mark the area as "Indian Land" on their maps from the date of the order, and on January 30, 1943, they ordered Land Field Agent A. W. Simington to make a detailed survey of the land and called his attention to the attempts renewed by the Havasupai Tribal Chairman, Dean Sinyella, to regain plateau land for the Havasupai. The author of the order, W. Barton Greenwood of the Office of Indian Affairs, instructed Simington, "you should prepare a report and a map of the lands which may be used as a basis by this office for recommending legislation that certain lands be set aside and reserved as an addition to the

Havasupai Indian Reservation . . . as early in this session of Congress as possible. . . . Be sure to keep in mind that the reports must contain ample information upon which recommendation for the enactment of legislation can be based." [70] The stage was set for the Havasupai's third attempt to return to the plateau, one that was backed by all the government agencies involved except the National Park Service.

Simington's instructions advised him that Dean Sinyella had written the Office of Indian Affairs in 1940 to say that his people desired the return of the area "from Grand Canyon Park down Coconino Wash to West Triangle Tank, then on to Long Point past Black Tank, and on to Kiska [Kisaha?] Tank, and on to the Walapai [Hualapai] Reservation line." Subsequently the Truxton Cañon Superintendent had written in 1942 to describe a rather different area, and Simington was to resolve the discrepancy. According to Simington's instructions and the Examiners' Report, the forfeited railroad lands would correspond to the present south rim portion of the Grand Canyon National Monument and the Kaibab National Forest west of Cataract Canyon.

Truxton Cañon Superintendent John O. Crow, who much later, in 1972, was to become Deputy Commissioner, responded to the Office of Indian Affairs' instructions to Simington that he felt the rights of the Havasupai antedated either the Park or the Forest Services, and he indicated an area corresponding roughly to the tribe's grazing permit lands which he felt should be returned to them. He noted additionally, "the officials of the Forest Service have expressed a willingness to relinquish all of this area to the Indians, and, in fact, for all practical purposes now consider the area as Indian land. . . . No opposition would be offered by the State and County officials to any move to add land to the reservation as recommended. These officials have been most sympathetic to the needs of the Havasupai." [71]

Simington worked extremely fast and by March 20, 1943, sent his report to Allan G. Harper, Acting Director of Lands in the Office of Indian Affairs. After extensive survey Simington had determined that obtaining all the lands described in Dean Sinyella's 1940 letter would be impossible, as it included "thousands of acres of State and privately owned land that is not for sale even if funds for the purchase could be appropriated." He outlined instead a proposal to return 264,959 acres by withdrawing the 30,700 acres included in the railroad grant area and 18,400 more from the Grand Canyon National Monument's even-numbered sections. He suggested a further withdrawal of 68,500 acres from Kaibab National Forest and 133,400 acres of Havasupai permit area from the Grand Canyon National Park. Simington proposed return of another 5,760 acres of public domain and 5,120 acres of state land. All this would be consolidated with the existing 518.06 acres and the 2,560 acres withdrawn for tribal use in 1940. Simington also noted:

> There will be no difficulty with the Forest Service as they now consider all land west of the Havasupai drift fence as belonging to the Indians. . . . As for the part within the Grand Canyon National Park, I am unable to say

what attitude the Park Service will take; they have no developments on this area and make no use of it while the Indians do use it for grazing.

Simington continued:

> The land needs of the Havasupai is [sic] something that can be stated in a very few words. There are forty families and to make them self-supporting will require 4,000 head of cattle. At an average of six head per section will require 666 sections or 426,240 acres.

> At the present time these Indians use 33,963 acres of the Kaibab National Forest. . . . On the Grand Canyon National Park, 30,290 acres are used. . . . Other government lands used [Grand Canyon National Monument] are 16,840 acres. . . . The totals in use are 786 head of cattle on 81,093 acres. It can readily be seen that to make these Indians self-supporting in the cattle industry an additional 345,000 acres will be necessary. There is no hope of securing this land at this late date. The very best that can be done is to attempt to secure the proposed reservation as shown on the attached map.

Simington added:

> Should there be any controversy over the National Park area included, at least an effort should be made to include the part back from the Canyon rim and shown on the map as Coconino Plateau.[72]

He concluded by reporting that Dean Sinyella, speaking as an individual, had agreed to this proposal, as had Mr. Crow verbally.

However, by April 30 Arizona Congressman John R. Murdock commented on a pending bill to return only the relinquished railroad lands to the Havasupai in recognition of the May 28, 1942, departmental ruling, "The Indian Reservations don't need this land, and I believe it can be put to better use for other purposes, such as grazing." [73] What Murdock thought the Havasupai had in mind is hard to conjecture. It is not hard to conjecture, however, that Murdock probably hoped the released railroad lands would be added to the State of Arizona.

The next week the Park Service released its views on the return of Park land to the Havasupai over the signatures of Frederick Law Olmsted, Harold C. Bryant and Harold M. Ratcliff. Their May 4 report considered at length Havasupai rights on the plateau as outlined in the railroad examiners' report and offered additional economic, social and spiritual reasons in support of transferring land to the Havasupai, concluding:

> That the morale of the Tribe would be greatly improved by the mere fact of their getting back even that much of their ancestral country as a Reservation of their very own, to which they could admit outsiders on suffrance instead of themselves being admitted to it only on suffrance.

Then the report continued with a lengthier list of reasons *against* any transfer of land to the Havasupai, despite the reasons they had already listed *in favor*. The Park objected to placing Park lands (whether forcibly stolen from the Havasupai or not) under the jurisdiction of an agency "having statutory authorization to utilize areas under its jurisdiction for industrial, commercial or other economic objectives," even though they both shared administrative control by the Interior Department and even though, by their own statement, "We are fully in accord with the essential objectives toward which the proposal was aimed."

The authors of the Park report also stated the Simington proposal would remove from the Park so-called "research areas" on the Great Thumb, regardless of the admitted fact that the Havasupai had long continued to use this area and no real "research" was going on there. The authors reaffirmed the Park Service's determination to have the Park's western boundary include Havasu Canyon because, "The view down into Havasupai Canyon from Manakacha Point and other places on its eastern rim will remain uniquely interesting and beautiful for centuries to come—perhaps long after the last of the Havasupais shall have passed away." Again this notion of the Havasupai as some sort of Park attraction; again the waiting game until the Havasupai—the "doomed race"—die out.

The Park Service report proposed simply continuing tribal permits on Park Service areas. Any water developments allowed on Park land would remain minimal, however. The authors recommended what was to become a familiar theme, that the tribe should expand onto land elsewhere to the south of the federal lands surrounding their reservation, in effect leaving the Havasupai village within the Park and the ancestral plateau lands of the Havasupai still under Park and Forest Service administrative control. The Park report did hold out the possibility of adding Forest land to the reservation; this they did not seem to find objectionable.

The report stated a willingness to see the National Monument land south of the river returned to the Havasupai, except for the points on the north, since "Superb views of this unit of the Grand Canyon are obtainable . . . from the rim on the south side especially at and near Yumtheska Point." The report cited a number of other notable views from areas they were loath to surrender and then admitted:

> Because of present difficulties of access, few of the visitors interested in the scenery of the Grand Canyon country have ever seen these notable views from near the rim of this part of the National Monument; but, with the development of better roads from the southwest *on which the Indian Service is engaged* [italics ours], it is reasonably to be expected that, under such regulations as the Indian Service may prescribe, considerable numbers of visitors will be enabled to reach these superbly scenic points of view; and it seems in accordance with sound established public policy that provisions for these recreational visitors when they reach these notable view points should remain where they have been placed by Congress, under the jurisdiction of the Park Service, rather than be transferred to the jurisdiction of the Indian Service.[74]

By September 13, 1943, Park Service Director Newton B. Drury sent a memorandum to the Indian Commissioner saying the Park Service would have to oppose any transfer of Park land until the building of Bridge Canyon Dam. He blandly concluded perhaps the transfer could be made at "a more favorable time."

On October 21 H. M. Critchfield, Director of Lands for the Office of Indian Affairs, reported to Supt. Crow that his conversations with the Park Service had fairly convinced him that "If this area is useless to the Indians, if no water can be developed at reasonable cost, then it seems to us that we should cease to work for the addition of the monument and park lands to the Havasupai Reservation." [75]

That the Havasupai effort should be so easily dashed for the benefit of the Park Service overwhelmed Crow, and he erupted on October 27 in a long and angry letter to the Commissioner of Indian Affairs:

> I am surprised to note the intimation that I had agreed with the conclusion that no water could be developed on the area at reasonable expense and that the land would be of little use to the Indians or to anyone else. . . . At the time of our only conference with the local officials of the Park Service at Grand Canyon on April 28 and 29, this argument was advanced by the Park officials in spite of the fact that apparently no survey had been made by them and they were unfamiliar with the area. . . . They were not even aware of the presence in the area of some ten earth-filled tanks built by the Indians themselves without assistance and by using only their primitive equipment. Some of these tanks were built over 30 years ago and have proven successful. We are convinced that water can be developed along this line as several promising tank sites have been observed. These tanks and most of the prospective sites cannot be seen from the automobile trails but must be visited by horseback or foot transportation.
>
> During the month of July a party from this Agency . . . spent four days on the area. . . . It was our unanimous opinion that considerable use of the area could be made by the Indians with the assistance of the Indian Service.
>
> . . . This area . . . represents the only area we have or will possibly ever have the slightest chance to obtain for these people. This land and other land nearby should never have had any status but Indian ownership. . . .
>
> You refer in your letter to conferences held in the field during July and asking for a report from me on these conferences. If such conferences were held during July we have no knowledge of them.
>
> However, on April 28 and 29, a conference was held at Grand Canyon. . . . As a result of this discussion, a report was later prepared and signed by Superintendent Bryant, Mr. Ratcliff and Mr. Olmsted.
>
> The objections of the Park Service to our proposal are listed in this report beginning on Page 4 as follows:

1. Establishment of a precedent for:
   (a) reducing the area of a national Park, and
   (b) transferring that area to a bureau who has no paramount interest in conservation.

2. Specific objections:
   (a) exclusion of 40 miles of the river from the Park boundaries,
   (b) area proposed for withdrawal is of different type from that found elsewhere
   (c) area includes one of two "research areas" in the park and the "primitive area" protecting it
   (d) exclusion of beautiful Havasupai Canyon from Park.

3. Objection stated verbally in conference but omitted from written report:
   (a) that the Indian Service has entered into a conspiracy with the Bureau of Reclamation to gain control of the Colorado River in order that additional power dams could be built.

To an Indian Service Administrator, constantly confronted with economic problems of a group of practically landless people, these arguments seem most inadequate. The general theme of the Park Service objections would lead one to believe that to turn land over to the Indians and Indian Service would be to abrogate the Government's Conservation policy. This is a false impression and a slighting one to the Indian Service in view of our policy on Conservation. Emphasis is placed by the Park Service on the fact that the proposed action would remove from the Park, Canyon scenery "superlatively worth preserving in a natural condition forever." Yet in another section of the report it is said that "The views down into Havasupai Canyon from Manakacha point and other places on its eastern rim will remain uniquely interesting and beautiful for centuries to come—perhaps long after the last of the Havasupais shall have passed away." The inclusion of this area in the Indian reservation would not, could not, cause these views to be exhausted and when the last Havasupai has passed away, the area should be restored to the Park, richer in historical background by virtue of having been the home of a vanished race. As for objection No. 1 on the list, admittedly the greatest objection, and in fact the only valid objection in the list, that of setting a precedent by reducing the size of a national Park, *it cannot be dangerous policy of any Government to restore rightful lands taken from a minority group—taken from them without their consent or even their knowledge* [italics ours].

The language in the Congressional Act of 1919 creating the Grand Canyon Park expressly recognizes the prior rights of the Havasupais in the area set aside. The spirit of this language, however, has not been adhered to. It was not long after the establishment of the Park until a band of Havasupais living at Indian gardens on Bright Angel Creek [sic] were removed by subterfuge and with other bands pushed westward to what is now known as the Havasupai drift fence. There is small wonder that we, and the Havasupais, fear that justification will be advanced to deprive them of even the small 500-acre reservation they now occupy. There is certainly precedent for this fear.[76]

Crow may or may not have been aware that in fact the Park Service had already advanced this very proposal in 1940. Despite Supt. Crow's best efforts at persuasion, the Indian Service withdrew further support from the Havasupai under the Park Service's pressure. While Crow was still desperately searching the United States Statutes, Congress ended on March 4, 1944, the new Tribal Council's first effort to continue the long-standing work of the Havasupai traditional chiefs to regain 264,959 acres of their people's land. On that date the United States Congress acted to recognize only the administrative withdrawal in 1940 of the four sections of desert canyon around the seep spring—2,539 acres of land located thirty miles away.

Perhaps mercifully, Mánakaja had died February 24, 1942—late enough to know about the Supreme Court's decision in U.S. v Santa Fe but too soon to see that the government would fail to apply it to the Havasupai. Nothing further was said of the odd-numbered sections of land within Havasupai territory which the railroad had forfeited. Congressional action would have been needed to convey any even-numbered sections of this area to the Havasupai, but the odd-numbered sections the Supreme Court had by implication already conveyed to them.

The winter of 1942–1943 Clark and Ethel Jack spent the last winter of the Havasupai in Indian Gardens. The National Park Service had hired Clark to maintain the Bright Angel Trail, and he decided to take his wife to live down by the spring for a final winter, where she herself had grown up. She remembers most of all the loneliness where once her grandfather, Burro, had farmed and laughed with his family. They never returned.

Ethel became gravely ill after her stay at The Place below The Spruce Trees and began to sink despairingly week by week. Her father called the healer Allen Ákaba to help her, and four times Allen Ákaba came to her to sing and take the sorrow and sickness from her soul. On the fourth visit he placed an eagle feather in her hair and said he could do no more. That night Ethel felt she must die and began to slip away. While she was unconscious that night she heard horses coming up the canyon from the falls. Soon she saw two horses arrive and stand outside the house, a sorrel and a beautiful, slim gray horse. Her father went out to them and soon called her to come out and mount the gray. She asked weakly how she could do that. He told her she must come out to the horses by herself and told her to walk slowly and she could make it. She found she could rise then, and when she reached the gray it knelt like a cow so she could mount it. Then it stood.

Her father held the horse while he gave her last-minute instructions. He gave her a quirt but told her just to hold it and not to touch the horse with it or say anything to the horse, for it knew where to take her. He told her she would never be ill again and released the horse. Ethel says the horse rose into the air and began to travel through the sky toward the east. Before long she could see a place below with many houses and lights. Grass and trees grew everywhere.

Never had she seen such a place. She says it appeared that she was seeing it through a little window as she descended. Then she was standing among the trees in a wonderful place, smiling. Then her dream ended, and she awoke in her father's house in Havasu Canyon. She remembers she felt reborn.

No one could understand the miraculous recovery that followed. She told them of the dream, as she did others over the years, but no one could decipher its meaning, so she kept the dream to ponder. She never became ill again; only 31 years later was Ethel Jack to discover the message of her dream.

Four years after Ethel's sickness Wa tahómja died. The great *wa jemátv* above Pasture Wash began to fall away until its massive stacked timbers stood open to the wind, the sun casting them into the pattern of a black star upon the earth where he had lived.

Immediately after the war Congress passed the Indian Claims Commission Act. This momentous 1946 act was designed to settle for good all further Indian land claims and complaints against the United States Government by encouraging all Indian tribes to file claims with the newly created Indian Claims Commission for lands unjustly expropriated from them by actions of the United States Government. The act gave Indian plaintiffs a deadline of 1951 to submit their suits; then the suits would be adjudicated, and each plaintiff would receive a financial settlement for the tribe's lost lands. The act made no provision for returning any land.

An unexpected flood of claims ensued, and the government extended the life of the act another ten years to handle the deluge. Several tribes went beyond the expected procedure and filed claims for which they expressly refused to accept money; they simply asked the Claims Commission to substantiate their legal right to the lands they had lost.

The Indian Service had apparently lost heart for the Havasupai fight to return to the plateau and persuaded them to begin a legal claim just under the original 1951 deadline. Neither the Bureau of Indian Affairs nor the lawyer retained for the tribe, Royal D. Marks of Phoenix, offered the Havasupai any encouragement to file for any lands still claimed and desired for return without compensation, although some of the Havasupai complained throughout the lengthy adjudication that they had little use for money when their land was gone.

In 1951 and 1952 the Arizona Commission of Indian Affairs, led by member Dr. Leo Schnur, considered pushing for legislation to restore the Havasupai's permit areas to them but dropped the idea because they feared such an effort might hinder the tribe's legal suit. Schnur pointed out to local newspapers the Park Service viewed the Havasupai as "mere squatters."

In 1952 the American people elected Eisenhower to the Presidency, and he ushered in a new time of stress for Indian people throughout the country with his new policy of "termination." The new administration's intention was to end the special trust status of Indian land as quickly as possible to bring native Americans into the "mainstream" of American life. Before this experiment was halted it brought ruin or dispersion to four tribes who actually were "terminated" and social and spiritual disruption even to those who managed to resist actual termination. The Havasupai would before long number themselves among those drastically affected by the pressure to leave the reservations; in fact, the Havasupai were being pushed from two directions.

In 1952 National Park Service headquarters in Washington notified Grand Canyon Park Superintendent Harold C. Bryant that he would have to demonstrate some valid, existing Havasupai right to use Park land for such use rights to be continued. On May 6, 1953, after a thorough search of his records, Dr. Bryant responded to Park officials by quoting from the Park's own May 4, 1943, report:

> There has been no legal extinguishment of the rights of the Havasupai Tribe to occupancy and use of those parts of their aboriginal territory the legal title to which has remained continuously in the United States and which are now included in the National Park, the National Forest and the National Monument; and in the case of the National Park those rights were even expressly recognized by the Congress of the United States in the Act of 1919 creating the Park by the provisions of Section 3 authorizing the Secretary of the Interior "to permit individual members of said tribe to use and occupy other tracts of land within said park for agricultural purposes." [77]

By the next year Dr. Bryant retired, and his successors at Grand Canyon renewed the pressure on the Havasupai. In 1955 Park officials informed the Havasupai families at Grand Canyon they could remain only if they were employed. After passing this information along, the Grand Canyon officials held a conference at Grand Canyon with the Bureau of Indian Affairs' Truxton Cañon Agency Superintendent, Wesley T. Bobo. Within a short time of this conference, the Grand Canyon Park and the various concessionnaires began terminating practically all Havasupai jobs within the Park, and Park officials once again began dismantling homes at the Havasupai residence camp. The Bureau of Indian Affairs had a truck available to haul the dispossessed and their belongings away. Effie Hanna remembers that the truck hauled old people, children and all and unceremoniously dumped them in the snow at Topocoba Hilltop, where a rugged, 14-mile trail led down 2,300 feet to Havasu Canyon. It was winter, and she remembers concealing three families in her cabin at the residence area to protect them from a like eviction. Her husband, Henry, was among the few who had kept his job at the canyon.

Those who were abandoned at Topocoba were too tough to freeze. They were also too angry to forget.

9.

THE TRACK

OF

THE CAT

Late in the year you number 1952 Swèdeva's spirit passed from the earth, and his lumber cabin in the trees above his well stood empty.

Dasjígva had presented him no children; so while he yet lived among us he named me, Jóla, whom you call William Little Jim, as his successor and only heir. I am son to his half brother. I am also no fool; I had the inheritance set down by your law in your courthouse beneath the Snowy Mountains at the place you call Flagstaff. My inheritance included the permit to live by my uncle's well.

No sooner had Swèdeva gone than the men of the Park came to us still living there at The Spruce Trees. They told us to show why we should live at The Spruce Trees and use land of the Park any longer. The men of the Park said if we could not prove our right there, then we would have to leave the Park.

And it was so that we already held in our hands the paper bearing the pencil-written words of the man who called himself "Perry E. Brown, Chief Ranger at Grand Canyon." On the day he called November 16, 1947, he had

Swèdeva at Havasu
Havasupai subchief

Courtesy Wayne Paya 1942

used that paper to tell Arthur and Eleanora Kaska that they could not keep their own home at our camp at The Spruce Trees. Even now those who understand the writing can say his words which he set there. Here, see it:

"This is your last warning. Get the damn shack down."

Now my uncle was gone, and the boss men of the Park were saying this to all of us.

The time was the Moon of Staying at Home, near the time you say your *jízes* was born. Even he could get no room from you to be born.

White Man on Tiptoes, the man of the Park who called himself Carl Lehnert and had for his woman the sister of the Kolbs, called us all together at our new meeting hall. There White Man on Tiptoes told everyone he had received a paper from Wá sendon saying we the Havasupai would have to move our horses and our families from the lands of the Park. White Man on Tiptoes did not want us to feel we had done anything wrong; he told us the paper had come from the big bosses in Wá sendon and was not his idea.

I came late with my friend Múlo, and the people told us of White Man on Tiptoes' words. I wanted to see this paper he spoke of, but White Man on Tiptoes told me, "I don't have it here to show you. But we want you out in about a week." He told us we would all have to go back to Blue Creek. I asked him if I would have to go, too, and White Man on Tiptoes told me, "No; you have Big Jim's permit. You can stay there as long as you want."

At that time I was not myself with my uncle gone. He had lived around The Spruce Trees for almost a hundred winters, and I could not see the place any more until my sadness was gone. When I heard my permit was all right, I got my things together to travel to my son Ernest and stay at Little Verde among his wife's people the Yavapai. The place lies far to the south toward the Home of the Dark People [Phoenix].

Lorenzo and Harriet and the others tried to get me to stay; they said I must put my sadness behind me and hold my hand against the men of the Park. But I had my sorrow to follow; it is the way. I left while the Wood Bearer was still in the sky. The snow lay heavy on the land.

After I left some of the people went to Doctor Bryant [the Grand Canyon Superintendent] and begged him to help them keep their homes; most of them had no land at Blue Creek. Doctor Bryant knew us all for many years and heard our words when we went to him. He looked hard among his papers. On the day you call May 6, 1953, he placed in their hands a paper he had sent to Wá sendon. The paper told them we could stay.

But by the time of snows in the year you number 1954, Doctor Bryant was gone, too. He did not die. No. He said he was old and would not work at the Park any more. This may be so. He was a friend, for he stopped Wá sendon from chasing some of us from our homes. Some of us.

I lived with my son yet among the Yavapai. When I returned I went again to stay at my uncle's cabin by the well there near The Spruce Trees, and soon my son Ernest came with his family to stay with me there. Scarcely another winter passed, and the men of the Park again were telling us we would have to leave the Park. When we showed them Doctor Bryant's paper words, the men of the Park said the paper was about another place but they changed their words to us to say this: As long as we were working for money there at The Spruce Trees, we could stay.

Soon after these words from the men of the Park, one after another of us lost his work there. We had done nothing wrong, they would tell us. They just didn't need us for a while. And the men of the Park came to tear down the home of each one there at The Spruce Trees. Yes, and trucks came for us and our things, and they hauled us out. Soon it was my turn, and they told me I was too old to work. Too old! Even now I am stronger than most of them were who sent me away.

And when the snow left in that year—was it the one you number 1960?—the men of the Park sent out a great yellow machine that shook the earth with its noise and sent up a black smoke. For it was planting time, and all of us had gone to Blue Creek to make our farms. And the machine left the print of its banded tracks across the softening earth. The track of the cat, for that is what you call it, led to the place where my uncle had spent forty winters by his well. Yes, and the yellow cat of the Park pushed into the old cabin and crushed it like an egg, for it was but a home and had not the strength of a rock or a tree. The men of the Park piled up the pieces and set them ablaze. The smoke rose straight.

Lorenzo had gone before the cat of the Park and taken a saddle and some small things out for me. That was all. Had he not foretold it?

Before the snows came I returned and found a new pain to fill my heart. Only the blackened earth and broken dishes showed where the "Home of Big Jim" had stood. Even his well along the place you call Bright Angel Wash they had filled with dirt. Those men were fools! Could they know what they had done?

And I followed the track of the cat yet farther, to the Farms, where it led to another circle of blackened earth by my uncle's earth dam just inside the Park fence. Yes, even the little earth lodge was gone. Less than an hour's walk south through the Farms Wa tahómja's camp still stood; it was beyond the Park fence, where the cat of the Park could not go.

I would stay. I would build another place; for had they not said, "You have Big Jim's permit. You can stay there as long as you want"?

Yet in half the cycle of the moon the Park sent their men to tell me the permit was no good because I had abandoned the place. What of the permit of Big Jim? It was no different from our camp over the waste ditch at The Spruce Trees.

At last I became stone inside, and I told the men of the Park, "Don't say some others told you to say this. It's you; you're saying it. You, and the ones like you, brought this to the place that was my home and the home of my uncle before me. You cannot hide it!"

Yes, and that day I left the place and have never looked upon it again. I played there as a boy and raised my own children there.

Even then Wa tahómja's son Elmer, he who was lost in the snow, and Clark Jack, who had been our Chairman, had planted their last gardens at the Farms. By the year of the destruction they, too, were gone, and all of Wa tahómja's camp there by the Farms was fallen empty. But it stood beyond the reach of the cat, and they tell me the camp still stands, even as Wa tahómja had said it should be—the great lodge should stand always, to remind us. I would not know, for I have not turned my eyes to the place again.

I went back to my son at Little Verde and stayed with him many winters before returning here to Blue Creek. Here by my friend Múlo I built this small house and here I stay. My permit still lies in my son's hands. Once I thought papers were words and promises; I know now they are only paper, and you have no time for paper.

All is gone that tells us of my uncle. We see only the pieces of stone and dishes that still look from the earth in that place where he once sang with the wind among The Spruce Trees. Out in the piñons stands the brown stone where we laid him in the earth. Perhaps some day the cat of the Park will wipe that, too, from the earth.

And now enough. I cannot say more.

10.
THE
LONG WAY
BACK

In 1955 the Bureau of Indian Affairs was finally able to carry out Hamley's threat, and the little Havasupai school did not open for the first time in sixty years. The new push for assimilation into the "mainstream" justified perfectly the need to send Havasupai children out into the white world—at age six. The Bureau demonstrated that attendance figures had fallen so low that they could no longer justify operating a local school. They also claimed the Havasupai offered their children an unwholesome moral atmosphere. Charles F. Allen, criminal investigator for the Bureau, visited the Havasupai for two days in 1955. During that time he admitted the village to be quiet and peaceful; nevertheless he felt compelled to report the Havasupai to lack any semblance of law and order, as they did not have a court, and added:

> Under the influence of alcohol, the men of the tribe, who are natural horsemen, take up their pastime of roping and raping the women and girls of the tribe, not always against their will.[78]

Sinyella
Havasupai subchief

Courtesy Lorenzo Sinyella 1920

The Bureau lacked even hearsay to justify such a crude judgment, but they let it stand as a reinforcement for their decision to close the school.

Children left home for nine months at a stretch, and many individuals tell of being away from home for years at a stretch. The Havasupai were desperate and tried approaching all the surrounding communities to see if their children could at least go there instead of to the 350-mile-distant Indian school at Fort Apache. Williams, Ash Fork and Seligman were all approached, but all replied they could not accept nonresident children, as they provided no tax support to the school. The tribe approached the school at Grand Canyon Village, which educated primarily the white children of Park Service employees; but Havasupai living at Grand Canyon at the time report the school there did not make Havasupai children welcome. They tried to obtain federal funding to build their own school on the plateau or in some nearby town but received the reply that no federal funds could be used to build a tribal school on nontribal land. Every avenue seemed blocked.

Some children simply did not go to school at all except to attend the informal classes that Mrs. Collins, who had been hired as a Bureau teacher when the school was closed, conducted in her home.

Then in 1956 the Bureau of Indian Affairs began its formal program of relocation from the Havasupai reservation. The aim was to encourage young Havasupai to leave their homeland and resettle them in urban, industrial areas. People who wished to apply for this program were screened and then sent to relocation centers in Los Angeles, Oakland, Chicago, Dallas and other cities. Scott Momaday has ably depicted the anomie and dejection these dislocated people fell into in the blank impersonality of America's cities in his *House Made of Dawn*.[79] Some few Havasupai chose to try resettlement, but nearly every one, disillusioned and lost, returned to Arizona if not to the Havasupai reservation itself.

For some years the Bureau of Indian Affairs had also encouraged Havasupai to relocate to the Colorado River reservation, where the government had once thought of forcing them to live, and take up life as farmers. A number of families also tried this, but every one of them returned to his home as well.

Early in the 1930s a prospector named W. J. Johnson had established residence on the Havasupai reservation itself. He owned the patented mining claims between Havasu and Mooney Falls adjoining the north end of the 1882 reservation boundary. The area included the Havasupai cremation grounds as well as the actual mining operation near the mouth of Carbonate Canyon.

By the Second World War a Seligman merchant named E. F. Schoeny had acquired the Carbonate Canyon mining claim from Johnson. The mine was of very low productivity, and little activity went on there. A few Havasupai farmed small plots in the narrow, nearly sunless gorge where they had once cremated the dead, and they, Johnson and later Schoeny, had put up several cabins on the ground between the two falls and rented them to visitors. As demand for lead soared during the war Schoeny had a man named Sanderson reopen operations on his claim, and about eight or ten Havasupai worked out the war years in Schoeny's lead mine.

Following the war the mining operation quickly went broke and closed down again. Once again the Havasupai were left the only real users of the area. They now began to turn the cabins to use by renting them out to the few campers and visitors who came to Havasu Canyon in those days. In return for the use of the cabins, the Havasupai Tribal Council paid Schoeny a share of whatever income they could derive from this arrangement. The operation also allowed the Havasupai to keep an eye on the few artifacts that the miners and previous visitors had not already carried off.

The National Park Service had never been able to establish a clear claim to this Havasupai area because of the original 1880 Presidential intention to make it part of the Havasupai reservation. Apparently during the 1950s the Park Service began quiet negotiations with Schoeny to buy the claim and add it to the Park that way without alerting the Havasupai.

Despite earlier Havasupai attempts to reclaim the falls from Schoeny, in mid 1957 the National Park Service achieved a settlement and paid him $15,000 to add his mining claims to the Grand Canyon National Park. Grand Canyon Park officials then fenced off the 62-acre area and destroyed the cabins there.

At the time Dean Sinyella's son Juan was Tribal Chairman, and he and Tribal Secretary Lemuel Paya wrote strong pleas for help to Senator Barry Goldwater and to former Arizona Governor Howard Pyle, who had become administrative assistant to President Eisenhower. In their letters, written August 25 and 26, 1957, Juan Sinyella and Lemuel Paya asserted the area taken from them was rightfully Havasupai and asked, "What recourse do we have?"

Apparently neither Goldwater nor Pyle felt they had any, for they offered no measures to rectify the seizure. After fencing the area off from the reservation, Grand Canyon Park officials made little serious effort to protect either its remaining artifacts or its fragile sustenance until it was too late to save either fifteen years later. Instead, they made it into a public campground.

By 1960 the Havasupai had reached a low point in their history. Their children were torn from their families during their most dependent post-infancy years and cast into a boarding school for incorrigibles, as Fort Apache was in those years. The Bureau allowed other reservations their own day schooling, and only problem children were shipped off to Fort Apache—problem children and Havasupai children. The tiny Havasupai children had their money and clothing stolen and found no one to protect them except the older Havasupai children. They learned to be hard and crafty; few of them had the time or the opportunity to learn to be Havasupai. They were constantly in and out of trouble, involved in drinking violations, fighting and theft. The pressure fell most unrelentingly on boys, and the number of them who graduated from high school during those years can literally be counted on one hand. Girls, comparatively more sheltered, withstood the experience somewhat better, but even many of them dropped out through pregnancy or simple school violations. It seems surprising so few of them did seek physical relationships with their men under this lonely, stressful situation.

At Grand Canyon headquarters the Park Service had adopted the policy of tearing down the cabin of any Havasupai family who was forced to depart the camp there for loss of work or any other reason. The little camp shrank with each departure or death until only five cabins remained where ten families had once lived.

In Havasu Canyon, the Bureau of Indian Affairs was openly encouraging the Havasupai to abandon their little reservation and on occasion simply shelving resolutions passed by the Havasupai Council. No amount of effort on their own behalf seemed to bring any results.

Morale was extremely low. Drinking and fighting became rampant within the little canyon village. The Bureau had long discouraged and finally banned the traditional gambling get-togethers. The late summer Peach Festival had become an occasion for drunkenness and violence. Suicide, an act almost unknown among the practical and industrious Havasupai, began to occur.

Anyone present during those years of the early sixties with a group of men drinking can attest to the morosity and bitterness that surrounded it. Young boys would go off alone in the rocks to drink up cheap sweet wine and brood for a day or two whether to turn the gun they had brought along against themselves. Though hatred and violence was not always self-directed, it was nearly always directed against Havasupai. Frequent occasions arose when individuals would stand off the village with a rifle or run through town threatening to use a knife on anyone encountered during an alcoholic bout. Gas and glue sniffing became widespread among young people, and their parents in despair ceased offering them any direction.

After ten years the Indian Claims Commission in 1961 reached an initial settlement of the Havasupai claim for some three million acres of stolen lands, but the eastern portion of this overlapped lands claimed by the Navajo Tribe, who had begun moving into Havasupai territory in the 1890s. The Navajo had been drifting westward even since Kit Carson's destruction of their Cañon de Chelly farms in early 1864. The case went back for further adjudication.

Seeing the Havasupai in that year of 1961 the casual observer might well have felt inclined to agree with Dama Margaret Smith's premature assessment of the Havasupai in 1921 as the "doomed race" (see p. 130), but any such assessment had to ignore the extraordinary resilience and determination of the Havasupai. The Havasupai had become used to battling, and the strongest of them knew they could still rally their people to overcome even this despair. Those strong persons began to lead the way back.

On October 11, 1962, Chairman Earl Paya and the Havasupai Tribal Council unanimously approved resolutions 9-62 and 10-62 once again demanding the return of all Havasupai grazing allotments on the National Forest and National Park lands. The Havasupai asked for the restoration of 78,720 acres from the Kaibab National Forest and 166,522 acres from Grand Canyon National Park, on all of which the tribe had exercised exclusive use since 1908.

The Bureau of Indian Affairs attached to the resolutions a justification stating, "The Havasupai Tribe is rather reluctant to accept large sums of gratuitous money for their sustenance and improvement. They would rather accept the lands in question and develop them to the best of their ability as rapidly as possible." [80]

Finally in September of 1964 the Havasupai achieved the first big victory in their fight to reestablish their shattered lives: the reopening of their school. By the early 1960s the tribal effort to reopen their little day school had attracted attention from several private individuals and a number of government officials. In September 1964 the Bureau of Indian Affairs relented and reopened the Supai Day School, but with only two grades. Children still had to leave the canyon by eight or nine years of age to attend Fort Apache. Though the school reopened, the nine year experience left lasting scars on the Havasupai by uprooting and embittering nearly a whole generation of their young people.

The next step came November 14, 1964, when Vice Chairman Reed Watahomigie, grandson of Wa tahómja, and the Tribal Council passed resolution 15-64 "that the National Park Service be requested to relinquish administrative control over the Park Campgrounds located [on the former Schoeny mining claim] adjacent to the Havasupai Reservation to the Havasupai Tribal Council." [81]

On March 13, 1965, Chairman Earl Paya contacted Arizona Congressman George F. Senner, urging him to sponsor legislation to return the lands outlined in the 1962 and 1964 resolutions. Senner replied, "I fully appreciate the need the Havasupai people have for these additional lands. . . . You may rest assured that I will certainly do everything possible to be of assistance." [82]

That same year the Bureau of Indian Affairs assigned a new Superintendent to the Truxton Cañon Agency, Charles Pitrat, a fairly passive man but one who was not opposed to seeing the Havasupai strike out on their own.

This they proceeded to do, for that year the Havasupai also received their first approach from the newly established Office of Economic Opportunity, the "War on Poverty." Dr. James Wilson, the Sioux head of OEO's Indian Division, visited the Havasupai reservation along with R. Sargent Shriver, then the head of OEO. They explained they could provide the Havasupai assistance in a new form: If the tribe could convince OEO to grant them funds, the Havasupai community itself would make the decisions about the management and use of these funds.

By 1966 the Havasupai had begun a Community Action Program, which largely aimed to organize the resources of the Havasupai themselves, and a Head Start preschool program for their children. The first directors of both the Community Action Program and the Head Start were non-Indian. Nonetheless, the tribe saw a striking difference: the tribe hired these people and could deal with them as employees rather than as masters. In the spring of 1968 the Havasupai Tribal Council took another step and hired a Havasupai as Community Action Director, and today a Havasupai still operates the program for the tribe.

During the postwar years the Havasupai established a number of tribal enterprises, including a tribal store and a tourism enterprise to coordinate the opportunities for local horse owners to earn money bringing in tourists and supplies. Havasupai people manage these enterprises.

All these enterprises operate under the Havasupai Development Enterprise, run by a General Manager, a tribal employee. This position has passed through a number of hands, local and nonlocal, but has run mostly under the management of the non-Indian Ted Shaffer. Shaffer grew up with the Havasupai as a young man in the mid-thirties, when his father was the local agent for the Office of Indian Affairs. Shaffer returned to the Havasupai after the war, and, except for brief periods, has never left them. His sympathies lie completely with the Havasupai, and his efforts provided much of the impetus behind the effort that was to grow from Earl Paya's work to regain land by Congressional action.

During Shriver's visit the Havasupai presented their complaints against the Park Service and acquainted him with their desperately long fight to regain some of their plateau lands. They had an opportunity to do likewise with another visitor who was to prove the most important the tribe received in 1965, Arizona Congressman John Rhodes of Phoenix. After hearing the Tribal Council's feelings, Rhodes contacted Shriver on January 10, 1966, to see what Shriver might suggest to help the Havasupai in their fight. Shriver forwarded Rhodes's inquiry directly to the Secretary of the Interior. Not until March 1 did Rhodes receive any reply, and that from the Deputy Assistant Secretary of the Interior, who claimed that:

> During the last several years the Havasupais have developed their tourist industry considerably with the assistance of the National Park Service. The Superintendent of the Grand Canyon National Park has been in constant contact with tribal officials concerning comprehensive recreational planning of park lands, as well as reservation lands, for the benefit of visitors of Havasupai.

> One of the problems that has affected the economy of Havasupai is the tremendous number of range horses that the Indians have kept over the years resulting in a gradual depletion of the range. . . . We appreciate very much your interest in the Havasupai people and we assure you the Department will make every effort to cooperate fully with them.[83]

[By the next year, when the Park finally bothered to make an aerial survey of the "tremendous number of range horses," they discovered the Havasupai were keeping 23 horses on the Park grazing lands above Havasu Canyon.]

Rhodes, somewhat angered by the offhand reply he had received, wrote directly to Interior Secretary Stewart Udall on March 15 to say:

> In the letter of March 1, it is set forth that the Havasupai people are able to use lands in the Grand Canyon National Park for grazing purposes. This is in accordance with the facts as I know them. However, it does not

represent a situation which is satisfactory to the Havasupai, nor one which allows them to develop their resources for the future.

In order for the grazing lands in the National Park to be utilized by the Havasupai, it is necessary for reseeding and for the development of water resources. The Park, of course, is not willing to do this. The Havasupai Tribe would certainly like to do it, even though it is recognized that they would need at least temporary help from the federal government in order to provide the necessary facilities. . . . There is a considerable acreage of land on the South Rim which could be ceded to the United States in trust for the Havasupai, without harming the Park.[84]

Rhodes continued his pressure and by 1967 had interested Arizona's third Congressional district Representative, Sam Steiger, in the Havasupai's long fight to regain their land on the plateau. Ted Shaffer began an extensive correspondence with Steiger to acquaint him with the tribe's 1962 resolutions. Steiger studied these and decided the Havasupai would gain little by adding that part of their permit below the rim along the Colorado River. Accordingly he proposed to return to them all their grazing lands above the rim as well as the canyons leading into Havasu Canyon. This the Havasupai found acceptable and on July 30, 1968, Steiger introduced H.R. 19072 to transfer to the Havasupai some 173,400 acres of Grand Canyon National Park and Kaibab National Forest, representing all their grazing permits above the rim. Though his effort heartened the Havasupai immensely, it resulted in nothing. The House Interior and Insular Affairs Committee apparently did not take the bill seriously and gave it no hearing. Few of them had heard of the Havasupai. By the end of Congress's 90th session, the tribe realized that this attempt, too, had failed.

Astonishingly, 1968 also marked the first year that the Havasupai were able to vote in state and federal elections. Coconino County had never designated the Havasupai reservation as a voting precinct, and the Havasupai could only vote by registering and voting in other, distant communities. Martin Goodfriend, a California businessman long sympathetic to the Havasupai, finally persuaded the Coconino County officials in 1967 to appoint a local registrar in Supai and to designate it as a regular voting precinct.

Hoping to stall any further expressions of Havasupai discontent before they became public knowledge, the Park and Forest Service developed a joint grazing allotment use plan to be administered by the Forest Service and used by the Havasupai communally rather than individually as in the past. This eight-year plan specified that with $1,393,740 of reservoir, fencing and range improvement the tribe could be running 702 cattle and 341 horses on their permit by 1976. The plan included 38,319 acres of Park plateau east of Havasu Canyon, 16,741 acres west of it and a total of 43,088 acres of Kaibab National Forest plateau. The joint plan also specified, however:

Failure to comply with the provisions or obligations of a grazing permit may be considered as grounds for revocation or suspension of the permit in whole or part. So long as provisions of the permit are met and it is in the public interest to do so the permit will be renewed to the holder.[85]

Then a whole new complication entered the discussion. In December 1968 the Indian Claims Commission finally reached a compromise settlement of the Havasupai and Navajo claims and offered the Havasupai $1,240,000 for the government's deprivation of 2,257,728 acres of their former range. The government was offering them 55 cents an acre for land that included Grand Canyon National Park.

The tribal claims lawyer, Royal D. Marks, replied to the U.S. Attorney General, John Mitchell, on February 28, 1969, with an offer to accept the compromise and concluded:

> Should you accept the foregoing offer, we agree to make all reasonable efforts to obtain the approval of the Havasupai Tribe . . .[86]

Marks's contract stipulated he was to receive 10 percent of the settlement as his fee. This standard arrangement certainly did not encourage claims lawyers to have their clients sue directly for the return of land itself.

On May 13 Marks came to the Havasupai to present to the Tribal Council a report on the offered settlement. During the discussion he warned the tribe, according to the minutes of the meeting:

> If a settlement is not agreed on . . . the tribe then [may] hire . . . expert appraisers to hold additional hearing before the Indian Claims Commission. If the tribe [does] not agree on this settlement an appeal can be taken . . . it would take two to three years minimum . . . before we might have an opinion from the Indian Claims Commission.[87]

Marks then informed the Council their next step would be to call a general election for the tribal people to decide whether to accept or not to accept the settlement. The Council set June 14 as the date for this vote and sent out a notice to all tribal members on May 29 informing them that "A complete explanation of the proposed final settlement will be given by the Claims Attorney at the meetings, followed by a question and answer session in which members of the Havasupai Tribe will be encouraged to participate."

Eighty-five adults attended the June 14 meeting, conducted by Chairman Daniel Kaska, the strong-minded young tribal policeman and son of the first Chairman. The fate of the Steiger bill was on everyone's mind, and Daniel Kaska repeatedly urged those present not to accept the settlement, saying, "We want the land; we don't want money. What happens to our land if we take this money?" A number of others raised this question, and Marks assured the meeting that accepting the settlement would not affect their right to regain their permit lands or any other lands through Congressional action. Daniel Kaska protested again that the government could keep its money and give them the land. Marks advised the tribe this course was not available to them; if they chose to refuse the money, they would get nothing at all. The Bureau of Indian Affairs officials present corroborated this assessment of the situation. Both the lawyer and the BIA officials showed a certain amount of exasperation with the Chairman's stubbornness on this point and assured him he could not use the land claim to regain any of the land itself.

In fact the tribe had some very real alternatives. The Yakima of Washington had expressly excluded the 21,000 acres around Mount Adams from their cash settlement and asked the Claims Commission only to substantiate their right to this area. The Oklahoma Cherokee had submitted their claim in such a way that they would use their $3.75 an acre settlement to buy back the very Indian school lands around Chilocco they were claiming. The Havasupai did not learn of these arrangements.

The matter was then put to a vote, and 52 people voted to accept the settlement. Ten voted to refuse it, including Chairman Daniel Kaska.

The claims lawyer then traveled to Washington July 22 to present the outcome of the referendum; the Chairman accompanied him. It was the first and only direct contact the Havasupai Tribal Council made with the Indian Claims Commission during the entire 18-year process. The Commission's report of the meeting says only that

> Mr. Kaska testified, among other matters, that the meeting of adult Havasupai voters held on June 14, 1969 was well attended and that the terms of the proposed settlement were understood and fully approved by those persons present and that the vote taken at the meeting was a fair and representative reflection of the views of the Havasupai Tribe.[88]

The "other matters" discussed, Daniel Kaska remembers, included a closing question from one of the Commissioners as to whether the Havasupai had realized before voting that acceptance of the settlement could affect their right to their aboriginal land. Daniel says he assured the Commissioner they had not realized this.

The Commission approved the settlement, and the Havasupai were now required to submit a plan for use of the settlement funds which would be subject to approval by the Bureau of Indian Affairs, the Secretary of the Interior and finally the U.S. Congress, who would then have to appropriate the money. The Congress finally did this in 1971, but the Havasupai were then required to develop a census in order to distribute the 25 percent of the settlement that was to go to individuals. Each of the adults among the 425 recorded members of the tribe would receive $651.37 for the loss of their entire birthright, save their few acres of Havasu Canyon. Not until September 1973 was this money finally distributed.

The remainder of the funds the BIA-developed use plan devoted to resource development and investment. The BIA held these funds in trust and required the Havasupai to submit a further detailed plan for each use of these funds. Each plan was subject to approval by the Bureau of Indian Affairs and the Secretary of the Interior. In effect, Congress had voted a block increase in BIA funding for the Havasupai reservation; by no means did they appropriate a settlement to the Havasupai themselves.

Among the development plans designed by the Bureau were proposals to carry out range developments on the Havasupai permits on the plateau. The Park Service and the Forest Service saw it differently, and Grand Canyon Superintendent Robert R. Lovegren wrote the Havasupai, "We understand the Havasupai tribe will receive compensation for past iniquities involving lands unjustly appropriated from them. The land claims have now been settled and are not a matter for continuing conjecture." [89]

Upon the completion of the settlement the National Park Service began developing what they called "A Master Plan for Grand Canyon National Park" which proposed to incorporate in the Park all the Havasupai permit lands surrounding the Havasupai reservation. The maps for this "Master Plan" did not even show the existence of the Havasupai reservation; the area was treated as part of the National Park.

The Park Service set the rent of the Havasupai cabins at Grand Canyon Park headquarters at $18.50 a month and continued to provide neither maintenance nor repair. They increased their pressure on the remaining Havasupai there to move out of their special-use area and rent apartments in the Park village. Finally Park Service employee Gary Howe came out in early 1971 to talk with the Havasupai still living at the peaceful 160-acre camp in the pines and reported the following things:

1. These people desired and enjoyed the separateness of the camp and did not necessarily want to live in the village proper.

2. They do not mind the lack of modern facilities such as electric ranges, indoor water, indoor restrooms, and the cramped quarters.

3. They did want to have the buildings and area fixed up and brought up to their standard i.e. a wood stove that hasn't burned or windows with glass, etc.

4. They were willing to clean up the outside area and rid it of junk and old cars.

5. Each person pretty much stated that they could not afford an increase of rent that would be necessary if they were moved to other quarters.

6. Most were thoroughly disenchanted with N.P.S. maintenance of the area and some said that previous maintenance personnel had outwardly disliked Indians. This feeling had resulted in their complete avoidance of asking N.P.S. for any maintenance assistance.[90]

Howe concluded with a set of recommendations to the Park administration urging the construction of a heated bath house (as residents had no bathing facilities), new stoves for the houses and heater for the recreation building, fixing the holes in the walls of the cabins, replacing windows with glass rather than the past Park practice of replacing with plywood, painting, fixing broken doors and routine repair. In May Ranger Warren Hill recommended Howe's report to the Park Superintendent. The Park's response was only to step up its pressure on the few camp residents to vacate the area.

The government was shifting its emphasis from development to preservation of federal lands, but now federal officials cited preservation as a block to returning the Havasupai's land, just as they had cited development possibilities in the preceding decades. Through the vagaries of policy the Havasupai had constantly pursued their moderate and careful use of their plateau lands to provide themselves animal protein and a livelihood.

Suddenly they faced their most desperate battle yet to keep their land.

ECHOES

101. My House 1973

102. Mona Lee 1973

103. *Minnie Marshall 1973*

104. *Oscar and Pearl Paya 1973*

105. Unloading the Mail 1973

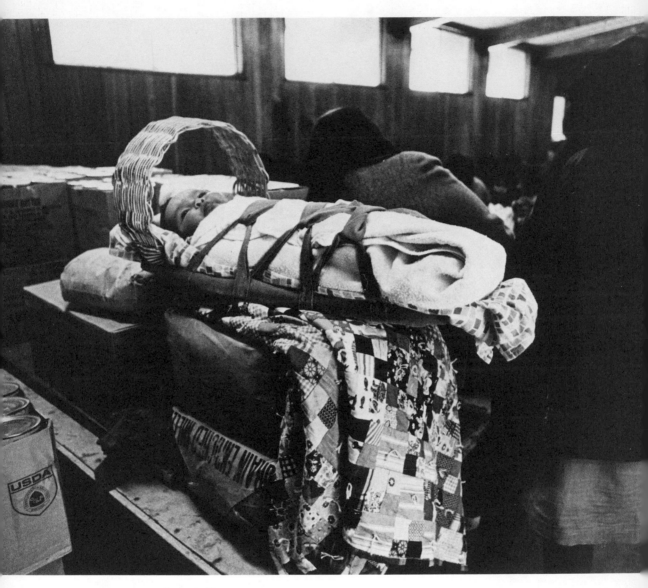

106. On Commodities 1970

107. *Perry's Family 1973*

08. *Wayne and Jewell Paya*
   with Annalita, Suzanna, Anthony
   and Anjanette 1973

   le

109. *Playing Indian 1970*

le

110. Bela and Friend 1970

111. Havasu Falls 1973

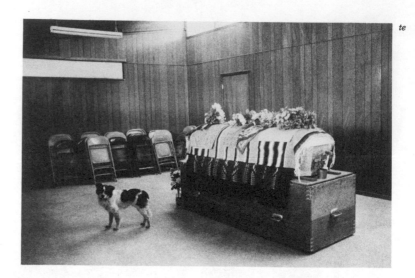

112. His Dog 1970

114. Gilbert Marshall 1973

113. Summer Afternoon 1973

te

te

te

117. *Under the Juniper: Plateau 1973*

118. *The Visitor 1973*

119. *National Park Service Campground:*
Havasu Canyon 1973

120. *Daniel Kaska: Plateau 1973*

le

121. Havasupai Home: Plateau 1973

122. *Exiled in the Public Interest 1973*

11.

I AM
THE GRAND
CANYON

When word of the Havasupai land claim settlement of 1969 reached the Grand Canyon Park officials a Park Service and Sierra Club team quietly went to work on their plan, one which would incorporate all the Havasupi permits into the National Park and limit the tribe to the same restrictive conditions everywhere that they already endured on the Park permits.

The Grand Canyon officials and their Sierra Club collaborators went through three drafts of their plan before it came to the attention of the Havasupai. Finally, the tribe's new attorney, Joseph R. Babbitt of Flagstaff, obtained a copy of the third draft, prepared in January 1971 and slated for release in the spring. The plan was called "A Master Plan for Grand Canyon National Park" and proposed incorporating into the Park the Forest Service lands where the Havasupai generator station stood on Long Mesa, upper Havasu Canyon and Moqui Trail, and the Havasupai's only topside outpost at Hualapai Hilltop, site of the tribal warehouses and horse pens. The Master Plan stated:

259

Yul gesyó
Mary Wescògame

Courtesy Kolb Collection 1950

The charm and beauty of Havasu Canyon is attracting more and more people, who threaten the area with results of their heavy impact on a limited, rather fragile environment. With extensive development on the reservation, the Havasupai may lose the charm and beauty of their environment and ultimately the qualities that attract the visitor . . .

Resource management, visitor use, recreation, grazing, and similar plans will be made with the Havasupai Tribal Council, the Bureau of Indian Affairs, and the U.S. Forest Service.[91]

The Havasupai Tribal Council had only to consider the way the Park had developed the Master Plan itself to wonder whether they would in fact cooperate any better in developing any subsequent plans. They saw that the Master Plan maps did not even show the existence of the Havasupai reservation, but rather depicted it as part of the National Park. They read further:

There is a continuing concern for providing sufficient camping capacity for tourists who are within and moving through the region. . . . Private campgrounds are meeting some of the demand. Indian reservations offer a great potential for this and other recreational activities. . . . The trail for Hualapai Hilltop to Havasu Campground will be managed for high visitor use.

Addition of Cataract [Havasu] Canyon . . . will give Park protection to this scenic and scientific area rim to rim. . . . The Moqui Trail, an old Indian trail used for centuries by the Havasupais and other tribes, is also located within this addition.[91]

The Tribal Council immediately held a discussion with Grand Canyon Park Superintendent Robert R. Lovegren. Lovegren listened sympathetically to their concern and said he would see if any adjustments could be made in the Master Plan. He also let them know the Park Service would be holding public hearings on the Master Plan at Grand Canyon May 18.

The forceful Chairman Lee Marshall, grandson of Mánakaja, decided he would bring all the feelings of the tribe together and pour them forth at the hearings, though the Park had not originally scheduled any time for the Havasupai to testify.

After hours of speeches and presentations at the May hearing, Lee Marshall finally gained his turn. He began by pushing his glasses down and looking around the room with a bemused smile, then began, "I heard all you people talking about the Grand Canyon. Well, you're looking at it. I am the Grand Canyon!" He complained that those so concerned with the fragile ecology of plateau grasslands were blind to the human ecology of natives of the Grand Canyon and predicted the Master Plan could threaten the very existence of the Havasupai.

He then replied to the Park's Master Plan with what he called "A Master Plan for Grand Canyon Village by the Havasupai Tribal Council":

We want our freedom from the park lands and forest lands which surround our reservation. Land doesn't talk; wild plants don't talk; wild animals don't talk; even the beauty of our canyon doesn't talk, but our Great Spirit and mother nature have a way to care for them.

Wild plants, wilderness, forests, wild animals and fowls of the air were put on this mother earth for a purpose; that purpose was that men could gather and eat and save what they can.

Even our ancestors' bones are dug up, placed in glass containers and displayed on shelves to tell a story to canyon visitors of prehistoric creatures roaming our lands.[92]

He continued that the tiny canyon reservation would soon become a jungle of government housing, inhabited by people existing only on welfare. He proposed instead the return to the Havasupai of their traditional use areas to provide a modest cattle business, a place to live and jobs for the young. He asked the return of the Park Service campground and the Havasupai residence area at the Park village. He said the Park must again treat the Havasupai preferentially in employment.

Southwest Regional Park Director Frank J. Kowski admitted, "The Havasupais might have some good points there." He said their objections could be considered in writing the final draft of the Master Plan.

In July Superintendent Lovegren contacted the Havasupai to inform them he would be amenable to returning 60,500 acres of Park land to them. The area he proposed would include 41,300 acres around Topocoba Hilltop and 19,200 acres of the National Monument to the west. The Council, though they saw this as a step in the right direction, faced several problems with the offer. First, the Park was proposing to take the Great Thumb Mesa and the residence camp at Grand Canyon away from them. Second, there was no mention of returning any Forest lands.

When the Council approached Kaibab Forest Supervisor Keith Pfefferle about this matter, they met a much less interested audience than they had with Lovegren. Seeing the Havasupai over a barrel, Pfefferle radically altered the Forest Service's 1943 attitude on returning Forest lands. He said Forest Service regulations did not permit his agency to give up land without receiving land in return. Since the Havasupai had nothing to trade, the Forest Service could not return any land to them. He offered to continue their permit so long as it should continue to be in the public interest to do so.

On August 7, 1971, the Council called in the old people to determine what they must do to provide the self-sufficiency and independence the tribe was seeking. After an all-day discussion, the tribal people led by Lee Marshall and Juan Sinyella finally hammered out their counterproposal, and it was essentially what they had been requesting for more than a half century. They wished the return of Park and Forest permit areas, including Pasture Wash. The tribe still felt their own presence there had not been terminated by the 1917 action allowing white ranchers to use the area as well. The Council asked the return of some 200,000 acres of private lands located within the 1866 Atlantic & Pacific Railroad grant to the south of them. Finally Lee Marshall said he could not permit the Park Service to drive away the Havasupai people still living at Grand Canyon Village: "We want the Indian Village forever." In effect, the tribal request was for the very amount of plateau land that A. W. Simington had seen in 1943 as necessary to their self-support.

Havasupai representatives then went to the Park Service and the Forest Service with their counterproposal August 18 and September 30. Neither Service would consider the tribal plan. After some weeks, the Park and Forest Services finally conferred with each other and on December 14, 1971, they proposed a trade between each other. If the Havasupai wanted a contiguous reservation they would need to get Long Mesa to the west of Havasu Canyon from the Forest Service. The Park proposed trading their Havasupai permit areas east of Havasu Canyon to the Forest Service in return for putting Long Mesa into the Park. The Park would then give Long Mesa to the Havasupai. The result would be to give the Havasupai a reservation including only the waterless semidesert west of Havasu Canyon and Havasu Canyon itself up to its east rim. All the valuable grazing permit land on the east side of the canyon would remain under Forest Service control—all except the Great Thumb, which the Park Service would retain but close to further tribal use.

A November 5, 1971, news story in the *Albuquerque Journal* expressed the government attitude toward the Havasupai proposal all too well:

> The darndest attempted land grab started since the Blue Lake law involves not New Mexico Indians, but the tiny Havasupai Tribe in Grand Canyon. The Havasupais, who number less than 250 people, own 580 [sic] acres of land in the bottom of Grand Canyon. They want Congress to give them 280,000 acres of land now controlled by the Forest Service and National Park Service. And they also want title to thousands of acres of Bureau of Land Management lands.

Several months of waiting and talking followed until any hope of agreement collapsed when Keith Pfefferle spelled out more clearly what would happen with the tribe's use areas on the east side of the canyon in a letter to them April 24, 1972: ". . . it was logical that the Tribe continue to have 'free' grazing use on these lands as they now have; however, binding commitments to any exclusive use, other than grazing . . . use of this land, could not be made." [93] Again the veiled threat of revocation "in the public interest" loomed. Again the right to reside on the plateau was dismissed.

In desperation the Council on May 13 appealed to Secretary of Agriculture Earl Butz and Secretary of Interior Rogers C. B. Morton for their intercession:

> . . . we fear to go ahead under the present arrangement. What if the Forest Service should find it necessary "in the public interest" to pull it all out from under us?

. . . We care more deeply for the beauty of our land than Sunday hikers or professional environmentalists because this land is part of us, and we live on it. . . . We are human beings with the right to survive, not rocks or dust. This is not a zoo. . . .

We have seen our people driven from acre after acre and spring after spring. We can be reduced no more; we cannot surrender this too. We still live, and we are determined to live on our own. . . .

We have managed with this reservation since 1882 because we believe someday we would have a second chance. The chance has come, and we expect to have to live with the outcome as long as we lived with the 1882 outcome. Our people need some of the room they used to have to live. We can no longer live in this crowded condition. Ninety years is enough.[93]

For the Interior Department, Assistant Secretary for Public Land Management Harrison Loesch replied on May 30, "I have asked both the Bureau of Indian Affairs and the National Park Service for comments on your letter so that I may better advice [sic] Secretary Morton as how best to deal with the questions you have raised. You will be hearing again from us." [94] They never did.

For the Agriculture Department, J. W. Deinema replied on June 2 for Chief Forester John R. McGuire, "We are expecting a report soon on this matter from Regional Forester William D. Hurst. When his report is received we will make a careful review of the case, including consideration of the points you have raised. We will reply further to your letter after that review." [94] They never did.

When a copy of the Havasupai letter reached Leonard Garment in the White House, Garment wrote on July 5 that he was having special minority affairs advisor Brad Patterson check "to find out what Interior thinks about the Havasupais . . ." [94] The Havasupai never received any further report on this, but they felt they already had a pretty good indication what Interior thought of them.

By August Tribal Attorney Joe Babbitt again attempted to start talks with the Park Service and Forest Service, but now neither would negotiate any further. Finally Babbitt wrote Pfefferle on October 20, 1972, citing the Railroad Examiners' 1942 report to support his opinion that "the free use permits are the administrative method of recognizing Indian rights to use and possession and that the Forest Service could not dispossess the Indians or give the use of the lands to others." Babbitt concluded, "The Havasupai Tribe would ask that the Forest Service reassess its position and consider a relinquishment of Indian Grazing lands for an Indian Reservation." [95]

The Forest Service simply replied that they did not see it that way.

By November the Tribal Council learned that within a matter of months Senator Barry Goldwater would be offering, in Congress, the plan to expand the Park, and on December 12, 1972, they sent an urgent telegram to him asking him to meet with them on the Havasupai reservation. As soon as he saw the telegram Goldwater contacted the Tribal Council to tell them he would meet with them on January 27, 1973. Two days before Goldwater was to arrive, the

Tribal Council met in special session and adopted the following resolution spelling out what they wanted and prepared a position paper explaining their attitude more fully. The entire Council signed the paper—Chairman Oscar Paya, Vice Chairman Clark Jack, Ervin Crook, Augustine Hanna, Lloyd Hanna, Stanley Manakaja and Leon Rogers.

When he arrived, Goldwater listened closely to the arguments of the Tribal Council and asked a number of detailed questions which showed him to be quite well informed on their situation. Finally he looked at the gathered Councilmen and said, "We are in better shape to get land than we have been in many years. . . . I can promise you at least a favorable hearing on your proposal, and I think we can work it into the bill."

For the first time since the days of Henry Ewing and John Crow a government official was speaking as an ally.

Senator Goldwater then informed the large crowd of tribal people gathered, "I have no hesitancy offering the whole ball of wax. I hope we would have no trouble getting your wants met. I promise to put in everything you ask for, but I can't promise you'll get it." He said he would do everything he could to regain the land for the Havasupai Tribe, and the crowd broke into unaccustomed applause.

During the crucial month preceding actual introduction of the bill, heavy rain and snow closed all access roads to the Havasupai reservation from February 8 to March 19, and not until April 6 did the roads remain passable all the time. The Havasupai were unable to get in or out of their canyon prison for nearly two months to try and gain support for the return of their lands under the Goldwater bill.

After two months of tense waiting in Havasu Canyon, the Havasupai learned that Senator Goldwater had introduced the expansion plan to the Senate as S 1296 on March 20. When Goldwater mentioned the expansion of the Havasupai reservation, he cited their position paper frequently:

> The bill includes a very significant proposal for restoring the Havasupai tribe of Indians some of their sacred and ancestral lands. This tribe of some 300 individuals includes the remaining descendants of a people who once lived on millions of acres in the Grand Canyon and the Coconino Plateau in northern Arizona. In fact, the eastern neighbors of the Havasupai, the Hopis, depict the Havasupais in their ancient tradition as the keepers of the Grand Canyon and its sacred places.

> . . . today there is only about one acre for each person to live and work on. Here the Supais are left with no economic land base and may pass into extinction absent the return of some of their essential plateau lands and sacred places.

> . . . I am impressed at the youth and vision of the new Council members of the Havasupai Tribal Council. I believe these leaders have the energy and the will to guide the Havasupai back into a self-sustaining people with tribal control over their own lives.

RESOLUTION NO. 1-73
OF THE GOVERNING BODY OF THE
HAVASUPAI TRIBE OF THE HAVASUPAI RESERVATION
((A FEDERALLY-CHARTERED INDIAN CORPORATION)
SUPAI, ARIZONA

WHEREAS, the havasupai people's historic occupancy of some three million acres of the western portion of Arizona's present Coconino County is widely established, and

WHEREAS, the Havasupai people were in 1882 reduced to a state of near landlessness by their restriction to a 518-acre reservation, and

WHEREAS, places sacred to the Havasupai people remain on lands now held by others, and

WHEREAS, the Havasupai people require some restoration of their ancestral lands to support themselves, and

WHEREAS, the Havasupai Tribe has negotiated for 55 years to regain some usable lands from its traditional holdings, and

WHEREAS, the Havasupai Tribe was in 1943 all but promised return of repossessed railroad indemnity-grant lands and federal permit lands, and

WHEREAS, the Havasupai Tribe is again engaged in negotiations with the federal government for restoration of former tribal areas presently reserved by the government for tribal use;

NOW, THEREFORE, BE IT RESOLVED that the Havasupai Tribal Council and people request the return of all Havasupai allotments and permit areas presently under U.S. Park Service and U.S. Forest Service control, including the 160-acre Havasupai residency area at Grand Canyon; the return of the 1866 Atlantic & Pacific Railroad indemnity-grant lands; and the return of Havasu campground to the Havasupai Tribe as part of the Havasupai Reservation. This resolution expresses the true wishes of the Havasupai Tribal Council and people and supersedes any prior resolutions regarding restoration of former tribal lands.

C E R T I F I C A T I O N

I, the undersigned, as Chairman of the Havasupai Tribal Council do hereby certify that the Tribal Council of the Havasupai Tribe is composed of seven (7) members, of whom __7__, constituting a quorum, were present at a *Special* meeting held this __25th__ day of __January__ 1973; and that the foregoing resolution was duly adopted by the affirmative vote of __7__ for to __0__ against; pursuant to the Constitution and By-laws approved March 27, 1939 and amended July 22, 1967, June 18, 1968 and September 23, 1972.

Oscar Paya
_____
Chairma, Havasupai Tribal Council

ATTEST: *Reed Watahomigie*
_____
Secretary, Havasupai Tribal Council

The bill we are proposing would help this wonderful people to survive. They are the natives of the Grand Canyon and surely any bill relating to the ecology of the canyon should include protection of the human beings who live there.[96]

The next day Arizona Congressman Morris K. Udall introduced the House version of the Grand Canyon bill.

Meanwhile the Sierra Club and several other environmentalist groups began mounting a nationwide campaign of opposition to the Havasupai land return by spreading the word that the purpose of returning the land was so the Havasupai could either develop it or lease it to developers, trying to leave the impression that the Havasupai planned to put Disneyland on the plateau. One such "environmentalist" wrote the Tribal Council directly to say:

Restitution of your ancient lands cannot be the instrument through which to mete out justice . . . you must realize that opening the smallest portion of *our* [italics ours] preserved lands to commercial use creates the precedent through which the special interests will seek to destroy the entire structure of our national preserves. No such commercial use must be permitted. Not a single acre! . . . Obviously adequate grazing must be made available for your horses, but beyond that, nothing.[97]

The Sierra Club's Southwest Representative of Tucson announced to the Associated Press March 3, "If he [Goldwater] is transferring the land to Indians for the purpose of commercial development, I feel he is not making correct use of public lands."

The environmentalists' attitude about the Havasupai's land was most perplexing, for the Park Service had already begun the very sort of plans the Sierra Club was attributing to the Havasupai.

As early as 1970 the Park Service had quietly written off the South Rim as a preservation area and decided to devote it to mass tourism. The Park would maintain only the North Rim as a limited-use wilderness-type area and leased the North Rim concession to TWA's Utah Parks division, who would renovate the rustic cabins of the North Rim and preserve its bucolic atmosphere.

For the South Rim the Park Service hired ERA and ROMA, two Los Angeles–based firms, to plan the large-scale tourist development of the South Rim. ROMA was the very firm which had designed Disneyland. Phase I of the South Rim development would put up 100 new housing units for Park employees and two or three large new lodges for tourists. Upon the death of photographer Emery Kolb, the surviving Kolb brother, the Park would tear down his historic studio on the rim within ninety days. The Havasupai would be forced from their residency area to make room for further development.

Phase II of the South Rim development would move to the development of Indian Gardens, including the possibility of building a mock Havasupai camp there; and Phase III would move to the development of the south shore of the Colorado River itself.

In later planning meetings for the South Rim development during the summer of 1973, Park officials voiced their determination to draw a line across the base of the Havasupai permit on the Great Thumb Mesa and keep tribal people and their animals off the area. They stated they would not compromise on this point.

Of all this the Sierra Club said nothing.

Initial hearings on the Grand Canyon bill were scheduled for June 20, 1973, and the Interior Department released its carefully guarded recommendations on the bill the day of the hearings. The recommendations apparently caught even Goldwater by surprise. The report made only passing mention of the Havasupai, but the mention was most damaging:

> . . . to protect park-quality resources or to aid in management of the park . . . we also strongly recommend that any decision on transferring land from the National Park System, *as well as other Federal land* [italics ours], to the Havasupai Reservation be deferred for a year until the department is able carefully to review this proposition.[98]

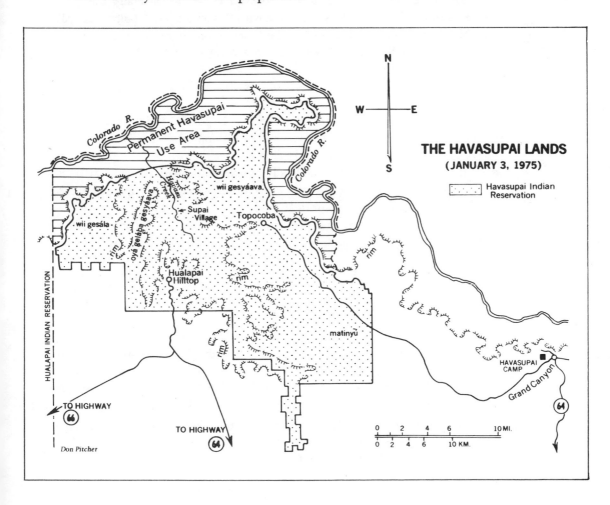

THE HAVASUPAI LANDS
(JANUARY 3, 1975)

Havasupai Indian Reservation

The Interior Department did not hesitate to recommend that Agriculture Department (Forest Service) lands be withheld from the Havasupai as well. No copy of this report was made available to the Havasupai until a month later.

The Tribal Council sent Vice Chairman Clark Jack and Councilman Augustine Hanna along with Joe Babbitt to present the Havasupai case at the hearing. Goldwater led off with a short presentation on the bill; when he came to the Havasupai expansion, he said, "When we consider that about 300 Indians live on a little over 500 acres, I don't think that is exactly fair in anybody's book and I do hope you can work out some solution which will help this fine people to survive."

When the Park Service witnesses began to speak, they showed very quickly they did not support even Lovegren's offer of 60,500 acres of Park land. (Lovegren had been transferred to another post within a year of making the offer.) Armed with the Interior Department report, Park Service Director Ronald Walker said the Park Service opposed deletion of any lands from the Park and indeed still wanted to add the Forest permit areas to the Park.

The Forest Service's Thomas C. Nelson came forward and said, "The Indian claim and public values associated with this area need detailed study. The National Forest lands for inclusion in the Reservation are presently used by both the Indians and the general public [He gave no indication how the general public used the area.] . . . The Administration plans to study the new [sic] Indian claim and the uses and values of this area and present its recommendation at a later time."

The Sierra Club's Southwest Representative spoke to tell of spending all of 180 days hiking in the Grand Canyon and of his opposition to expanding of the Havasupai reservation from any federal lands.

By the time the Havasupai finally spoke they were the only witnesses testifying in favor of the bill; nearly every other witness had opposed the bill because it would return some of their land.

Clark Jack spoke first and presented a lengthy written statement to the recorder, which stated in part:

> . . . We do not seek these lands to develop them into any big business, as some so-called environmentalists claim. This malicious report is designed only to get our land for themselves. There is no basis to this belief. We ask for these lands to give our people a home again on the plateau. Many of our people were born there. We love these lands where we gave birth, built our lives and returned our old people to the earth. Our old homes and burial grounds lie on these lands. Our historical, emotional and legal ties and claims to these plateau lands we have outlined are so powerful they are undeniable to any who view them. We invite you to view them.
>
> We believe the reservation we propose is the only one which can provide us with the essential plateau lands which would assure tribal control of our lives and sacred places forever.

Clark then spoke extemporaneously to point out that his people had always welcomed their friends and visitors at Grand Canyon and now they themselves were being barred from it. He said he had grown up there and always considered it his home. He was called to the Army and then returned to Grand Canyon to find his home was not a home after all but a Park, and he was going to have to leave it.

Augustine Hanna then testified at some length, saying in part:

> . . . We've had these permit lands all our lives, before most of us in this room were born. We have to have these lands returned to our people.

> . . . Not too many of you would stand the humiliation we stand every day; we live in a Park Service zoo. . . . We are the only ones who don't seem to matter, and we are human beings who have to support ourselves on this land. And we used to own it. . . .

> We still have old homes on the Great Thumb and dirt water tanks we made with horse teams some fifty years ago. Some of us were even born out there. We'd keep the Thumb open to backpackers and horse riders, but we really would like to keep roads off it for anything but emergencies. It's quiet there now, and it's the only place we are allowed to see out over the Grand Canyon. . . .

Finally, to answer all the statements that the Havasupai had already been paid for their permit lands under the Indian Claims Commission Act, Augustine Hanna said the Havasupai were ready to give back any money they might have been awarded for the permit lands to the government. He added that he did not feel that lands under continuous use and occupation could have been included in the claim against the government.[99]

A month later, a copy of the Interior Department report finally arrived through the Bureau of Indian Affairs. On seeing it, the Council wrote a heated reply, saying in part:

> . . . Four hundred of us are taking on the machinery of the United States government, and we intend to win. But it is a bit discouraging to find ourselves facing the B.I.A. across the lines when we expected them to stand shoulder to shoulder with us. . . .

> Apparently the Interior Department hopes we will give up and die off, and if that doesn't work they can study us to death, so that even our reservation can go into the National Park system. . . . Close your ears and make your studies, but we are not going to give up. And some day somebody besides Senator Goldwater is going to hear us.[100]

On July 29 Senator Goldwater in exasperation resigned from the Sierra Club, saying, "I don't believe the Sierra Club is actually interested in anything but demonstrating Sierra Club muscle, and as a result of this, I have resigned from the club—not that it will make one bit of difference to them." [101]

On August 3 the Park and Recreation Subcommittee decided to drop the expansion of the Havasupai reservation from S 1296 in favor of a study, as the Interior Department had recommended:

> . . . the Congress directs that the Secretary and the Secretary of Agriculture jointly shall, within no later than sixty days after the convening of the second session of the Ninety-third Congress, conduct a comprehensive study and make detailed recommendations to the Congress and the President concerning proposals for expansion of the Havasupai Reservation.[102]

On September 24 the United States Senate accepted this language, except that it extended the period of the study to one year, and passed the bill.

Numerous reasons were produced. Forrest Gerard, staff aide to the Senate Subcommittee on Indian Affairs, said, "We were caught up with other things at the time." [103]

Terry Emerson, Senator Goldwater's legislative assistant, said, "The substitute language was forced on us. We had no choice. Major opposition arose in committee from Senators responding to pressure from environmentalist groups such as the Sierra Club." [103]

One such group, the Tucson Audubon Society, had in fact seriously proposed to the Subcommittee on Parks and Recreation that, "No Park lands closer than one mile to the rim should be given to the Indians." [99]

Some Washington officials dismissed the Havasupai issue as no more than "a lot of emotional rhetoric." Others candidly admitted the purpose of a one-year study was to gain time to produce further excuses for maintaining the status quo.

Acting Commissioner of Indian Affairs Marvin Franklin said, "The battle for a favorable report on the Havasupai land return from the Interior Department was lost in the Office of Management and Budget [a euphemism for "White House"].[103]

After some months of delay, the House of Representatives announced they would hold their initial hearings on the Grand Canyon expansion plan on November 12, 1973. The Havasupai decided to send the fiery and eloquent Lee Marshall to present the tribe's case this time. When Lee arrived at the hearing he found the Interior Department was still recommending a study, despite the Tribal Council's numerous pleas and complaints:

> We also strongly recommend that any decision on transferring land from the National Park System, as well as other federal land, to the Havasupai Reservation, as proposed . . . be deferred for a year until the Department is able carefully to review this proposition. . . . The Department intends to begin immediately to evaluate this proposal, in cooperation with the Department of Agriculture, and expects to be able to make a recommendation within 12 months.[104]

The statement expressed no intent to consult with the Havasupai.

The entire front row of the hearing room was packed with Sierra Club members as the hearings began. Congressman Sam Steiger offered the initial testimony on the bill in place of sponsor Morris Udall. Steiger still maintained his support for the Havasupai, for when he came to the section regarding the enlargement of their reservation he said he would "lay my political life on the line" to see this enlargement carried out. He said this might alienate the cattlemen and environmentalists of Arizona, who outnumbered the Havasupai "about 5,000 to 1," but he said he did not care; the Havasupai cause was just.

When he completed his statement, Committee Chairman Roy A. Taylor of North Carolina said succeeding witnesses would have to limit their statements to four minutes apiece, as he would have to attend hearings on the national fuel shortage in the afternoon.

The Havasupai Tribal Council had prepared 24 detailed pages of evidence and history of their long land fight over the preceding ninety years. Their statement outlined the mismanagement and near destruction by the Park Service of some of the very lands the environmentalists wished to keep out of Havasupai hands and included maps, copies of former bills, their offer to the Indian Claims Commission to return part of their land claim settlement, and letters and excerpts of letters dating back to 1885 demonstrating the tribe's need for plateau land.

When the Park Service witness spoke he testified, among other things, that the Park Service had already begun their study of the Havasupai. Lee Marshall was outraged, for the Senate had carefully specified that the study must be made in cooperation with the Havasupai; in fact no government agency made any approach at all to the tribe regarding the study.

The Forest Service witness testified, as in June, that the general public used the lands proposed for transfer to the Havasupai and that the tribe had already been paid for them. He, too, recommended that the committee delete from the bill any additions to the Havasupai reservation.

The Havasupai witnesses then spoke and asked for all their written evidence to be placed in the record and expressed surprise that the Interior Department seemed to feel a study of the Havasupai's needs was again necessary, for the Department had in 1943 already studied the matter and determined that the Havasupai would need 426,240 acres to support themselves.

Lee Marshall then presented a terse and compelling summary of his people's feelings:

> All my life I've seen studies made about our land. You see how much land they've brought us. Now the Senate says, "Let's make another study." What for? People have done studies again and again. You can read about them.
>
> . . . after three generations of our people—and some of yours, too—have kept beating on Washington's door about this, what do we hear today? All these so-called environmentalists telling you to keep this land away from us to protect the plants and wild animals, which they just found out about. . . .

. . . The Park says they want to save the environment and archaeological places. They're not talking right. We have homes and burial grounds on our permit lands. We fear for them if we are not there to protect them. If the Park Service chases us off they will destroy everything that was ours and wipe out all trace of our people. If you think we lie, ask the Park Service what they did to our old homes at Grand Canyon in 1934. Ask them what they did to Big Jim's place . . . ask them what they did to our burial ground below Havasu Falls. That's how they protect things.

Lee voiced his perplexity at how people could ignore the Park Service's development plans for the South Rim and then wring their hands in concern that the Havasupai might some day make some sort of development somewhere. He concluded:

The National Park Service has to learn to be like Indians about the land before they understand the secret of saving the earth. We'll be glad to teach them. . . .

No other lands except our permit lands are available to us. Our permit lands are the heart of our homeland, and we are not leaving our home. . . .

. . . So hear us now and remember. We will go on grazing our animals on all our permit lands forever. We will go on keeping our homes on them forever. We will not be pushed from the plateau for Sunday recreation ever.

We have never stopped using these lands, and we will not go from them now. They belong to us.[105]

Finally after these hearings were concluded members of the Arizona chapter of the Sierra Club informed the Havasupai they would be willing to meet with them in Flagstaff on December 2. On that day, a snowstorm set in over northern Arizona, but the Havasupai had endured too much to let that stop them. The few reservation residents with trucks assembled a regular caravan through the snow, and one truck after another rolled up to the meeting place until 28 Havasupai representatives were gathered, including Chairman Oscar Paya, Vice Chairman Clark Jack and the formidable Lee Marshall.

The Sierra Club people said they did not oppose the Havasupai's using their permit areas; they just wanted to keep them in public ownership so "all the people" could determine how they should be used. The Sierra Club's Southwest Representative, who was present, said he simply could not approve of private land, and he viewed Indian reservations as private land. The Havasupai said they had never asked to decide how Sierra Club people used their homes. The Sierra Club people finally asked the Havasupai to list their dissatisfactions in writing, which they did December 5, trying to explain in detail where Sierra Club theorizing had been unrealistic:

"Public ownership" of land does not place the power of decision in the hands of some theoretical "people"; "public ownership" means in practice control by bureaucracy under the heavy influence of whatever federal administration happens to be in office. It is often misguided, arbitrary and venal. . . . The Havasupai fail to see why "all the people" should determine how the Havasupai are to use an area that has always been their homeland, just as they fail to see why "all the people" should determine how the citizens of Tucson use their homeland. The people who live in an area, know it and love it should determine its use.[106]

The following week the Sierra Club's Flagstaff group met and voted to change their position and recommended that the Arizona chapter's executive committee support the return of "appropriate federal lands" to the Havasupai.

Several other people who had attended the December 2 meeting representing the Sierra Club's Prescott, Phoenix and Tucson groups felt they should make a special effort to come to Havasu Canyon as well.

This group spoke with the Havasupai Tribal Council on December 31 and asked a number of detailed questions regarding Havasupai use and management of the plateau, and asked for Havasupai views on the management of the South Rim portion of the Grand Canyon National Park as well.

The Havasupai proposed the only lasting solution to the Park's management problems would be to staff it from top to bottom with Havasupai at the South Rim. Frequent turnover made the people managing the Park strangers to it; they said the Havasupai alone have a lifelong commitment to the preservation of the Grand Canyon because they live in it. While the reservation should still be enlarged to restore to the tribe its homes and burial places, the Havasupai should administer the remainder of the Park under existing Park regulations with the normal federal funding. This would provide the tribe meaningful, permanent employment in their own homeland and guarantee the best care for the Grand Canyon National Park.

Following these contacts the Arizona Sierra Club held several further discussions and finally on January 26, 1974, the Arizona chapter's executive committee resolved that they supported the enlargement of the Havasupai reservation from any source.

On March 4 the House Subcommittee on Parks and Recreation met to consider S 1296 as already amended and passed by the Senate. When they came to the study language on expanding the reservation, some committee members apparently felt even this went too far. Some of them expressed the opinion that the Havasupai might build factories right on the South Rim and said the whole proposal represented an intolerable precedent. Despite the best efforts of Sam Steiger, the committee decided to restrict the purpose of the study yet further—to a possible reduction of the tribe's use area to 100,000 acres!

> . . . the Secretary of the Interior and the Secretary of Agriculture shall within one year of the enactment of this Act jointly formulate, and thereafter expeditiously implement, a comprehensive plan allowing the

Havasupai Tribe the use of not less than 100,000 acres of Federal lands for various purposes, including but not necessarily limited to, economic subsistence, grazing, and limited residential purposes.[107]

This plan would leave the tribe with permits and, should the government take 100,000 acres as a ceiling figure, a 60 percent reduction even of those.

When word of the action reached the Havasupai, they were stunned. The bill was to go before the full Interior Committee and then to the House floor for final vote within a matter of weeks unless the Havasupai could do something.

Upon learning of the March 4 subcommittee action, William Byler of the New York–based Association on American Indian Affairs contacted the Havasupai Tribal Council immediately to offer the AAIA's full assistance in salvaging something from the setback. (The AAIA is a privately supported foundation to which the Havasupai had previously appealed for help in their fight.) Byler first put the Tribal Council into contact with a dedicated young Scottsdale attorney named Joe Sparks. Sparks, already noted for his work in environmental law, had been involved in several Indian land cases and had been instrumental in gaining federal recognition for the previously unrecognized Yavapai-Tonto Apaches of Arizona. Byler advised the Council that any hope they had of recovering from the March 4 blow would probably lie in Joe Sparks, so the Council sent Daniel Kaska to speak with him and bring him to talk with the Tribal Council.

After a quick conference with Sparks in Havasu Canyon in early March, the Tribal Council learned that the subcommittee action left them only the slimmest chance to save the lands they had sought so long. When the Council voiced their determination to commit all their meager resources to this last-ditch chance, Sparks told them they faced a long, uphill battle with defeat the most likely outcome but said he was ready to join them. The Council engaged Sparks then and there and dispatched him to Washington immediately to develop the legal groundwork for their comeback effort.

Within two weeks the Council sent Ethel Jack, a spokeswoman for their traditional spiritual beliefs, and Councilmen Leon Rogers and Augustine Hanna on their way to join Sparks in Washington.

When Ethel stepped from her cab at the old Capitol Hill Hotel she says she just stared across the street in surprise. Then a slow certainty took shape. For there in the park across the street, tree for tree, was the destination of her dream of 31 years before! (See page 215.) For this she had lived.

In another two weeks Daniel Kaska and Council members Earl Paya and Issa Uqualla joined the first group. Joe Sparks acted as general of the campaign, working his willing soldiers 16 and 20 hours a day. They spent weeks talking to Congressmen and government officials to explain how totally their situation and intentions had been misrepresented. Fortunately for the Havasupai, an extremely controversial bill on strip mining bogged down the House Interior Committee in amendments and disagreements, and the tribe gained nearly a month of time to make their case. It was enough.

On March 30 the Sierra Club's National Committee on Native American Issues resolved, in opposition to the Club's national directorate, that Congress should grant the Havasupai trust title to all 251,000 acres of their free-use area. On April 18 the *Washington Post* ran an editorial urging Congress to return the land to the Havasupai. On May 3, only a few months before his resignation, President Richard Nixon said that he and his administration, reversing their former stand, would urge Congress to grant the Havasupai trust title to all 251,000 acres of their free-use area:

> When Senators Goldwater and Fannin introduced a bill to enlarge the reservation, the departments of interior and agriculture took the position that a year should be devoted to studying the question.
>
> However, after consultation with Secretary of the Interior Rogers C. B. Morton and Agriculture Secretary Earl Butz and Indian Commissioner Morris Thompson, the Arizona congressional delegation and representatives of the tribe, I have concluded that the Havasupai have waited long enough.
>
> . . . We must remember that the conservation record of the American Indian stretching over the thousands of years he has inhabited this continent is virtually unblemished.[108]

Thus, by the first part of May 1974 the Havasupai had already swung the Nixon administration, many Congressmen and several influential daily newspapers over to support of their long and unswerving effort to regain their land. By the end of the summer these supporting journals were to include the *Los Angeles Times*, *The Wall Street Journal*, *The Christian Science Monitor*, the *San Francisco Chronicle* and *The Denver Post*. But the fight was only beginning.

By June it seemed only the Sierra Club's national directorate and a few environmentalist groups such as Friends of the Earth remained adamant. Though he no longer spoke for his Arizona colleagues, the Sierra Club's Southwest Representative continued trying to persuade Congressmen to withhold from the Havasupai trust title to any federal land. Finally, in desperation over the growing public support for the Havasupai cause, several of these groups began to use deliberate misrepresentation. In July Friends of the Earth bought a national advertisement making the clear implication that the Havasupai were "cigar store Indians" in the employ of land developers and that granting any federal land to them would be a national disaster of the first magnitude. Such tactics began to prove quite effective, though the ethics of their use remain at least a little perplexing to the Havasupai, who continue to believe the governmental process depends on truth.

In late spring John O. Crow learned of the renewed Havasupai fight and came out of retirement to lend his voice to the very effort he had furthered 31 years earlier. By mid July Crow, Sparks and the Havasupai had finally familiarized S 1296's House sponsor, Morris Udall, with the full sweep of the tribe's long campaign. Udall prepared amendatory language for the House

Interior Committee to grant the Havasupai trust title to their entire free-use area of 251,000 acres as part of S 1296.

The Sierra Club still had powerful friends. The Chairman of the Parks and Recreation Subcommittee, Congressman Roy Taylor of North Carolina, as acting chairman of the House Interior Committee, had the responsibility of scheduling his Park subcommittee's March 4 work for consideration by the full Interior Committee. When Taylor learned of Udall's decision, it became apparent suddenly that S 1296 simply would not be scheduled. Several weeks of desperate negotiation followed, with the Havasupai standing nervously in the wings. Finally Udall offered Taylor compromise wording to grant the Havasupai trust title to all that part of their free-use area beginning a quarter mile back from the uppermost rim of the Grand Canyon, an area of some 160,000 acres. The remainder of their free-use area, some 95,000 acres, from the quarter-mile setback down to the Colorado River, Udall proposed as a perpetual and irrevocable Havasupai use reserve under the administration of the National Park Service. As a compensation for his forced retreat, he also wrote into his proposal the return of some 15,000 acres of Pasture Wash upon the expiration of the Globe Ranch's existing permit there. This was the most daring and—for the Havasupai—most precious provision in his amendment. Not only might they finally regain their existing use area, but they now saw half realized what they had only dreamed of before: the restoration of the homes and farms they had lost in 1917. Taylor finally decided to allow the Interior Committee to consider this amendatory language.

Udall's amendment was presented to the Interior Committee July 31; by a vote of 24 to 11 they agreed to it. Startled by this turn of events, certain opponents on the staff of the Interior Committee objected that a quorum was not present to approve the entire bill and in this fashion managed to delay final Interior approval until August 14.

A furor followed from the Sierra Club and its friends, who held a Washington press conference September 12 to announce the opening of a nationwide campaign to stop the Havasupai land return. Sierra Club newsletters began to appear across the country within weeks urging that Congress refuse to return *any* public land to the Havasupai.

As the opposition campaign mounted, the bill still had to be filed with the House Rules Committee and cleared by them for a House floor vote. The election would be coming up November 5, and Congress would go into recess from mid October to mid November. With thousands of letters of support for the Havasupai still coming in from across the nation, the opponents' best tactic was simple delay. The House Interior Committee staff received the assignment of writing up the Committee decision of August 14. The Committee staff simply delayed filing this report with the Rules Committee until September 25th. As election day recess approached and the days of October passed one by one, the Chairman of the Rules Committee stated he intended to go home to campaign at the end of the first week of October.

This promised disaster. A lame-duck session would return after the election in late November to do perhaps three or four weeks of cleanup business. The Havasupai had to achieve House passage before the recess, or the chance of action on S 1296 would be lost. The following year, the 94th Congress planned to revamp its committee structure so that Indian land bills would likely have to go through the unsympathetic Agriculture Committee instead of the Interior Committee. The Havasupai's best and likely last chance lay in S 1296.

The Havasupai had one powerful friend in the House besides Udall; upon the accession of Gerald Ford to the Presidency, Arizona's John Rhodes had become House Minority Leader. Rhodes remembered very well his friends in Havasu Canyon and their fight, which he himself had joined in 1965. Joe Sparks had Rhodes intercede for the Havasupai with the Rules Committee Chairman to hold a further session, and on October 8 the Rules Committee, with no dissenting votes, recommended S 1296 to the House for a floor vote. By then the House had announced its intent to recess on October 11, only three days later.

John Rhodes bent his every effort to accomplish the vote before the recess, as the environmentalist campaign was beginning to confuse many supporters of the Havasupai land return. Finally Rhodes persuaded House Speaker Carl Albert to schedule the Grand Canyon bill for October 10.

During that entire day environmentalist lobbyists had been working on Congressmen with a story that the Havasupai were planning extensive developments of their homeland, including the location of a highway and two tramways into Havasu Canyon, a railroad across the plateau and an effort to dry up Havasu Creek. As Congressmen filed into the House chamber that evening for the vote, people stationed at each entrance informed them the Havasupai had a signed agreement with the Marriott Hotel Corporation for a giant resort complex and that Joe Sparks was representing Marriott.

When the bill was presented, an acrimonious, hour-long debate followed. Ethel Jack who by then had, along with Leon Rogers, become the Havasupai's Washington spokesman, was in Washington alone at the time and had sat in the House gallery most of the day, simply keeping vigil.

Congressman Taylor, in presenting S 1296, stated his opposition to the Havasupai land return, saying that it needed further study. John Seiberling of Ohio followed him to say that the Havasupai had already been paid for their land by the Indian Claims Commission in the amount of "approximately $10,000 per family." He stated further:

> . . . if we give title to thousands of acres of the Grand Canyon . . . it would also open the door to possible commercial exploitation of the Grand Canyon by interests who may not have the same view that we have about the preservation of that tremendous and unique national asset.[109]

Sam Steiger, John Rhodes and Morris Udall responded with lengthy statements of support for the Havasupai, Udall saying in part:

> . . . This is not a giveaway of national park land. It is simply a protection of this tribe in the legitimate, honorable uses they have had. . . . Congress

has the responsibility and the power to create, add to or abolish Indian reservations as it sees fit. The Indian Claims Commission is not authorized to grant land, only monetary consideration for land taken illegally by the United States or others from Indian tribes. The question here is one of need, and the committee concluded that the tribe indeed needs a larger land base.

Thomas Foley of Washington and John Dellenback of Oregon then rose to speak at length against the transfer of land to the Havasupai, pointing again to the Indian Claims Commission settlement and to purported plans to develop the area (notwithstanding the Interior Committee's language precluding such development and the Havasupai's frequently expressed willingness to abide by reasonable environmental restrictions). Both Foley and Dellenback urged the Havasupai would be more benefited by improved health and education programs than by returning their plateau homeland. Dellenback concluded one statement by saying, "The proposal to give this land to the Havasupai—however great their needs—is a very bad amendment which we should not adopt." Seiberling chimed in, calling the proposal to return the Havasupai winter lands a "dangerous precedent."

Then, by surprise, Congressman Ketchum of California rose to give one of the most telling speeches of the entire debate:

> . . . It seems we have a great many Indian experts around this place all of a sudden and I certainly do not claim to be one of them. . . . There is a great deal of hassle going on about these 459 Indians who have been locked into about 518 acres. We ought to be really proud of that. . . . We are trying to give them back the land to give them the one thing they do not have right now—pride. We have been talking here tonight about whether we ought to make arrangements to give them medical clinics, we ought to make arrangements to give them this and give them that, and that is precisely what they do not want. These people have pride. . . . Can we imagine that they will jeopardize the Forest Service and the Park Service of the U.S. Government? Are they going to do this with tomahawks? . . . Give them the land and with it their pride.

Steiger castigated the Sierra Club for the tactics they had adopted against the Havasupai, and Dellenback rose again to defend the representations of the Club, whom he characterized as "sincere, earnest, good people." Steiger responded:

> . . . As far as my overgenerous description of the Sierra Club, that is purely a judgment call, and I thank the gentleman for defending them. I am sure his record is clear because he has defended them and I cannot think of a group who needed defending more.

Udall stated in this regard:

I have fought a lot of fights with the Sierra Club. I have been with them most of the time, but the tactics they use with this plan are really unfair and are unworthy of their fine organization.

Craig Hosmer of California later added:

. . . what have they [the Sierra Club] done? They [have] come in [to] jump on some poor Indians, less than 500 Indians . . . They oppose the bill on the grounds these natives of America would spoil the environment. How mixed up have we managed to get?

As the Congressmen moved toward the vote on S 1296, Seiberling rose again to say:

Why should they [the Havasupai] want to put residences on the national parkland? The only fertile, productive land is the land they already have, the land on the bottom of beautiful Havasu Canyon. The plateau land above, which is part of the national park, is a desert. I would be very surprised if there are going to be any residences up on the plateau. . . .[109]

Carl Albert then called for a voice vote and said the noes appeared to have it. John Rhodes demanded a recorded vote, and the recorded vote showed that the Havasupai land return amendment instead had passed by 180 to 147. Then the House passed the entire bill by a voice vote. The Havasupai had achieved the most significant victory in their 66-year campaign with Congress for the return of their homeland—passage in one house of Congress; but much work still lay ahead of them.

After the election recess, a Senate-House conference committee would have to meet to iron out the differences between the Senate version of S 1296, which provided only a study of the Havasupai question, and the version of S 1296 the House had just passed. The time would be extremely short, as Congress would adjourn by Christmas. Failing a conference agreement and ratification of the agreement in both houses of Congress before adjournment, the Havasupai would have to start all over again against even worse odds than they already faced.

The election had already cost the Havasupai terribly, as they had lost 19 of their House votes. Congress faced many large national issues, including an energy bill, the Soviet-American Trade Act, the strip-mining act and the confirmation of Nelson Rockefeller as Vice President. Weeks dragged by without the naming of any conference committee members until December 3, when Arizona Senators Goldwater and Fannin prevailed upon Senator Alan Bible to recommend Senate conferees to Henry Jackson and Mike Mansfield. Again certain elements of the House Interior Committee showed their distaste for the land return by delay, failing to recommend the House conferees for another week.

Finally, on December 12 and 13 the conferees were able to meet and discuss S 1296. By then sizable opposition had arisen to the return of Pasture

Wash to the Havasupai, and Joe Sparks, Leon Rogers and Ethel Jack faced the heartbreaking prospect of losing this precious area again, when they thought they had finally regained it. They had spent days taking around photographs of their remaining homes in Pasture Wash to prove their claim to it. On December 13 the conferees reported their settlement, and the Havasupai land return remained intact as Udall had presented it. The Havasupai were at last safe from further amendment. Each House can vote only yes or no on a conference committee report.

Once again, the House Interior Committee staff had its chance to prevent passage, however. House rules require that a conference report must lie over for three days after submission before a confirmation vote. By December 13 it was announced that the House would devote December 19 to the confirmation of Nelson Rockefeller. So the Committee staff, who was given the assignment of writing and submitting the conference report, simply sat on it again. Ethel Jack and Leon Rogers by December 17 were sitting in the Committee room all day to ask every few minutes if the bill was ready yet. Not until 6:30 that evening did Interior Committee Chairman James Haley accede to John Rhodes's and Barry Goldwater's appeals and finally file the report.

At that late date, the only chance left to present the conference report to the House for confirmation would be on the following day under a special waiver of the rules allowing all conference reports to be considered on the day of filing. After the House leadership passed such a waiver, John Rhodes gained a place on the schedule, and Morris Udall presented the conference report about 6 P.M. on December 18. Carl Albert called for a voice vote; by a large margin the ayes had it.

The report was rushed over to the Senate immediately, and Senators Paul Fannin, Barry Goldwater and Henry Jackson, without difficulty, obtained final Congressional confirmation within the hour.

Finally the long Havasupai fight seemed to be over; only Presidential signature was required, and the Havasupai had taken that for granted ever since the Nixon statement of May. The bill was presented to President Ford on December 24, giving him until January 4 to sign the measure to prevent its defeat by pocket veto. The days again began to pass with no word of the signature. By January 1 Joe Sparks learned that an examiner in the Office of Management and Budget would recommend that Ford veto S 1296 on the grounds that the Havasupai land return would upset the work of the Indian Claims Commission. On January 3 the OMB made the veto recommendation official.

Shock descended upon the people in Havasu Canyon. Rhodes and Goldwater were incredulous; they had received continuously positive signals from the White House on S 1296, and now it looked as if all the bitter debate and months of work were to be overturned. Both men began making repeated contacts with the White House in the day remaining, and Interior Secretary Rogers Morton went to see Ford personally to state the position of the Interior Department that, for the sake of the Havasupai, S 1296 should be signed.

Finally on the morning of the last day, January 4, President Ford called John Rhodes to inform him that he had signed S 1296 into law the evening before. S 1296 had become PL 93-620.

Acting in complete peace and working always within the law, the determined Havasupai had persisted in their belief for 66 years; and they finally overcame every obstacle and surmounted seemingly impossible odds because they had at last touched the decent instincts of the people of the United States.

For Congress and for Indian people, the enactment of PL 93-620 was historic because by it the government had returned the largest amount of land ever restored to a single tribe. For the Havasupai the enactment was more than historic. It was fulfillment. Their beloved winter homeland is again reunited with them. Their long nightmare is over.

Fannie and Lorenzo

Courtesy American Museum of Natural History 1913

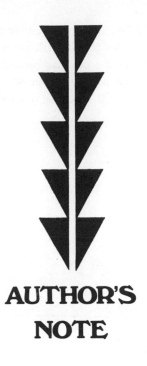

AUTHOR'S NOTE

At the time of writing, the Havasupai are busily engaged in developing a use plan for their returned lands that will preserve in every way possible the wild nature of their home, as PL 93-620 requests them to do and as they themselves have always wished to do. They are showing great enthusiasm over the task. The people have elected Leon Rogers to be Tribal Chairman.

On the plateau, several families have already returned to winter residence, and others are assembling lumber to repair their cabins on the beloved land. Some Havasupai have taken up temporary residence in tents among the once-forbidden piñons.

Many of the individuals described in "A Season on the Plateau" still live. Some are gone. The person from whose life I distilled Baa vam nyuéva hija is a very old man now but still vigorous and keen-minded. He can be by turns merry, reverent and wistful when he tells of his life in the times of snows, of a year which began and still begins with *sal j'ála'*, of a life which government rangers temporarily interrupted—but did not end.

Baqí has died now, but Baa is surrounded by her children and grandchildren. He harbors no bitterness for the difficult years of his young manhood and middle age. He forgives all, for the day has returned when he may ride again with the people to the plateau before the snows. Perhaps he may ride first, because he is old and knows how it was, and open the fences before them.

BIBLIOGRAPHY

BOOKS AND MANUSCRIPTS

COUES, ELLIOTT, trans. and ed., *On the Trail of a Spanish Pioneer; The Diary and Itinerary of Francisco Garcés*, F. P. Harper, New York, 1900.

CURTIS, EDWARD S., *The North American Indian*, J. Pierpont Morgan Library, New York, Vol. II, pp. 97–102 and supplement to Vol. II, plates 72 and 75.

CUSHING, FRANK H., "The Nation of the Willows," *Atlantic Monthly*, **50**, September and October 1882 (now published as a book by Northland Press, Flagstaff).

DOBYNS, HENRY F., and EULER, ROBERT C., *The Ghost Dance of 1889 Among the Pai Indians of Northwestern Arizona*, Prescott College Press, Prescott, Arizona, 1967.

DOBYNS, HENRY F., and EULER, ROBERT C., *The Havasupai People*, Indian Tribal Series, Phoenix, 1971.

DOBYNS, HENRY F., and EULER, ROBERT C., *Wauba Yuma's People*, Prescott College Press, Prescott, Arizona, 1970.

ELLIS, RICHARD N. ed., *The Western American Indian: Case Studies in Tribal History*, University of Nebraska Press, Lincoln, Nebr., 1972.

EMERICK, RICHARD, *Recent Observations on Some Aspects of Havasupai Culture*, University of Pennsylvania M.A. thesis, 1954.

HUGHES, J. DONALD, *The Story of Man in the Grand Canyon*, Grand Canyon Natural History Association, Arizona, 1967.

ILIFF, FLORA GREGG, *People of the Blue Water*, Harper & Brothers, New York, 1954.

JAMES, GEORGE WHARTON, *The Grand Canyon of Arizona*, Little, Brown & Co., Boston, 1910.

JAMES, GEORGE WHARTON, *In and Around the Grand Canyon*, Little, Brown & Co., Boston, 1900.

JAMES, GEORGE WHARTON, *Indian Basketry*, Henry Malkan, New York, 1909. (Reprinted by Dover Publications, New York, 1972.)

JAMES, GEORGE WHARTON, *The Indians of the Painted Desert Region*, Little, Brown & Co., Boston, 1903.

JOSEPHY, ALVIN M., JR., *The Indian Heritage of America*, Alfred A. Knopf, New York, 1968.

KNOBLOCH, MADGE FOSTER, unpublished manuscript of personal experiences on Havasupai Reservation 1931–1933, on file in Havasupai Tribal Collection, Supai, Ariz.

KROEBER, ALFRED LOUIS, ed., *Walapai Ethnography*, Memoirs of the American Anthropological Association, number 42, 1935.

MC KEE, BARBARA, and MC KEE, EDWIN, *Havasupai Baskets and Their Makers*, Northland Press, Flagstaff, Arizona, 1974.

REYNOLDS, CHARLES R., ed., *American Indian Portraits; from the Wanamaker Expedition of 1913*, The Stephen Greene Press, Brattleboro, Vermont, 1971.

SMITH, DAMA MARGARET, *I Married a Ranger*, Stanford University Press, Stanford, California, 1930.

SMITHSON, CARMA LEE, *The Havasupai Woman*, University of Utah Anthropological Papers, number 38, April 1959.

SMITHSON, CARMA LEE, and EULER, ROBERT C., *Havasupai Religion and Mythology*, University of Utah Anthropological Papers, number 68, April 1964.

SPIER, LESLIE, "Havasupai Ethnography," *Anthropological Papers of the American Museum of Natural History*, New York, **29**, Part 3, 1928.

SCHWARTZ, DOUGLAS W., *Havasupai Prehistory: Thirteen Centuries of Cultural Development*, unpublished Ph.D. dissertation, Dept. of Anthropology, Yale University, New Haven, Conn.

WAMPLER, JOSEPH, *Havasu Canyon: Gem of the Grand Canyon*, Howell-North Press, Berkeley, California, 1971. First edition 1959.

WATKINS, T. H., ed., *The Grand Colorado*, American West Publishing Co., Palo Alto, California, 1969.

WHITING, ALFRED F., manuscript 3 (unpublished), on file at the Museum of Northern Arizona, Flagstaff, circa 1940.

ARTICLES AND REPORTS

BARBER, ABE and COHEN, FELIX, *Examiners' Report on Tribal Claims to Released Railroad Lands in Northwestern Arizona*, May 1942, on file in Havasupai Tribal Collection.

DAVIS, A. E., "The Wallapais," *Alta Arizona*, May 13, 1882.

Depositions of Big Jim, Billy Burro, Supai Mary and Allen Akaba (before the Indian Claims Commission, Docket 91, Grand Canyon, Arizona, August 4, 1950), on file in Havasupai Tribal Collection.

GOODFRIEND, MARTIN, *In Supai . . . Life with Added Meaning for All*, report to the Havasupai Tribe and the Bureau of Indian Affairs, Santa Monica, August 1969.

HOOVER, J. W., "Modern Canyon Dwellers of Arizona," *Journal of Geography*, 27:7, October 1929.

JOHNSTON, JAY, "Indian Shangri-La of the Grand Canyon," *National Geographic*, March 1970.

MEADOR, BRUCE S., and ROESSEL, ROBERT A., JR., *Havasupai School Survey*, Indian Education Center, Arizona State University, Tempe, May 1962.

Petitioner's Proposed Findings of Fact and Brief (before the Indian Claims Commission, Docket 91), Royal D. Marks, Attorney of Record, on file in Havasupai Tribal Collection, Supai, Arizona.

SCHROEDER, ALBERT L., "A Brief History of the Havasupai," *Plateau* (Museum of Northern Arizona), 25:4, 1952.

SCHWARTZ, DOUGLAS W., "The Havasupai 600 A.D.–1500 A.D.: A Short Cultural History," *Plateau* (Museum of Northern Arizona), 28:4, 1956.

SCHUFELDT, R. W., *Some Observations on the Havesu Pai Indians*, U.S. National Museum Proceedings, U.S. Government Printing Office, Washington, 1891.

Survey of Conditions of the Indians in the United States, hearings before a subcommittee of the United States Senate Committee on Indian Affairs, third session Seventy-first Congress, 1931, pp. 8740 *et seq.*

SPIER, LESLIE, "Havasupai Days," *American Indian Life*, Parsons, Elsie Clews, ed., Viking Press, New York, 1922.

WILDER, CARLETON S., "Archæological Survey of the Great Thumb Area, Grand Canyon National Park," *Plateau* (Museum of Northern Arizona), 17:2, 1944.

NOVELS AND OTHER BOOKS GIVING AN INTENSELY PERSONAL VIEW OF AMERICAN INDIAN LIFE

BERGER, THOMAS, *Little Big Man*, Dial Press, New York, 1964.

CORLE, EDWIN, *Fig Tree John*, Pocket Books, New York, 1972.

CORLE, EDWIN, *People on the Earth*, Random House, 1937.

KROEBER, THEODORA, *Ishi, in Two Worlds*, Univ. of California Press, Berkeley, 1961.

KROEBER, THEODORA, *Ishi, Last of His Tribe*, Parnassus Press, Berkeley, 1964.

LA FARGE, OLIVER, *Laughing Boy*, Houghton Mifflin Company, Boston, 1929.

MOMADAY, N. SCOTT, *House Made of Dawn*, Harper & Row, New York, 1968.

SANCHEZ, THOMAS, *Rabbit Boss*, Alfred A. Knopf, New York, 1973.

STORM, HYEMEYOHSTS, *Seven Arrows*, Harper & Row, New York, 1972.

TALAYESVA, DON C., *Sun Chief; the Autobiography of a Hopi Indian*, Yale University Press, New Haven, 1942.

WATERS, FRANK, *The Man Who Killed the Deer*, Farrar & Rinehart, New York, 1942.

Bibliography

NOTES

1. 1974: LIFE IN A NARROW PLACE

1. Letter written by W. P. Hermann, Grand Cañon Forest Reserve Supervisor, on November 9, 1898, to Binger Hermann, General Land Commissioner, Department of Interior; on file in National Archives (NA) and Havasupai Tribal Collection (HTC).

2. The reader with an interest in Havasupai basketry is directed to *Havasupai Baskets and Basketmakers* by Edwin McKee, to be released by Northland Press, Flagstaff, Arizona; and *Indian Basketry* by George Wharton James, reprinted by Dover Publications, New York.

3. Smithson, Carma Lee, *The Havasupai Woman*, University of Utah Anthropological Papers, number 38, April 1959, p. 83.

4. See, for example, Whiting, Alfred F., manuscript 3 on file at the Museum of Northern Arizona, Flagstaff, circa 1940.

5. Dobyns, Henry F., and Euler, Robert C., *Wauba Yuma's People*, Prescott College Press, Prescott, Ariz., 1970, p. 19.

6. Dobyns and Euler, *op. cit.*, p. 5.

7. Cushing, Frank H., "The Nation of the Willows," *Atlantic Monthly*, **50**, September 1882, pp. 362–374.

8. This discussion of prehistory draws on a number of sources. The reader is directed especially to Alvin Josephy's *The Indian Heritage of America* for a good general discussion. Material relating specifically to Havasupai prehistory includes books and articles by Henry F. Dobyns and Robert C. Euler, Douglas W. Schwartz, and Albert L. Schroeder.

9. Josephy, Alvin M., Jr., *The Indian Heritage of America*, Alfred A. Knopf, New York, 1968, pp. 152–158.

10. James, George Wharton, *Indian Basketry*, Henry Malkan, New York, 1909, p. 212.

11. Euler, Robert C., "The Canyon Dwellers," *The Grand Colorado* (T. H. Watkins, ed.), American West Publishing Co., Palo Alto, 1969, p. 25.

12. See especially Schwartz's *Havasupai Prehistory: Thirteen Centuries of Cultural Development*, unpublished Ph.D. dissertation, Dept. of Anthropology, Yale University, New Haven, Conn. and Euler's work with Dobyns, especially *Wauba Yuma's People, op. cit.*, and Euler's "The Canyon Dwellers," *op. cit.*, for the Cohonino/Havasupai connection. The reader is also referred to the discussion by Carleton S. Wilder, "Archæological Survey of the Great Thumb Area, Grand Canyon National Park," in *Plateau*, **17**, no. 2, October 1944.

13. Iliff, Flora Gregg, *People of the Blue Water*, Harper & Brothers, New York, 1954, pp. 200, 201.

14. See, for example, Sitgreaves, L., "Report of Expedition down the Zuñi and Colorado Rivers (Senate Ex. Doc. 59, 32nd Congress, 2nd Session, 1853); Ives, Joseph C., "Report upon the Colorado River of the West" (House Ex. Doc. 90, 36th Congress, 1st Session, 1861); Beale, E. F., "Wagon Road from Fort Defiance to the Colorado River" (House Ex. Doc. 124, 35th Congress, 1st Session, 1858); Cushing, Frank H., "The Nation of the Willows," *op. cit.*; Hrdlička, Aleš, notes on file with Smithsonian Institution, 1897; Powell, J. W., *Explorations of the Colorado River of the West*, Washington, 1875; Whipple, A. W., "Report of Explorations for a Railway Route near the Thirty-fifth Parallel, etc." (*Reports of Explorations and Surveys . . . from the Mississippi River to the Pacific Ocean*, 3, U.S. Congress, Washington, 1856).

3. THE INVASION BEGINS

15. Spier, Leslie, "Havasupai Ethnography," *Anthropological Papers of the American Museum of Natural History*, **29**, Part 3, 1928, p. 104.

16. *Ibid.*, pp. 99–100.

17. Cushing, *op. cit.*

18. Spier, *op. cit.*, p. 101.

19. *Petitioner's Proposed Findings of Fact and Brief* (before the Indian Claims Commission, Docket 91), Royal D. Marks, Attorney of Record, p. 20.

20. Cushing, Frank H., "The Nation of the Willows" (part II), *Atlantic Monthly*, **50**, October 1882, pp. 541–559.

21. *Ibid.*, pp. 541–559.

22. Dobyns and Euler, *Wauba Yuma's People*, p. 50.

23. *Ibid.*, p. 72.

24. *Depositions of Big Jim, Billy Burro, Supai Mary and Allen Akaba* (before the Indian Claims Commission, Docket 91), Grand Canyon, August 4, 1950, pp. 36 and 46.

25. HTC (Havasupai Tribal Collection).

26. *Petitioner's Proposed Findings, etc., op. cit.*, p. 44.

27. *Ibid.*, p. 44.

28. *Examiners' Report on Tribal Claims to Released Railroad Lands in Northwestern Arizona*, Abe Barber and Felix Cohen, May 1942, p. 47.

29. *Depositions of Big Jim, etc., op. cit.*, pp. 57–59.

30. NA (National Archives).

31. *Petitioner's Proposed Findings, etc., op. cit.*, p. 54.

32. NA.

33. Dobyns, Henry F., and Euler, Robert C., *The Ghost Dance of 1889 among the Pai Indians of Northwestern Arizona*, Prescott College Press, Prescott, Arizona, 1967, pp. 37, 38 and 41.

34. Schufeldt, R. W., *Some Observations on the Havesu Pai Indians*, U.S. Government Printing Office, 1891, p. 388.

35. Davis, A. E., "The Wallapais," *Alta Arizona*, May 13, 1882, p. 31.

36. Dobyns and Euler, *The Ghost Dance of 1889, etc., op. cit.*, pp. 45–46.

37. *Ibid.*, p. 58. For this entire discussion of the ghost dance among the Havasupai we are heavily indebted to the pioneering work of Dr. Dobyns and Dr. Euler.

38. Knobloch, Madge Foster, unpublished manuscript, HTC.

39. HTC and NA.

40. NA and HTC.

41. NA and HTC.

42. NA and HTC.

43. *Nineteenth Annual Report of Indian Rights Association* for year ending December 6, 1901, Indian Rights Association, Philadelphia, 1902, pp. 21–29.

44. Iliff, Flora Gregg, *op. cit.*, p. 191.

45 *Ibid.*, p. 210.

4. BANISHMENT

46. *Depositions of Big Jim, etc., op. cit.*, pp. 38–39.

47. Recorded by Richard Emerick in *Recent Observations of Some Aspects of Havasupai Culture*, University of Pennsylvania M.A. thesis, 1954, appendix p. 53.

48. Iliff, Flora Gregg, *op. cit.*, p. 193.

49. *Depositions of Big Jim, etc., op. cit.*, pp. 17–19.

50. NA and HTC.

51. Spier, Leslie, *op. cit.*, p. 209.

52. Hoover, J. W., "Modern Canyon Dwellers of Arizona," *Journal of Geography*, **27**, October 1929, p. 7.

6. IN THE PUBLIC INTEREST

53. NA and HTC.

54. NA and HTC.

55. NA and HTC.

56. NA and HTC.

57. NA.

58. NA.

59. NA and HTC.

60. Smith, Dama Margaret, *I Married a Ranger,* Stanford University Press, Stanford, California, 1930, pp. 86–89, 97–103.

61. *Depositions of Big Jim, etc., op. cit.,* p. 49.

8. A VALID POSSESSORY RIGHT

62. Report on file at Museum of Northern Arizona, Flagstaff.

63. NA and HTC.

64. NA and HTC.

65. *Survey of Conditions of the Indians in the United States,* hearings before a subcommittee of the United States Senate Committee on Indian Affairs, third session Seventy-first Congress, 1931, pp. 8740 *et seq.*

66. HTC.

67. HTC.

68. Supreme Court of the United States, October 1941 term, *United States of America* v. *Santa Fe Pacific Railroad Company,* decision written by Justice William O. Douglas.

69. *Examiners' Report on Tribal Claims, etc., op. cit.,* pp. 47–53, 56–57.

70. HTC.

71. HTC & Bureau of Indian Affairs, Truxton Cañon Agency files.

72. HTC.

73. *Conconino Sun* (Flagstaff), April 30, 1943.

74. on file at Grand Canyon National Park headquarters, Grand Canyon, Arizona.

75. HTC.

76. HTC.

77. HTC.

10. THE LONG WAY BACK

78. Meador, Bruce S., and Roessel, Robert A., Jr., *Havasupai School Survey,* Indian Education Center, Arizona State University, Tempe, May 1962, p. 32.

79. Momaday, N. Scott, *House Made of Dawn,* Harper & Row, New York, 1968.

80. HTC.

81. HTC.

82. HTC.

83. HTC.

84. HTC.

85. Bureau of Indian Affairs, Truxton Cañon Agency files.

86. "Additional Findings of Fact" (Before the Indian Claims Commission, Docket 91), p. 327.

87. HTC.

88. "Additional Findings of Fact," *op. cit.,* p. 339.

89. Letter on file with J. R. Babbitt, attorney, Flagstaff.

90. Internal memorandum on file at Grand Canyon National Park headquarters, Grand Canyon, Arizona.

11. I AM THE GRAND CANYON

91. *A Master Plan for Grand Canyon National Park*, Robert R. Lovegren *et al.*, National Park Service, January 1971, third draft.

92. Copy with Lee Marshall, also reported in *Daily Sun* (Flagstaff), May 19, 1971.

93. HTC.

94. HTC.

95. Letter on file with J. R. Babbitt, attorney, Flagstaff.

96. *Congressional Record*, March 20, 1973.

97. HTC, letter written to Havasupai Tribal Chairman Oscar Paya, March 8, 1973, by chairman of Arizonans for Quality Environment (name withheld to protect privacy).

98. Report to Senate Interior Committee Chairman Henry M. Jackson, June 20, 1973, by Interior Department Asst. Secretary John Kyl.

99. Quotes are all taken from *Hearing before the Subcommittee on Parks and Recreation of the Committee on Interior and Insular Affairs United States Senate Ninety-third Congress, 1st Session, on S. 1296*, U.S. Government Printing Office, Washington, 1973.

100. HTC.

101. *Arizona Republic* (Phoenix), July 29, 1973.

102. Report to Senate Interior Committee Chairman Henry M. Jackson by Park and Recreation Subcommittee, August 3, 1973, in referring S. 1296 to full Interior Committee.

103. American Indian Press Association reports NV232 and NV233 by Karen Ducheneaux.

104. Report to House Interior Committee Chairman James A. Haley, November 9, 1973, by Interior Department Asst. Secretary John Kyl.

105. From testimony presented before Subcommitte on Parks and Recreation of the Committee on Interior and Insular Affairs United States House of Representatives, November 12, 1973.

106. HTC.

107. House Interior Committee preliminary report by Park and Recreation Subcommittee, March 4, 1974.

108. Statement by President Richard M. Nixon in Phoenix, Arizona, May 3, 1974.

109. All statements on October 10 debate taken from *Congressional Record* for October 11, 1974, H 10436-10451.

INDEX